RED STAR
IN ORBIT

RED STAR
IN ORBIT

✩

James E. Oberg

Random House · New York

The evaluations and opinions in this book are those of the author and cannot
be construed to reflect policies of NASA, of any other government agency, or
of the McDonnell-Douglas Aerospace Corporation, the author's employer.

Library of Congress Cataloging in Publication Data
Oberg, James E. 1944–
Red star in orbit.

1. Astronautics—Russia. I. Title.
TL789.8R9O24   387.8   80–6033
ISBN 0–394–51429–7

2 4 6 8 9 7 5 3

To Sergey Korolev

Acknowledgments

This book, the result of nearly a lifetime's interest and a full decade's active research, represents only an overview of the major aspects of this subject. Much more work is needed, particularly in the Soviet Union (where honest space history research is stonewalled), with the large numbers of recent Soviet emigrants and defectors, and within the recently declassified records of U.S. and West European intelligence agencies.

The research which led to this book involved a net of amateur investigators around the world. First and foremost are the people of the Kettering Group of amateur radio listeners who have decoded and deciphered telemetry from many Soviet satellites. Their chief, Geoffrey Perry, is the apotheosis of the dedicated, talented English "amateur" scientist, and mention must be made of other colleagues, such as Sven Grahn of Sweden, Richard Flagg of Florida, Mark Severance and Joe Durapau of Texas.

Credit is also due to other Soviet space watchers, such as Charles Patrick Vick, David Woods, Saunders Kramer, Theo Pirard, Maarten Houtman, Michael Cassutt, Joe Bruman, Leonid Vladimirov, Joseph Rowe and Henry Gris (in particular for permission to quote from his translation of Ryumin's space diary). Special mention must be made of Charles Sheldon II of the U.S.

Library of Congress and Fred Durant III of the National Air and Space Museum; of NASA help from historians Lee Saegesser and Eugene Emme; and of help with illustrative material from Mike Gentry and Les Gaver of NASA. (Special photo work for this book was done by Eric Jacobs.) I wish to thank William Shelton for the donation of his boxes of files on the first ten years of the Soviet space program, and Mrs. Lloyd Mallan for access to her late husband's unique Soviet space material.

Many friends and colleagues made helpful suggestions while reviewing various drafts of the manuscript. Among them I want to especially thank my wife, Cooky, and my editor, Bob Loomis, along with Pinky Nelson, Shannon Lucid, Wayne Hale, Lonnie Schmitt, Doyle McDonald, John Hubisz and Keith Lawler. Others —who cannot be named for a variety of reasons—shared insights, experiences and observations which contributed to this book.

James E. Oberg
Houston, Texas
October 15, 1980

Contents

Foreword by Tom Wolfe   xi

1. At Home in Orbit   3
2. The Birth of Sputnik   14
3. The Nedelin Catastrophe   39
4. Man and Woman in Space   50
5. The Voskhod Follies   74
6. Death and Disaster   87
7. The Moon-Race Cover-up   111
8. The Long Climb Back   128
9. Secret Space Cities   150
10. The Salyut-6 Breakthrough   162
11. Guests in Space   183
12. Through the Zero-G Barrier   202
13. Things to Come   222

   Appendices
   Biographies   239
   Guest Cosmonauts   246
   Soviet Man-Related Space Shots   248

Contents

Annotated Bibliography   256
Sources of Current Information   260
Open Questions   261

Index   265

Foreword by
Tom Wolfe

I am particularly fond of two pictures in this book. In one
we see an official portrait of the Soviets' first group of cosmonauts, taken in 1961, just after Yuriy Gagarin, the one with
the necktie, had become the first man to go into space. The
older man in the jacket is the great Soviet rocket engineer,
Sergey Korolev. In the second we see the same scene, the
same frozen slice of time, identical in every detail save one:
a cosmonaut has vanished. The wall behind him has been
airbrushed in (not 100 percent successfully) to fill up the
ghostly space his mortal hide once occupied. Moreover, as
we learn from James Oberg's text, our poor phantom voyager
was in all likelihood dematerialized not because of defection
or scandal but simply because he had washed out of the
Soviet space program, and reminders of his existence were no
longer considered edifying. It is as if NASA were to have
doctored its official group photographs of the seven Mercury
astronauts to remove all visual trace of Deke Slayton after
he developed an irregular heart rhythm and was scrubbed
from the Mercury program in 1962.

What we are looking at is an especially small-minded example of what Orwell referred to, in *1984,* as throwing history "down the memory hole." The process could also become enormous and grotesque, however, as Oberg's excellent chapter on the Nedelin disaster demonstrates. In October of 1960, three years after Sputnik-1, the Soviet space program suffered the worst accident in the history of rocketry. Thanks to the overzealousness of Field Marshal Mitrofan Nedelin, missile chief for the Soviet military, a rocket explosion on the launch pad took the lives of dozens of the program's best engineers, technical specialists and Nedelin himself. For five years the Soviets managed to suffocate all news of the catastrophe. A garbled version appeared in *The Penkovskiy Papers* in 1965. Nothing more came out until 1976, after the emigration of Zhores Medvedev. Now, more than twenty years after the incident, Oberg is in a position to bring us the first full account—or as full an account as can be found outside the memory hole.

Oberg has widened considerably the breach in the wall of secrecy around the Soviet space program that was first opened by Leonid Vladimirov in *Russian Space Bluff,* a book that was dismissed out of hand at NASA and throughout the scientific community until practical experience (in the Apollo-Soyuz flight of 1975) corroborated most of it. It was Vladimirov who first told the story of Korolev, the rocket genius who was responsible for the Soviet Union's initial space triumphs, starting with Sputnik-1. Even his name had been an official state secret. Oberg expands our information concerning this early period and brings the story forward to the present and to what appears to be the Soviets' new grand strategy for space: a permanent orbiting station with military as well as scientific uses.

Oberg is not only a space engineer but a scholar who reads and speaks Russian. His approach to the Soviet program is always measured, never polemical. The skill with which he sifts hard data from hearsay and reconstitutes bits of information from his researches is an exciting process in itself. He is doing the work that Soviet historians should have embarked upon years ago but did not and, of course, never will.

RED STAR
IN ORBIT

1
☆

At Home in Orbit

For the third time in three years, cosmonaut Valeriy Ryumin felt the thrill of the final moments of a half-million-mile space chase. The rendezvous target now lay visible ahead of his spaceship: a starlike jewel above the curved horizon. His instrument panel reported that radar lock-on had been established. The range was just over twelve miles, closing at two miles per minute.

Ryumin, a forty-one-year-old civilian cosmonaut, relayed navigation data to his command pilot, Major Leonid Popov. After a full day of flight, the orbital rendezvous was still proceeding flawlessly and within an hour the two men expected to be linking their Soyuz-35 spacecraft to one of two mooring hatches on the Salyut-6 space laboratory.

But there could be no relaxation until that linkup had been made—as Ryumin knew well from personal bitter experience. On his first attempt to visit the Salyut-6 in October 1977, his Soyuz-25 spaceship had suffered a mechanical failure in its grappling latches, and the mission had been aborted. In February 1979 he had been given a second chance

and had been able to board the space station without incident. But two months later he had been watching through a
porthole as two more cosmonauts made their final approach
for a planned week-long visit; suddenly the flame of their
rocket engine flickered, changed color and died—their mission, too, was aborted at the last moment. Counterbalancing
these two failures, Ryumin knew, were the seven successful
manned linkups (and ten successful robot supply-ship linkups) during the two and a half years of operation of this, the
sixth Salyut space station. The odds of a successful linkup
were good, but Ryumin was by nature a worrier.

His own successful second space mission had ended just
eight months before, when he had returned to earth (along
with his command pilot Vladimir Lyakhov) after spending
half a year in space. During those 175 days the two-man crew
had busied itself with both research and applications activities, photographing earth's surface and atmosphere, producing unique zero-gravity industrial products such as semicon-
ductors, glass ampules and thin metal films, and testing new
techniques for space life support and space navigation. They
had broken all previous flight records (and had in fact *doubled* the longest American endurance run on Skylab), but
even more important, their medical tests and techniques had
smashed the last dragon standing on the road to interplanetary flight: the fear that prolonged exposure to space conditions could cause the body's bone calcium to leak away,
weakening the skeleton to the point of physical collapse
under even the gentlest of stresses. But it didn't happen—the
six-month flight in 1979 showed that decalcification, as the
insidious bone-decay process was called, eased off after three
months in space. That easing off had not been detected by
American astronauts because they had not stayed up long
enough.

Such a space mission should have been more than enough
for any man, and it should then have been the turn of other
cosmonauts to fly into space. Eventually, of course, Ryumin

could have expected to fly again, much later—three years, four years later, perhaps, taking his turn in normal crew-assignment rotation.

But that last landing had been on August 19, 1979, and now it was April 10, 1980. He had leapfrogged the normal wait and had been sent on the first ever back-to-back double space mission.

As the Soyuz passed high above a lonely radio relay ship in the south Atlantic, Ryumin reported on the condition of the spacecraft. The radio operator in Mission Control in Moscow was a thirty-eight-year-old fellow cosmonaut named Valentin Lebedev who, but for a stroke of bad luck, would have been aboard the Soyuz-35 himself—while Ryumin would have been working the radio in Mission Control. Only weeks before the launch, Lebedev had broken his knee in a trampoline mishap, and the only available cosmonaut qualified to take his place with flight commander Popov had been Ryumin. Space doctors confirmed that all physical effects of his recent six-month space flight had disappeared. So, with only a few weeks of warning, he was to blast off again for an even longer space expedition.

After all, that was why Ryumin had originally volunteered to be a cosmonaut seven years before: he wanted to fly in space. Before then, he had been a design engineer in the spacecraft-construction bureau, which was responsible for building the Salyut series of space stations, and he had frequently traveled to the Soviet Central Asian space port at Tyuratam for rocket launchings. In 1973 the opportunity came for him to actually fly—rather than just watch—and he grabbed for the chance: he was picked for cosmonaut training.

A sharp-featured man whose black hair had all the texture and composure of an old steel brush, Ryumin had one physical disability as far as space flight was concerned: he was nearly six feet tall, almost too big to fit comfortably inside Soviet manned space vehicles. But Ryumin had an answer to this: before he had studied electrical engineering at college, he had served in the Red Army as a tank commander—and had learned to squeeze himself into very small spaces. Whatever the effectiveness of that argument, Ryumin was soon accepted for flight training with half a dozen other engineers.

He had proved his worth, first as a member of the Mission Control Center team, then as a cosmonaut communications officer aboard an oceangoing tracking ship. In 1976 he was picked to be on the first crew scheduled to visit the new Salyut-6, and when that linkup failed in October 1977, he was reassigned to the six-month-long follow-on mission in 1979, which was entirely successful.

Now it was just eight months later and Ryumin was on his third space flight and his third visit to Salyut-6. The empty space laboratory was just ahead of them, soaring two hundred miles above earth's surface at a speed of five miles every second; the two-man Soyuz-35 chase ship was approaching from behind and slightly below, with intermittent bursts of its rocket engine slowing it down as the range dropped.

"Dawn, this is Dniepr," radioed the pilot Popov, using the standard call sign for mission control ("Dawn"), and a mission-unique code word for his own flight. (As in many of the earlier missions, this was a geographical place name, in this case the Dniepr River.) "We have the station in view."

The final approach was made as the two vehicles neared earth's shadow so the Salyut could appear bright against a black background. The cosmonauts soon could make out the structure of their future home: a stepwise-tapered cylinder, twice as broad at one end as at the other and four times as long as its greatest breadth. The Salyut's most visually striking features were its three solar-power wings sprouting from its midsection. The wings were silver and glinted in the sunlight; the body itself was covered with dark-green padding dotted with various metal gadgets protruding through that fabric covering. At both ends of the main body were the docking ports, but the cosmonauts could see that the rear port, at the thick end, was already occupied—a robot freighter, Progress-8, had been docked there for two weeks. On board were five thousand pounds of food, water, rocket fuel, spare parts, camera film and other equipment and supplies needed to reopen the Salyut and keep the men provisioned until the next cargo shipment could be sent up.

Ryumin lost sight of the Salyut during the final hundred feet—the only view forward was through the docking periscope, and Popov was staring into it intently. It was Ryumin's job to read off the range and rates from dials on the instrument panel. Forty feet, two feet per second . . . twenty feet, one foot per second . . . ten feet . . . five feet . . . contact! A probe in the nose of the Soyuz was now implanted in a guide cone mounted at the docking part; Ryumin flicked a switch and the probe pulled back into a recess, pulling the Soyuz and Salyut together until a three-foot-diameter tunnel mouth on one vehicle was flush against the other tunnel mouth. Latches lined around the mouth ring were triggered next, and electrical connections were made as plugs slipped into matching sockets.

The cosmonauts relaxed and exchanged congratulations with the Mission Control Center in Moscow. The most difficult task was over, although more hours of work lay ahead before they could enter the station. (The time would be mostly taken up with checking the airtightness of the tunnel into the Salyut, and with confirming via instrument readings that the atmosphere within the station was still breathable.) When Ryumin finally opened the hatches into the Salyut, turned on the lights and floated through the tunnel, he reported with delight, "There's no change—it's just like we left it!"

It was past midnight before the men unrolled the sleeping bags hung along the "ceiling" and crawled into them. They still were full of nervous energy, and the strange sounds of the spacecraft—the hums, whirrs, clicks and disconcerting creaks—kept waking them up. Physical adjustment to weightlessness also made them uncomfortable: they suffered from dizziness, nasal congestion and headaches, and after their first night's fitful sleep on board, they faced breakfast with no appetite and not a little nausea. But Ryumin knew the discomfort and clumsiness would pass in a few days, and he encouraged Popov to take things easy. There was going to be plenty of time!

There was a lot to be learned about living aboard the Salyut, but Ryumin was the best man in the world—and out of it—to be the teacher. As the days passed, he showed Popov all the aspects of life in space that could only be talked about down on earth: how large the station really was when you could point your head and body any direction that was convenient; how the zero-gravity toilet really worked and how easy it was to make an embarrassing and time-consuming mess; how one's arms tended to float in front of one's face while sleeping (one cosmonaut had experienced momentary terror when he awoke to perceive two open hands reaching for his throat—the hands were his own); how to fill a trash bag with the day's garbage and toilet filters without wasting space or spilling anything—and how to keep the ejected trash bag in sight out the window for hours as it slowly drifted away to eventual incineration; how to do complex free-fall calisthentics and gymnastics that would have made Olga Korbut weep with envy to see.

Besides following the official checklists for "de-mothballing" the Salyut, Ryumin made his own personal alterations to the living arrangements in the space station. He unhooked his sleeping bag from the assigned cranny on the ceiling and attached it to a bare section of the floor—since the planned sleeping space was too short for his six-foot length and he knew that in the absence of weight his spine was going to stretch a few more inches over the coming months. He detached the guitar from its improvised storage space, unwrapped it and began tuning it carefully. (It had been a surprise shipment to fellow-cosmonaut "Sasha" Ivanchenkov two years before, when engineers noticed that the cargo hold of a scheduled robot supply ship had some excess volume left over.) Ryumin carefully taped the large photographs of his wife and children onto convenient wall surfaces. The station's library of technical manuals and instruction books was carefully laid out across one entire passageway wall, the documents held in place by elastic cords crisscrossing the panel.

Amid the hectic work involving the reactivation of the space station, the cosmonauts had to take a few hours off for a special space ceremony. April 12 was Cosmonaut Day, the nineteenth anniversary of the first manned space flight. The crew sent ceremonial greetings to earth during which Popov told a live nationwide broadcast: "April 12 marks the date on which mankind's most cherished dream came true and also marks the triumph of Soviet science and technology." The young cosmonaut intoned the words reverently, conjuring up memories of that glorious day in 1961 when twenty-seven-year old Major Yuriy Gagarin rode the spaceship Vostok once around the world in one hundred and eight minutes.

During rare, quiet moments later in the flight, Ryumin had reasons to contemplate other Vostok anniversaries over the years. Only a year before, he himself had been aboard the Salyut on his second space mission; it had been the first Cosmonaut Day since Gagarin's flight that another cosmonaut had been in space. Now in 1980 this was the second year in a row in which Russian cosmonauts had been able to send Cosmonaut Day greetings live from outer space.

Considering the pace of the Soviet manned space effort, Ryumin might have been able to conclude that a new pattern was being established. The odds were that cosmonauts would be in space on the next Cosmonaut Day, too, and the next, and the next.

In fact, as Ryumin considered the recent successes of the Salyut-6 space station, the time could not have seemed far off when Soviet cosmonauts would always be in space, when there would never again be a day that there were not people in orbit above earth. Space would become permanently occupied—and Russians would be the ones to do it. They had believed in the dream, symbolized by Cosmonaut Day, and they had worked and suffered to realize that dream.

In the near solitude of space (Ryumin liked to spend some time every day off in a small compartment by himself), the cosmonaut may have been able to feel the ghostly presence of many of his space-faring predecessors who had paid terrible prices—often with no progress to show for it. Some of these men he knew only by reputation and others had been lifelong friends. Amid the successes of his own space mission, their fates could have reminded him of the human costs of the past.

There was Anatoliy, slated to be Russia's third man in space in 1962, who stoically refused to cry out as the centrifuge overloads tore his internal organs apart—and who, thus crippled, was discarded from the space program, his face erased from official cosmonaut group portraits . . .

There was Volodya, who, having accepted one space challenge too many, reported by radio on his efforts to straighten his plummeting capsule's tangled parachute—until the radio signal was snuffed out simultaneously with his life . . .

There was Yuriy, transformed before his death at thirty-four from a personable, cocky jet pilot into a demigod to be worshiped, emulated and protected from all risk and adventure until his own attempts to break out from the protective walls around him went just a little too far . . .

There was Ivan, a cosmonaut candidate of exceptional promise, whose parachute didn't open on a simple training jump one autumn—and whose name therefore never became a household word, whose soon-forgotten grave lies bereft of the wreaths of flowers which continuously bedeck the memorials to fallen "real" cosmonauts . . .

There was Dmitriy, spending the best ten years of his life watching and waiting as his younger colleagues literally climbed toward the stars—only to be told at the end that he was now too old and he could leave, thank you very much . . .

There was Pavel, dying on an antiseptic hospital operating table, his dreams of the moon turned into an agonizing nightmare of tension and heartbreak, which at last broke his body as well . . .

There was Vadim, who helped design the space equipment which ultimately killed him—and who probably spent the last moments of his life working out a way of fixing the fatal flaws which had left him and his shipmates trying to breathe vacuum . . .

There was Vladimir, cursing the broken space equipment which had frustrated two of his space linkups, returning to earth bent on reforming the whole cosmonaut training program—and succeeding, to become the kind of politically minded bureaucrat he had once despised . . .

There was Vasiliy, a tragic hulk of a man whose double background in medicine and test piloting made him the foremost candidate for space-station duty—but who was smashed down by a wave of unbelievably bad luck until he was stalled in his own bitterness, condemned to a desk job to train lesser men for space missions he had been denied.

Their full names filled a roster of men who had been in the vanguard of space exploration, and who had suffered an appallingly high casualty rate. Anatoliy Maslennikov, Vladimir "Volodya" Komarov, Yuriy Gagarin, Ivan Korniev, Dmitriy Ivanov, Pavel Belyayev, Vladislav "Vadim" Volkov, Vladimir Shatalov, Vasiliy Lazarev—good Russian names which have faded from the headlines into the dusty history books, or which, for "reasons of state security," cannot even now be published. But Ryumin knew many of them, and knew of the others—and he remembered their courage and their confidence, and their commitment to space travel.

It all reminded Valeriy Ryumin in 1980 that the heights through which Salyut-6 was both metaphorically and actually flying were, above all, a triumph of men rather than of machines or of ideologies. The boosters and capsules had often faltered and failed, crushing or suffocating or burning the frail human bodies inside, but there had always been more men willing to take the next flight. The vain pursuit of temporary political advantage, or of brief public glory, had frequently sent the space engineers and cosmonauts down long, dangerous detours, but the men had remembered the real goals, however often their course had been marked by blood or twisted by "orders from above." Now, nearly twenty years after the first Soviet manned space shots, the program seemed finally to have come out right. This time, the men, the machines and the political directives were all running harmoniously and parallel toward a common goal.

And that was a real reason for special celebration of Cosmonaut Day 1980. The Soviet manned space program had survived and finally triumphed over obstacles both technological and political. The goal—permanently occupied space stations in orbit above earth, as a stepping stone to flight to other worlds and the establishment of large space colonies—was within reach. The failures and tragedies involving many of Ryumin's predecessors had in some ways helped bring the goal into focus; the successes and triumphs of Ryumin's generation of cosmonauts had gone on from there, and fulfilled the dreams.

Since months of work aboard Salyut-6 lay ahead, Ryumin wanted to get off on the right foot with Mission Control. On the morning of their first day aboard the space station, he had held a large cucumber up in front of the TV camera and addressed an astonished Moscow space center: "We looked at our kitchen garden when we came on board yesterday, and we picked an excellent harvest," Ryumin announced, revealing the unexpected news that seeds left in the garden had sprouted and grown during the eight months he had been away. "We've eaten one already because we had to check on the quality. I must say it was excellent."

The ground specialists were astonished and grabbed their blueprints and logbooks. Could the garden have been left on accidentally? Weren't all the seeds accounted for? Hadn't Ryumin followed the proper procedure the previous August during the "power-down" of the Salyut?

Their consternation and confusion lasted only a few moments. Popov drifted into view on the TV screen and, together with Ryumin, began laughing out loud. Everyone soon realized it was Ryumin's idea of a joke. "We brought this beauty up in our luggage," he confessed, biting into it with gusto. A relieved laughter echoed in the control center.

The mood had been set. The mission was going to be tough on the men and the machines, but the men were upbeat—and the machines, while worn and in need of repair, could be handled by Ryumin's experience and Popov's enthusiastic energy.

2

☆

The Birth of
Sputnik

During the first week of October 1957, an international scientific conference was drawing to a close in Washington, D.C. One of the attendees at that conference was an American scientist who was born in Russia and had served as an officer in the tsarist navy until the Bolshevik Revolution forced him to flee. Constantine, as I will call him, was a long-time enthusiast of space exploration. He had read all of the works of Konstantin Tsiolkovskiy, Nikolay Rynin and other Russian space visionaries, and he chose the subject of space flight at the conference to tease the Soviet scientists.

The hundredth anniversary of Tsiolkovskiy's birth had been marked only a few weeks before. "Poor Tsiolkovskiy is turning in his grave," the ex-tsarist officer taunted. "His hundredth birthday has passed without even one Russian artificial earth satellite in orbit. Under the Tsar we would have had several of them long before now and would have celebrated the anniversary with a flight to the moon."

Most of the Soviet scientists took no offense at his ribbing, but one official, after attempting to restrain himself, finally blurted out, "Just you wait and see!" Constantine, sensing that he had touched a nerve, pressed his attack: "That's easy for you to say, but you are returning to Moscow next Sunday"—that would be October 6, just two days away. The man retorted, "It will be before then—you'll eat your words." Constantine, surprised by the man's confidence, realized he had uncovered something significant.

Suspicions that the Soviets were about to embark on some spectacular space venture had been aroused even before the conference, ever since they had claimed that, like the Americans, they, too, were preparing to launch scientific satellites as part of the International Geophysical Year. Two months before, they had announced the successful flight of an intercontinental ballistic missile, an ideal booster rocket for such a space probe; only days before, they had quietly released the radio frequencies at which their *sputnik* (Russian for satellite) would soon be transmitting.

Other people at the Washington conference also came to the conclusion that something would soon break. Walter Sullivan, a *New York Times* science correspondent, had picked up several such rumors and had researched all the earlier hints and speculations. Late that Friday afternoon he submitted a story to the New York news desk for publication in Saturday morning's edition (October 5). The space shot, Sullivan had written, could come "at any time." The dateline on his story was Friday, October 4, 1957. The story was never printed.

Instead, in Saturday's *New York Times,* under a three-level full-page banner headline saved for particularly earth-shaking events, was the news from Moscow: the satellite, Sputnik-1, had been launched late Friday, Moscow time; probably it had happened at about the same time that Sullivan was drafting his article and Constantine was teasing his Russian colleagues. Sullivan did not learn of the launching until late that evening; however, the Russian official's blurted boast had intrigued Constantine so much that he passed the story to some friends of his at the Naval Research Laboratory outside of Washington. They immediately tuned in their radio equipment to the frequencies which had been published a few days earlier—and within hours were picking up the signals from the satellite even before its launching had been announced in Moscow.

The launching of Sputnik-1 is a convenient milestone at which to mark the birth of the space age and the subsequent space race between the United States and the Soviet Union. But to appreciate all the dimensions of that fascinating development, the roots of Sputnik must be traced in detail. How it was launched—that was a technological question soon answered. Who were the men who had launched it—that, too, was answered, although this question was more difficult. But why was the project carried out? Only after a quarter century can we really answer that question.

The careers of two exceptional men are intertwined in the development of the Sputnik project and the subsequent space-flight explosion, which took men to the moon only twelve years afterward and set up permanent outer-space outposts within a quarter of a century. These men were Nikita Sergeyevich Khrushchev, the former miner, party bureaucrat, purge master and canny political manipulator, and Sergey Pavlovich Korolev, the engineer, pilot, GULag survivor, rocket magician and, finally, master of the embryonic Soviet space program. The Sputnik and the space age were born from the combination (and often conflict) of these two men's needs and capabilities.

The life of Korolev falls into several distinct phases. It has been frustratingly difficult to untangle the threads of adulation, cover-up and falsehood that have been wrapped around him by official biographers. The first phase of his life, which can be styled his "apprenticeship," has been described in a fairly straightforward manner even in the official chronologies—but it stops abruptly in 1938, when Korolev (then aged thirty-two) was swallowed up into the monstrosity of the GULag Archipelago so vividly documented by Robert Conquest and Aleksandr Solzhenitsyn. For the next fifteen years of his life, the most that Moscow has made available is a careful selection of isolated impressions and half-truths, with many years passed over in silence. Korolev emerges again as a real person in the mid-1950s, but with one particular drawback: while he was alive (he died in 1966), Khrushchev kept him anonymous, referring to him only as the "chief designer" and allowing him to publish only under the pseudonym "Sergeyev"; when his existence was finally acknowledged after a solemn state funeral, Khrushchev's turn had come to be deleted from the Soviet loose-leaf history books, and *he* was never thereafter referred to in relation to the development of the Soviet space plans in the 1950s. So a complete and honest appraisal of this relationship has never been published inside the Soviet Union.

Korolev's early life in the Ukraine, his studies at an aeronautics institute run by the great airplane designer Tupolev in Moscow and his amateur enthusiasm for flying homemade gliders have been well documented even in Soviet accounts. By the mid-1930s, just before his thirtieth birthday, he switched his spare-time enthusiasms from glider design to rocket propulsion research; he joined a small group led by the Latvian engineer Friedrich Zander. Their unofficial organization was named GIRD, which nominally stood for Group Studying Rocket Propulsion—but in recognition of the fact that they received no official support and had to acquire all of their materials from their own resources, they often jokingly referred to themselves as the Group Working for Nothing, which worked out to the same letters in Russian.

During this period, Korolev earned his living as a professional engineer designing aircraft in the bureau run by Tupolev, one of Russia's greatest aeronautical engineers and the creator of the line of aircraft bearing the Tu prefix—the Tu-20 *(Bear),* Tu-16 *(Badger),* Tu-56 *(Blinder)* and the supersonic Tu-144, as examples. But Korolev's enthusiasms were aimed at higher targets, and he avidly read books on rocketry and space travel. In 1934 he visited the home of Russia's revered space prophet, Konstantin Tsiolkovskiy (or Ziolkowsky—his father was a Polish lumberjack who had moved to Russia), and met briefly with the great man himself. Within a year, Tsiolkovskiy had died—but his dreams lived on in many Russians, including Korolev.

Rocketry research, meanwhile, took a great leap forward when it received the official blessing of Soviet Armaments Minister Mikhail N. Tukhachevskiy, who was intrigued by the possibility of rocket weapons. He was also apparently a genuine enthusiast about the concept of space travel, which, of course, would be accomplished by Soviet pioneers! So GIRD suddenly received a substantial budget and several full-time employees, first among them being Korolev, who was granted a commission of general-engineer (one star) in the Red Army.

Under the patronage of Tukhachevskiy, rocket research flourished. In 1933 the first free flight of a Russian-made liquid-fuel rocket took place at an army base near Nakhabino, outside of Moscow. Development continued for several years, spurred on by reports of the work of Robert Goddard in the United States (where it was ignored by the government and by the academic community) and of a group of German engineers. But this embryonic three-way space race ended disastrously for the Russian side in 1937.

The Stalin purges had been ravaging the nation's intelligentsia, while the collectivization drives were wiping out millions of peasants—but Korolev and his team no doubt felt safe under the wing of the highest-ranking Soviet military officer in the Red Army. But they were fooling themselves: Tukhachevskiy was suddenly arrested on June 10, 1937, and his whole staff followed him into prison and to their deaths. Stalin evidently suspected him of "Bonapartist" tendencies, believing perhaps that forty-three-year-old Tukhachevskiy planned to overthrow the Communist party and set up a military dictatorship. Stalin's distrust was also evidently fueled by falsified documentation implicating Tukhachevskiy, documentation prepared and planted by German agents. The politics of this episode remain obscure, but the effect on the fledgling Soviet rocket program was immediately obvious: annihilation.

All of Tukhachevskiy's favorite projects were automatically suspect since they no doubt would be staffed by numerous pro-Tukhachevskiy people. Stalin's secret police took no chances: everyone within reach was arrested. Korolev's life nearly ended—his official biographies stutter at this point and leap many years into the future.

A former fellow prisoner of Korolev's recounted how the future chief designer was initially interrogated by the secret police at Butyrskaya Prison in Moscow: "Your pyrotechnics and fireworks are not only unnecessary to our country but are actually dangerous," he was told. To protect the country Korolev was shipped off in a boxcar with a number and a life term. There were millions like him in those years, and most of them died.

Information about this phase of his life must be gathered from a number of independent (and, of course, unofficial) sources. However, defecting Soviet science writer Leonid Vladimirov has listed a series of oblique references which have made their ways into official books. Other sources are the *samizdat* underground newsletters which circulated in Moscow in the late 1960s and early 1970s. *Chronicle of Current Events,* number 10, issued October 31, 1969, criticized Politizdat (Political Publishing House) because a new book by A. Romanov about Sergey Pavlovich Korolev was deliberately incomplete: "There is no mention of the fact that Korolev was arrested and subjugated to repressive measures, nor of what became of Korolev's immediate teachers and close friends."

Throughout his prison term Korolev was described by former comrades as "absolutely firm, never disguising his contempt for the regime." Another Russian engineer who knew him in prison described him as "a cynic and a pessimist" whose favorite slogan was "We will all vanish without a trace." The closest any work has come to an official admission of this imprisonment was a fairly honest biography of Korolev by Yaroslav Golovanov, who made this suggestive comment when referring to Korolev's work in the 1930s: "He could not then by any means know that there would be many very hard times, sometimes cruelly unjust to him." Golovanov's ambiguity may have been fueled by Korolev's own utter refusal to discuss that period with strangers: "Several times I led the conversation round to his past," Golovanov wrote in 1967. "But as far as I remember, he did not like this theme and always tried to switch our talk in another direction."

Well could he have wished to avoid such themes, especially about the events of 1937. For months he had been packed in a boxcar heading eastward along the Trans-Siberian Railroad, only to be transferred at the Pacific coast into the crowded hold of a prison ship. The final destination was the east Siberian port of Magadan, staging area for the Kolyma gold mines, an infamous charnel house even by GULag standards. But back in Moscow a card with his number on it had been filed in a box in some police archive —and, as if by a miracle, he survived a full year at Kolyma before receiving a reprieve in the form of an order back to a special prison in Moscow.

As it turned out, Tupolev had saved him. The aircraft designer and his entire staff had also been arrested but had been locked up in a special prison, a *sharashka,* as the inmates called it, where they continued their engineering work on military projects. Korolev's time there was mentioned in Solzhenitsyn's documentation: "The father of space navigation, Korolev, was taken into a *sharashka* as an aviation scientist. The *sharashka* administration did not allow him to work on rockets and he had to do that work at night."

Tupolev had been instructed to gather together any other of his engineers who had been scattered throughout the GULag, and it was his request for Korolev (and the officiousness of some secret-police bureaucrat who was actually able to trace Korolev's sentence) that had snatched him to the relative safety of the *sharashka*.

Korolev spent several years in the prison near Moscow while World War II was ignited and Germany invaded Russia. As the Wehrmacht neared Moscow, the Tupolev group was evacuated (still under guard—there was always the chance they might try to escape and join the Nazis!) to Omsk. Korolev had been there for only a few months when he was transferred to Special Prison Number 4 (location unknown), where a group was working on rocket-assisted airplane takeoff systems, on bombardment rockets, on an in-flight emergency acceleration rocket for conventional aircraft and on pure rocket- and jet-propelled aircraft. The engineer in charge of the unit was Valentin Glushko, an old friend and colleague of Korolev's from the GIRD days who had somehow struck a deal with the secret police and was now a free man.

The team worked for four years on these projects, with Korolev serving as Glushko's deputy for flight testing. After the war ended, Korolev's position improved, although he was still nominally a prisoner serving a life term for treason.

He and Glushko were assigned to a new rocket group under the command of an opportunistic and ambitious engineer named Chelomey (or Chalomei—sources disagree on the spelling).

When Glushko went to Germany in 1946 to study captured V-2 equipment (the first trainload of material from Peenemünde had been hijacked by Americans and replaced with wrecked farm machinery), he took Korolev along— under heavy guard. They both attended a British-sponsored test launch of an extra V-2 from the Baltic town of Altenwaide ("Operation Backfire"), but Korolev's name had not been officially submitted to the British site commander—perhaps because the Soviet secret police would not let him out of their direct custody—so he was forced to watch the test from outside the barbed-wire compound.

When Glushko returned to Russia, Korolev remained in Germany (no doubt under appropriate supervision) to direct the repair of the underground V-2 factory at Niedersachswerfen and to coordinate the shipment of V-2 equipment to the Soviet Union. He escorted the last shipment back to Russia in the summer of 1946 and supervised some test firings at a Soviet missile range on the lower Volga River, not far from Stalingrad. Korolev then returned to the Russian zone of Germany, where he interviewed dozens of former V-2 engineers and technicians (he was self-taught in German and English). Having prepared a list of useful Germans, he turned it over to Soviet security forces—and on the night of October 22–23, 1946, soldiers rounded up everyone on the list for immediate departure for Russia. There they were split into numerous design teams and put to work on various research programs; most did not return to Germany until 1950–1951.

The Russians, meanwhile, pursued their own rocket research with their own surviving experts. The German teams were used for collateral research or to cross-check each other and confirm Russian developments, and were never integrated into the mainline Russian development program. The first all-Russian ballistic missile, code-named the R-1, was created under the leadership of Korolev in late 1947; somehow Glushko returned to his subservient position and was in charge of the rocket engine while Korolev directed the entire project. Eleven test flights in October and November 1947 marked the resumption of forward motion of Korolev's dreams for space flight. He was even called to the Kremlin to personally brief Stalin on the military missile program.

Golovanov, the most candid of the official biographers,

made a poignant commentary on Korolev's life during this period, a comment that could not be fully appreciated without knowing about the GULag years. "Korolev was a most exact reflection of an epoch," wrote Golovanov in 1968. "He has become part of it, it would seem, forever and imperishably. He knew all its triumphs and drained the cup of its bitterness to the dregs. Korolev's biography is the concretization of the history of our land in one man . . ."

After a few years of near freedom, Korolev may have been thrown back into prison. Some of his former colleagues have reported that he was sent back in a *sharashka* in 1948 (although other reliable sources make no mention of this second incarceration). These special prisons have been eloquently described by the Russian novelist Solzhenitsyn in his *First Circle*. (According to Dante, the first circle was the highest and least uncomfortable circle of Hell.) Many observers regard a peripheral character in Chapter 17, a man named Bobynin, to be based on Korolev himself during his second imprisonment. In one bristling retort to a Soviet army interrogator, Bobynin/Korolev expressed the thoughts which might have gotten him into prison in the first place—and certainly kept him there:

> "We could make you talk."
> "You are wrong, Citizen Minister!" Bobynin's strong eyes shone with hate. "I have nothing, you understand, nothing! You can't get your hands on my wife and child—a bomb got them first. My parents are already dead. My entire property on this earth is my handkerchief; my coveralls and my underwear are government issue. You took my freedom away long ago, and you don't have the power to return it because you don't have it yourself. I am forty-two years old [so was Korolev], and you've dished me out a twenty-five-year term. I've already been at hard labor, gone around with a number on, in handcuffs, with police dogs, and a strict-regime work brigade. What else is there you can threaten me with? What can you deprive me of? My work as an engineer? You'll lose more than I will . . ."

Only two circumstances need revising to convert the fictional Bobynin into the authentic Korolev. First, Korolev's mother was still alive (and, indeed, was to survive him by more than fifteen years). Also, his wife and child were alive—but separated from him. In 1946, upon regaining his freedom for the first time, Korolev had divorced his first wife, Oxana (or Xenia) Vincentini. (Their one daughter had been born about 1935.) She had apparently yielded to pressure and had denounced him while he was at Kolyma, and then had never communicated with him again. The next year, 1947, Korolev had remarried, to Nina Kotenkova.

Following Stalin's death in 1953, Korolev was rehabilitated, along with hundreds of thousands of other purge victims. In Korolev's case, he was offered membership in the Communist party, and whatever his personal feelings, he knew it would increase his political influence—so he accepted. Korolev was also quickly rewarded for his previous work by election to the Soviet Academy of Sciences, first as a corresponding member (there are about three hundred) and soon afterward as a full member (of which there are about one hundred and fifty).

His rapid rise in the post-Stalin years may not have been based purely on merit: it was Khrushchev's policy not merely to rehabilitate purge victims, but to promote many of them above others who had gone along with Stalin's regime, thus providing Khrushchev with cadres of ready-made loyalists who owed their new positions to him—and would *fall* with him.

The new field of military missiles was one which obviously required careful watching. Russia's need for modern rocket weapons had become indisputable, and even before Stalin's death, industrial organizations had been set up to produce the new equipment. In mid-1953 a new organization called the Ministry for Medium Machine Building was founded, with the sole purpose of directing the manufacture of missiles. Some junior members of the Soviet government were assigned to maintain liaison between the engineers and the politicians. One was Dmitriy Ustinov, a young but highly competent armaments manager; the other was Leonid Brezhnev, an engineer turned politician.

Khrushchev first met Korolev when the "collective leadership" which followed Stalin's death in 1953 tried to grapple with the issue of the new rocket weapons. Stalin had favored such rockets because Tupolev's airplane bureau had been unable to design bombers with ranges sufficiently great to reach the United States—powerful missiles promised to overcome this restriction. (Korolev had taken charge of the project after his rehabilitation.) But as Khrushchev later admitted in his memoirs, the new leaders had been kept in the dark by Stalin and knew very little about rockets at all: "Korolev came to the Politburo meeting to report on his work. I don't want to exaggerate, but I'd say we gawked at what he showed us as if we were sheep seeing a new gate for the first time. When he showed us one of his rockets, we thought it looked like nothing but a huge cigar-shaped tube, and we didn't believe it would fly. Korolev took us on a tour of the launching pad and tried to explain to us how a rocket worked. We were like peasants in a marketplace. We walked around the rocket, touching it, tapping it to see if it was sturdy enough—we did everything but lick it to see how it tasted. . . . We had absolute confidence in Comrade Korolev. When he expounded his ideas, you could see passion burning in his eyes, and his reports were always models of clarity. He had unlimited energy and determination, and he was a brilliant organizer."

This impression of Korolev was a common one. Biographers both inside and outside the Soviet Union seem to paint a consistent portrait of Korolev's character. For example, another official biographer, Pyotr Astashenkov, wrote: "Korolev combined an excellent theoretical background, scientific foresight and organizing ability with the determination to fight hard for his ideas." Romanov's 1968 biography was even more graphic: "I study the scientist: a high and handsome forehead, as though intentionally modeled by a sculptor in order to emphasize the unusual qualities of this uncommon man. Black eyebrows, on the straight side. Over-wide and deep-set brown eyes. Energy blazes in them. At different times I have seen them angry and kind, raging and mocking, determined and good-natured. But in many years of knowing the man I have never seen them empty or indif-ferent. The mouth is firmly delineated, the corners down-turned, the chin juts forward. Taken all together, the appear-ance of the person sitting before me conveys tremendous energy, power, authority."

A former colleague, writing in the freer atmosphere of Yugoslavia, where he had taken political refuge, cor-roborated that image: "Korolev had great authority and commanded respect from those with whom he worked," wrote Sergey Korda in an obituary in 1966. "A man of inex-haustible energy, he combined great talent, excellent engi-neering intuition and surprising creative boldness with out-standing administrative capabilities and high spiritual values."

But a few words of caution are in order. Golovanov, most honest of the official biographers, pointed out that "there is no need to idealize Korolev. He was tough and harsh but cold and daring, sly and cunning but not devious. He was blunt, but he knew his business. And the main thing about him was his ideal."

That ideal, of course, was space exploration. But to achieve that purpose, to send men into space, as he had been planning for years, and to send probes to the moon and nearby planets, he needed an immense budget—and Khrush-chev was the one he had to persuade. Getting funding for military missiles was one thing, but for space projects—that was an entirely different matter.

In 1956 his first attempts to get approval for an earth satellite project were rebuffed. As he later recounted it, "We closely followed reports on the building in the United States of an artificial earth satellite with the suggestive name of 'Vanguard.' At that time some people believed that this satellite would be the first in outer space. . . . We took stock of what we had, and decided that we could send a good hundred kilograms into orbit. So we went to the Central Committee of the Communist party. There we were told that the idea was attractive but needed more thought."

Even without approval for the satellite project, Korolev continued work on the R-7 rocket (in Russian, it was affectionately known as "ol' number seven," or *semyorka*), the giant missile designed to carry a bulky two-ton thermonuclear bomb more than four thousand miles, far enough to reach the United States. As it turned out, the *semyorka* was a very inefficient military missile but an excellent space booster, which is probably what Korolev had in mind all along.

To test this giant new rocket, with a lift-off thrust of more than one million pounds (three times that of its American counterpart, the Atlas), an entirely new missile test range was needed. Construction began in June 1955 near the Aral Sea, north of the small village of Tyuratam in Kazakhstan. The party secretary of Kazakhstan at that time was Leonid Brezhnev, and he took great interest in the development of the missile project. So did the American CIA: before the concrete on the launch pad was dry, U-2 spy planes were flying overhead to keep tabs on the project.

The first R-7 exploded on launch in the late spring of 1957. Several more attempts also ended catastrophically, and by July 1957 Korolev was facing serious criticism from rival rocket experts (particularly the engineer Chelomey) and from Moscow bureaucrats; his satellite project looked hopeless. According to a thinly disguised but highly sanitized semi-biographical movie (*The Taming of Fire*, Mosfilm, 1972), Korolev counterattacked: "You think only Atlas missiles can explode? We are building the most powerful machines in the world!" His reference to the Atlas explosion during its first launch on June 11 helps date this comment (if the comment is authentic) and the R-7 failures which preceded it; the statement must also have preceded August 3, when the first successful launch was finally accomplished. A second success followed a few weeks later, when the missile was sent full range into the Pacific near the Kamchatka peninsula (and not too far from the Kolyma gold mines where Korolev had slaved in 1938–1939).

Meanwhile, fireworks had also been going off in the Kremlin. The position of Khrushchev as "first among equals" in the collective leadership was rapidly deteriorating as his colleagues found unexpected unity in a common fear of Khrushchev's growing power. While using a campaign of anti-Stalinism to combat his rivals, and by flaunting the success of his bold (his rivals styled it "reckless") crushing of the October 1956 rebellion in Hungary, Khrushchev reached for total and undisputed power. The showdown came in June 1957, when several Khrushchev allies were absent from Moscow: the anti-Khrushchev forces on the Politburo demanded a debate on the ouster of Khrushchev from his official posts, and then voted six to one to replace him with Shepilov. (Malenkov, Molotov and Kaganovich led the fight against him, and when he appeared to have lost, Bulganin joined the opposition; loyalists Suslov, Mikoyan and others had been out of town on party business when the meeting was convened, as the conspirators had planned.) But Khrushchev maneuvered adroitly and delayed certain official actions until a full Central Committee meeting could be convened. Meanwhile, he called upon Red Army leader Zhukov to organize an airlift of loyalists (and detours of unreliables) from all over the Soviet Union to the showdown vote in Moscow—which he then won.

His victory, while sweet, must have been incomplete. No doubt he suspected continued disaffection within the party apparatus, even as he drove the leaders of the revolt into retirement or obscurity. No doubt he also feared having given Zhukov a taste of power, since Zhukov, the victorious general of World War II, was a far more popular figure than Khrushchev, not only among the armed forces but also within the party hierarchy itself. Lest Zhukov move to grasp full political power (as his American counterpart, Eisenhower, already had—or so Khrushchev may have reasoned by analogy), he was the next target for elimination.

At the same time, Khrushchev was genuinely concerned about perceived military threats from the United States. If Russians in general seem to be paranoid about foreign invasions, they have also really been the victims of countless such invasions and attacks. From the Russian point of view, the American bases near their borders, combined with belligerent statements from American officials, were cause for genuine alarm. A way of reducing Russia's susceptibility to attack was the development of a credible deterrent system, such as nuclear-tipped missiles—but such a deterrent is useful only so far as it is believable, and any Russian claim to have invented such a device would probably be laughed off along with previous claims to the invention of airplanes, steam engines, radio, tractors and decimal coinage.

In the light of these domestic and international problems, Korolev's proposal for a Soviet artificial satellite (to be launched by an R-7 missile with a reduced payload) suddenly became much more attractive to Khrushchev. First, it would signal to dissident political forces within the Soviet Union that Khrushchev was really leading the country to a glorious future; second, it would overawe the traditionalist "artillery generals" in the Red Army and allow a reorganization of the armed forces, including a reduction in obsolete ground forces (saving money and pulling the rug out from under possible opposition leaders); last, it would demonstrate in an unequivocal manner the existence of the long-range missile system, which was intended to discourage a potential attack from the United States. Under these circumstances, what had at first appeared to be a pointless diversion of technical resources suddenly became—as far as Khrushchev personally was concerned—a powerful idea. And so, as Korolev later recounted, "in the summer of 1957, the Central Committee [a euphemism for Khrushchev, who by that time exercised full power] finally endorsed the project." It should be noted that neither science nor world opinion seems to have entered into consideration.

If approval for the satellite project came after the first successful R-7 launches in mid-August, Korolev's team had only one month to go before the hundredth anniversary of Tsiolkovskiy's birth. (That anniversary would have meant little to Khrushchev anyway.) It took them, instead, about six weeks—and Korolev literally lived at the launch pad to accomplish this.

The concrete stand from which the satellite would be launched stood at the edge of a two-hundred-foot-deep, half-mile-wide pit, a natural bay in a high ridge which crossed the missile center. Railway lines ran south from the pad to an assembly building about a mile away; there the missile was assembled horizontally (from sections shipped by rail from Moscow) on a railroad flatcar before being hauled out to the pad, erected and fueled for launch.

Halfway between the assembly building and the pad was a grove of trees surrounding a natural spring. In that grove Korolev had built a small wood-frame house for his own personal use. He would meet there with his deputies, or would walk fifteen minutes to the assembly hall in one direction or ten minutes to the launch pad in the other direction. Workers knew that Korolev could—and did—drop in at any time of the day or night; he did not sleep much.

There were other workers at the missile center whom Korolev could not visit, even though he knew them well. They were the men who had poured the concrete, excavated the bunkers and erected the buildings in which the rockets were being assembled. But the color of their drab clothing, and the color of the uniforms of their guards, identified these men as *zeks,* political prisoners among whose ranks Korolev had spent many, many years. Their work, too, contributed to Korolev's dream of the conquest of space—and no record exists of how he felt about their presence or what he could do (if anything) for them. They, too, must have been on his mind in those hectic weeks.

A simple test satellite was thrown together in one of the smaller machine shops in the assembly building. It consisted of a radio transmitter hooked up to a thermometer and powered by a pack of chemical batteries. The object was affectionately known as the "PS," the preliminary satellite—and this caused some confusion among many newly arrived engineers, since Korolev himself was known to his men as "old SP," for Sergey Pavlovich. The two nicknames *"espeh"* and *"peh-yess"* were often mixed together indiscriminately in those weeks, their intimate interrelationship blending in the minds of the workers into one entity. It *was* Korolev, or a significant part of him, who would be riding on that rocket.

Finally the payload was attached to the nose of the rocket as it lay on its carrier inside the assembly hall. As the nose cone was slid into place, a technician flipped a switch on the PS, activating its radio system. Someone had brought a shortwave radio into the hall, and the *beep-beep-beep* of the future Sputnik echoed strangely around the suddenly silent rocket specialists. The nose cone slid into place and the radio receiver was turned off; the men surged back to action.

Korolev took his place inside the command bunker, a steel-walled room built right into the concrete launch pad, about three hundred feet from the rocket itself. Some men watched the rocket through periscopes, while others monitored dials and meters. Korolev sat at a wooden desk, a white lab coat over his work clothes and a microphone in his hand.

As the countdown neared zero, a lone figure suddenly appeared on the concrete apron and blew a series of long trumpet blasts before vanishing back to his duty post. Nobody ever revealed who it was, and it might have been Korolev himself.

The sun had long since set when the count reached zero after many exasperating delays. The firing command was given and an automatic sequence of pump activation began; moments later, the engines lifted off, dazzling the watchers at the periscopes and temporarily deafening the occupants of the control blockhouse. Then the PS was on its way; within four minutes it was only a tiny spot of light in the northeastern sky.

During the ascent, twenty separate engines in five long pods fired in unison. The central cylinder held the satellite in its nose, while four tapered cylinders were attached to its sides in "parallel staging." The tapered units exhausted their fuel first and peeled away like a flower unfolding its petals; the thicker central stage continued burning for another five minutes until it was soaring at more than 18,000 miles per hour, two hundred miles above earth's surface. Gravity still pulled the now freely falling PS back toward earth on a descending arc—but so great was its speed (as Korolev had calculated) that the horizon of a spherical earth receded from the falling object at the same rate. PS was in orbit above the atmosphere. It was 1930 hours Greenwich mean time (2:30 in the afternoon in Washington, and 10:30 at night in Moscow); an hour and a half later, the PS finished its first circumnavigation of its home planet, announcing its success to radio listeners via its distinctive radio call sign.

Korolev's rocket team assembled at the still-smoking launch pad to await the news from the tracking site. The soon-to-be-famous *beep-beep-beep* was played over the pad speakers and the men cheered. Korolev stood up on an improvised rostrum and addressed his colleagues with a speech that, although impromptu, had probably been part of his daydreaming most of his life. "Today the dreams of the best sons of mankind have come true," he told the crowd of engineers. "The assault on space has begun." It was a vindication of his long-standing insistence that space travel was possible; as a later biography put it, it "was the culmination of his efforts to persuade skeptics that rocketry and astronautics were not merely science fiction."

Khrushchev had just returned to Moscow that night from his vacation home in the Crimea. A few days later he described his own reactions to reporter James Reston, who noted that "Khrushchev's attitude on the launching of Sputnik . . . was almost casual." Khrushchev recounted that "when the satellite was launched, they phoned me that the rocket had taken the right course and that the satellite was already revolving around the earth. I congratulated the entire group of engineers and technicians on this outstanding achievement and calmly went to bed."

In contrast, Moscow spokesmen trumpeted the launching to extract all the propaganda they could muster. The original launch announcement had set the tone: "Artificial earth satellites will pave the way for space travel, and it seems that the present generation will witness how the freed and conscious labor of the people of the new socialist society turns even the most daring of mankind's dreams into reality." That was to be the propaganda theme: success in space implied superiority on earth.

Khrushchev moved to exploit the impact of the announcement, for the purposes of which he had originally approved it—but as the days went by, he seems to have been surprised by the depth of the feat's impact on the Western public. That would turn out to be a bonus, but his original short-range purposes were also fully met: his reorganization of the armed forces proceeded swiftly, and less than five weeks after Sputnik-1, he removed Zhukov from his post. Within a year he had completed the demobilization of a million soldiers from the Red Army, had replaced additional dissident generals (including the army Chief of Staff) and had set up an independent missile force coequal with the army, navy and air force. "We had to overcome resistance among the traditionalist generals," Khrushchev delicately worded it in his memoirs. To implement his new programs, he found loyal military officers who would obey him completely; one such man was Field Marshal Mitrofan Nedelin, a former artillery expert who was put in command of the entire Soviet missile forces and who thus became Korolev's operational commander. Nedelin's eagerness to fulfill Khrushchev's orders would lead to tragedy and to his own death—but that story comes later.

As far as the lesson Khrushchev had planned for the West, it also was completely successful: "When we announced the successful testing of an intercontinental rocket, some U.S. statesmen did not believe us," he crowed. "The Soviet Union, you see, was saying it had something it did not really have. Now that we have successfully launched an earth satellite, only the technically ignorant people can doubt this. . . . We can launch satellites because we have a carrier for them, namely the ballistic rocket."

In the long run, however, Khrushchev's exploitation of Sputnik (and the long string of subsequent Soviet space spectaculars) in an attempt to overawe the United States met with, at best, mixed results. It created some initial panic, but this was followed by American determination to spend whatever was necessary to "catch up"—and Khrushchev probably had counted more on a stunned paralysis than on the vigorous counterthrust that followed. His boasts about producing ICBMs by the dozens, "like sausages," led to the fears of the "missile gap," a theme with which the Democratic party ousted the Republicans in a squeaker election in November 1960.

Meanwhile, many people in the West sought excuses for their lag. Some blamed it all on Army-Navy rivalries, or on bad schools and materialistic values, or on politicians, industrialists, intellectuals, whomever. Some complained, "We got the wrong Germans," a misconception even Eisenhower nourished when he announced it was "German scientists captured at the end of the Second World War [who] doubtless played a big part in the Soviet achievement." (One self-styled expert even claimed that *sputnik* was really a German word, *sputt-nicht*, a farewell wish to the rocket to "sputter not"!) America's cosmic humiliations continued, with bigger and better Sputniks circling over the burning wreckage of American "flopniks" and "pfftniks."

Amid the near hysteria, some voices called out for calm, claiming that the effects of the Soviet space shots had been exaggerated. Senator William Fulbright, for example, wrote: "What about the prestige that Sputnik gave the USSR? It does not feed their people. It was a trick, a kind of gambit. It does not convert anyone to communism. So far as real prestige goes, it is nothing." The world, however, did not seem to operate in such intellectual terms: Sputnik made a big impact, at least according to surveys made by the U.S. Information Agency. In one report, "World Reaction to the United States and Soviet Space Programs" (done in mid-1960), the USIA wrote that most of the West believed that Moscow was ahead and would still be ahead after ten years. In countries such as England, France, Germany, Italy and Norway, space activities were reported in the context of a race between Russia and America. The report continued: "Within this rivalry, space achievements are viewed as particularly significant because of the strong tendency for the popular mind to view space achievements as an index of the scientific and technological aspects of the rival systems, and to link space capabilities with military, especially missile, capabilities."

The "missile gap," meanwhile, was a product of Khrushchev's boasts and American panic. Korolev's R-7 was an inefficient ICBM (and he had never intended anything different): it was too large to disperse into the countryside and had to be installed on rail spurs off the Trans-Siberian Railroad; it took hours to fuel and launch and could thus be caught on the ground by a sneak air attack; it required ground guidance stations, which could easily be bombed or sabotaged; with the smallest possible nuclear warhead, the operational version could barely reach targets in the northeastern United States.

After the success of the Sputnik, Korolev lined up a whole series of new space shots, and Khrushchev—satisfied with the results of the first launches and delighted with the consternation such accomplishments were having in the West—promised complete support. A series of larger satellites with genuine scientific value were prepared: first a dog was sent up, to demonstrate that a living creature could survive days of weightlessness; then an even heavier geophysical probe was put into orbit (after the first of what would be a long series of satellite launch failures). Even the moon became a realistic target, theoretically brought within range by the addition of an upper stage to the *semyorka*—but it took a series of launch failures starting in June 1958 to perfect the improved booster, and it was not until January 1959 (after the United States had had four launch opportunities of its own and missed all four times) that success was achieved. An even bigger upper stage was designed, and Korolev set his sights on Mars and Venus; the proven moon-rocket version was redirected toward an equally spectacular goal, manned flight into orbit—and back.

It was at this point, in 1959–1960, that the Khrushchev-Korolev alliance began showing the first signs of strain. The problem was that Khrushchev had a very precise idea of what he was spending money on space shots for: to create the image, both at home and abroad, of a powerful Soviet technology and of a progressive and efficient Khrushchev regime.

Space research as such did not interest him. Although one defector remarked that "he adored fireworks of all kinds," he never seems to have actually attended a space launch. Following the success of each project, Khrushchev ordered the cancellation of follow-on launchings of the same type, which, while promising to be more scientifically productive, would only appear to be "repetitious" and would not result in new gasps of shock and fear around the world.

At first Khrushchev timed his own political power plays to follow close on the heels of space spectaculars, but as time passed, he began scheduling his diplomatic moves in advance, while demanding that Korolev conform his own space-launch schedule to meet Khrushchev's convenience. In the three years which followed the launching of Sputnik-1, these policies led to a greater and greater divergence of goals —and since Khrushchev controlled the purse strings, it was Korolev who accommodated himself to the political demands.

One additional demand of Khrushchev's must have infuriated Korolev: the space-program chief designer, although no longer a condemned prisoner, was enveloped in even more effective chains. His identity was kept secret and he was forbidden not just to travel abroad (his political reliability was never trusted), but also to even correspond with foreign space experts. One case in particular must have frustrated Korolev, when Dr. Hermann Oberth of Germany, an old colleague of Tsiolkovskiy's and a space pioneer in his own right, asked to meet with him—and Khrushchev forbade it. Wrote Oberth: "I am old, and at one time I lost hope that I would live to see the space era. And then a Russian Sputnik was orbiting the earth. . . . Unfortunately, I am not personally acquainted with another man I respect, the one who constructed the powerful rocket. Probably if my colleague Mr. Tsiolkovskiy were alive—your esteemed fellow countryman with whom I corresponded—then he and I, on meeting the wonderful designer, would exclaim 'Bravo! Bravo! You have realized the dream which nourished our minds for many years and for whose accomplishments we did our best.' Mankind is grateful to this man for his achievement." But neither Oberth nor anyone else was ever able to greet Korolev personally.

Khrushchev refused to share the glory with anyone, even

Korolev himself. "It was important," wrote the defector Vladimirov in 1969, "that Khrushchev maintain the impression that the Sputniks were being launched by the 'Soviet people' under Khrushchev's leadership." Khrushchev justified the enforced anonymity by using it as an excuse to whip up spy mania and xenophobia among the Soviet population: "For those who created the rockets and artificial satellites," he promised, "we will raise an obelisk and inscribe their names on it in gold so they will be known to future generations"—but he then blamed the West for their present anonymity: "We value and respect these people highly and assure their security from enemy agents who might be sent to destroy these outstanding people, our valuable cadres." And so Korolev the top space engineer was still Korolev the prisoner, although his physical horizons had widened slightly; his mental horizons, of course, had never been restricted, even in the depths of his Siberian and *sharashka* exiles.

Korolev had moved into a new type of imprisonment—with genuine rewards, to be sure, but with new types of punishments as well. One of these punishments was that in order to meet Khrushchev's demands, Korolev was compelled by the Soviet military missile hierarchy (personified by Field Marshal Nedelin) to gamble with other people's lives. On the night of October 23–24, 1960, one such gamble would be disastrously lost—and dozens of Korolev's people would die horribly. Compared to the torture of these deaths, his memories of the Kolyma death camps must have paled.

3
☆

The Nedelin Catastrophe

Every twenty-six months, the elliptical planetary processions of Mars and the earth around the sun bring them into the same relative alignment. At that point a "launch window" opens, during which rockets from the earth can reach Mars for the minimum cost in fuel.

Such a launch window was open for several days around mid-October 1960, and it was a target too tempting to resist. Early that year Korolev had received permission to launch several probes toward the red planet at this first opportunity and to launch several more probes toward Venus when a similar window (available every eighteen months in that case) opened the following February.

As the launch time approached, the excitement over the upcoming Mars shot was impossible to conceal in Moscow —but it came out garbled: most observers felt that a manned shot was on tap, since several test versions of a prototype manned spacecraft had been launched earlier that year. Khrushchev helped whip up speculation when he arrived by ship in New York on September 19 for a tumultuous UN visit; one of the sailors from the ship, the *Baltika,* defected and told journalists that there were "spaceship models" on board, which Khrushchev evidently intended to present to the UN as part of a propaganda triumph.

But nothing happened in space. Weeks passed. In New York Khrushchev blustered and played the clown, pounding his shoe on the table when he didn't like the speeches he was hearing. There was no news from the space center in Kazakhstan.

Suspicions began to surface: on October 13, a *New York Times* correspondent in Washington reported that "the Soviet Union failed in an effort to bring off a spectacular space shot" during Khrushchev's visit, pointing out that the Soviet Union sent a rocket to hit the moon a year before (on September 12, 1959), just three days before Khrushchev had arrived for a summit meeting with President Eisenhower. (Khrushchev proudly gave Ike a model of the moon probe.) According to the newspaper's report, a fleet of Soviet space-tracking ships had been spotted, two in the north Atlantic and four in the eastern Pacific. But Khrushchev flew home from New York on October 13, after extending his stay several times. A few days later, word was received that the Russian tracking ships were also returning to port.

A sensational new aspect of the mystery appeared two weeks later when Moscow announced the death of its top missile general, Field Marshal Mitrofan Nedelin, in "a plane crash" on October 25. Nedelin had been the commander-in-chief of the newly organized Strategic Rocket Forces, a separate branch of the armed forces set on an equal footing with the army, navy, air force and air-defense forces.

Nedelin's death immediately was linked to the "failed space shot" by many experts. For example, Soviet-watcher Albert Parry speculated in mid-November that Nedelin may have been pressured by a furious Khrushchev into taking too many risks with one of his rockets: "Something or other, in addition to Kremlin tempers, may have blown up in his face." An Italian news agency of somewhat dubious reliability (but also with occasional exclusive "scoops") reported on December 8 that Nedelin had died on October 21 in a "catastrophic explosion" at an unidentified missile site, along with a hundred other soldiers and scientists, including the U.S.S.R.'s top atomic scientist, Dmitriy Yefremov, and the Deputy Chief of Staff of the Soviet armed forces, General Nikolay Pavlovskiy. And veteran correspondent Paul Ghali filed a story from "foreign diplomats in Bern" that a manned launch had actually failed in early October, killing its pilot, and that Nedelin, who was in charge of the rocket program, was severely reprimanded, resulting in his committing suicide.

This event was the subject of repeated "leaks" and "revelations" as the years passed. Each added new pieces to the puzzle—but were they independent corroborations, recycled rumors or deliberately confusing disinformation?

The controversial book *Penkovskiy Papers,* allegedly the diary of spy Oleg Penkovskiy, who passed precious Kremlin secrets to the West until he was caught in 1962, was published in 1965. According to the account (which some observers suggest was actually a compilation of different documents and interviews, not all connected with Penkovskiy himself), the missile that failed was powered by nuclear energy of some sort: "Present during the tests of this new engine were Nedelin, many specialists on nuclear equipment, and representatives of several government committees. When the countdown was completed, the missile failed to leave the launching pad. After fifteen to twenty minutes had passed, Nedelin came out of the shelter, followed by the others. Suddenly there was an explosion caused by the mixture of the nuclear substance and other components. Over three hundred people were killed. . . . What was brought to Moscow were not Nedelin's and other victim's remains, but urns filled with dirt." Nedelin received a state funeral and his urn (whatever it contained) was interred in a niche on the Kremlin Wall. "The rest of the victims were buried quietly, without any fanfare. A period of mourning was announced in cities where some of the scientists who perished had lived or gone to school. I know that a long mourning period was announced in the city of Dnepropetrovsk."

At about the time Penkovskiy was being executed in Moscow, and the documents which were supposed to be his diaries were being edited in Munich by defector Peter Deryabin (an ex-KGB man himself), the U.S. government released some "intelligence data" of its own concerning failed Russian space shots. Along with a series of unannounced deep-space probes which had been trapped in unstable low orbits in late 1962, two failed Mars probes were described; the rockets had been launched on October 10 and October 14, 1960. No details were ever given about the nature of the failures, although it was suggested that they had occurred high in the sky over Kazakhstan. One U.S. government source pinpointed the failure in the turbopumps of the new upper stage, which would have been switched on about ninety miles up.

The next account of the Nedelin disaster came directly from Khrushchev himself. His posthumously published memoirs, which most observers believe to be genuine, refer to the event explicitly: "As the incident was later reported to me, the fuel somehow ignited and the engine prematurely fired. The rocket reared up and fell, throwing acid and flames all over the place. . . . Dozens of soldiers, specialists and technical personnel [died]. Marshal Nedelin, the Commander in Chief of our missile forces, was sitting nearby watching the test when the missile malfunctioned, and he was killed." Khrushchev made no mention of any role he may have played in the disaster by pressuring Nedelin.

The most recent version of the disaster is given by émigré Russian biochemist Dr. Zhores Medvedev in 1976. (His reliability has been significantly enhanced by the eventual confirmation of his originally doubted claim of a Soviet nuclear-waste disaster in the Urals in 1958.) According to Medvedev, "Khrushchev's misuse of space research to boost Soviet political prestige led to an irreparable catastrophe. . . . Always obsessed with the idea of showing the Americans Soviet superiority in at least some areas of technology, Khrushchev issued a directive that a Soviet rocket to the Moon should be launched to coincide with the time of [his arrival] in New York."

Medvedev's account, published in the British magazine *New Scientist,* continued:

> The elite of Soviet rocket technology was, of course, at the cosmodrome. However, when the start was ordered and the button was pressed, the ignition did not work. According to safety regulations, any inspection could only take place after the fuel had been removed. This was a long process and would mean postponing the whole spectacle. Marshal Nedelin, who was in charge and under an obligation to fulfill the ambitious order, irresponsibly decided to investigate the fault immediately. The special ladders and platforms were moved to the rocket and dozens of engineers and experts started to explore the different parts of the multi-rocket system. Suddenly, the ignition started to work. The rocket fell because it was blocked by the ladders. All the men and women in the area were killed. They were some of the best representatives of Soviet space technology. . . . The government's attempts to hide the real story meant that the tragic death of many prominent scientists and technical experts passed without even short obituaries. The duplicate rocket was later launched and declared a great achievement. But this would not heal the wounds of those who had lost their relatives, friends, and colleagues.

Years, even decades, passed before such information leaked out. One other tiny piece to the puzzle had been the brief notice in December 1975 in a provincial newspaper that the fifteenth anniversary had just passed of the death of Ivan Gvay, "a top Soviet rocket expert"—yet this man's name has *never* appeared in any official Soviet space history. Since his death took fifteen years to announce, the chances are he was yet another victim of the Nedelin disaster. As for Nedelin himself, a recent biography (*Nedelin: First Chief of the Strategics,* by V. F. Tolubko; Moscow: Young Guard Press, 1979) no longer even mentions the plane-crash cover story: it closes with the words "on October 24, 1960, this remarkable man . . . in the full bloom of his strengths and talents, tragically died in the performance of his official duties."

What can we make of these fascinating and perplexing reports? There can be no final answer, but the existence of a tragic pad explosion in October 1960 seems strongly established, and the tragedy was evidently a direct result of intense Kremlin pressure for a new space spectacular.

But how about the contradictions and garbled claims of those reports? Penkovskiy's version of a "nuclear" missile is clearly an error introduced by the death of atomic scientist Yefremov, which now appears to have really been of natural causes—and entirely coincidental. Medvedev's description of the launch as a "moon shot" is probably also a later amalgamation of the real moon shot that Khrushchev had ordered to mark his first New York visit one year earlier—and a "duplicate" rocket's success he mentions was, therefore, probably the Venus shot, which was successfully launched (after the first try broke down at the edge of space) the following February to much fanfare, which ceased when the probe fell silent halfway to its target planet.

But *when* did the explosion take place? Was it before the two high-altitude failures of October 10 and October 14, while Khrushchev was in New York, or was it closer to the official date of Nedelin's death, October 24? Intuitively, the disaster smacks of the desperation which would accompany a last chance after two flops—and it does not seem possible that two more launches could be made *after* such a terrible tragedy. Yet the tracking ships reportedly headed home immediately after the second failure, according to newspaper reports in mid-October.

The determination of this item of data would help define Khrushchev's precise role in the tragedy, along with Korolev's. We do know that in later years it was standard practice to allocate *three* rockets to each launch window. Therefore a third (and catastrophic) Mars shot on or about October 21–24, with Nedelin and Korolev still cringing from Khrushchev's rage following his empty-handed return from New York on October 15, is entirely plausible—but it remains just that, a plausible guess.

The handful of facts, speculations and known technical details allows us to reconstruct the disaster in the absence of any direct eyewitness accounts. The following scenario attempts to be consistent with the known evidence, filled in with informed interpolation and reasonable speculation.

By the time the rocket countdown had reached zero on October 23, 1960, the sun had already set. (That's known because of the navigation constraints on any launch window for a Mars-bound spacecraft.) When the rocket did not ignite, the ground crew sat still and waited. (That's common sense with any size of explosive, from a cherry bomb on up.) Korolev was chief designer, the head of the rocket engineers—but Nedelin was the military officer in charge of all of Russia's military missiles, and he outranked Korolev in whatever dispute followed. Hours might have passed before Nedelin gave the fatal order: go out and inspect the rocket right here on the launch pad. It probably was near midnight.

One vignette comes to us courtesy of Khrushchev's posthumously published memoirs. Korolev's chief deputy on the launch pad was Mikhail Yangel, a Siberian-born Soviet engineer of German ancestry. Yangel was a courageous man: he had infiltrated the Von Braun V-2 bureau at Peenemünde during World War II, serving as a spy for the Red Army (although the Soviets evidently never told the British or the Americans what he discovered). But now, fifteen years later, standing under a million pounds of fuel and armed explosives, Yangel apparently felt his nerves get the best of him —he had to have a cigarette.

For such a contingency, the rocket engineers had built a small fireproof hut near the pad. Yangel entered the hut and sealed the door. It was just as he was lighting his cigarette —according to Khrushchev's memoirs—that the rocket propellant ignited. Yangel was thrown to the ground by the concussion, but survived; everyone else in the open at the launch pad was killed. Many were simply incinerated or blown off the apron into the two-hundred-foot-deep flame pit; others beyond the reach of the flames were struck dead by the shock wave of the blast (reportedly, their bodies were completely undamaged). The detonation must have lit up the midnight sky for a hundred miles around; the thunder of the explosion would have echoed over the steppes.

Besides Yangel, the only other survivors near the pad would have been the few men who had remained deep inside the control bunker with Korolev—even though they would also have been shaken up severely. There's some question whether or not the survivors would have been able to open the outer safety doors after the blast—the doors might have jammed or might have been blocked by wreckage and bodies. But rescue squads from the fire-fighting unit, as well as volunteers from the night shift at the rocket-assembly building a mile away, could have arrived quickly.

The scope of the ghastly accident may have been slow to unfold, since all sources of artificial illumination at the pad would certainly have been destroyed—although scattered fires would have burned for hours. By the headlights of trucks and by hand-held lanterns and flashlights, the rescuers would have searched for survivors. Slowly the bodies of the dead would have been located and gathered into a makeshift morgue—perhaps the floor of the spacious assembly building itself. By sunrise, the wreckage would still have been smoking; the time would have come to find the fragments of bodies, the pieces of bone, the charred teeth. Eventually the duty roster that night would be checked to see how many people were completely missing—their bodies literally burned to ashes in the flames of a volcanic funeral pyre.

How high was the death toll? We just do not know. The underground reports ranged from "forty" to "several hundred," with the more likely count probably tending toward the lower figure. There would hardly have been enough work at the rocket itself for more than a few dozen specialists.

Also present was Nedelin's military staff, since as a reassurance (and a show of bravado) he had ordered some chairs to be set up right next to the rocket. That was where he was, with his aides, lieutenants and other staff officers, when his military career came to a close.

There may have been some work for the medical teams, since there probably were a few survivors in need of hospitalization. But all accounts agree that the number of those killed outright far exceeded the number of those merely injured: the people had mostly been standing too close. (There were few duties for people at the pad except duties right up near the rocket itself.)

Korolev's bitterness over the loss of so many of his friends and coworkers could only have deepened a few weeks later when he received the reports from Simon Kosberg's office. Kosberg had been in charge of developing the upper-stage booster engine, which was supposed to extend the range of the *semyorka* rocket to allow the launchings of interplanetary probes. Building such a rocket engine capable of starting itself in space under conditions of weightlessness was an extremely difficult technical project, since (among other problems) the propellants would be floating around inside the tanks and would not feed evenly into the fuel lines and pumps.

Kosberg's analysis probably reached the same conclusion as a study by American technicians who had eavesdropped on the radiotelemetry signals from the unsuccessful launches on October 10 and October 14. In both cases, the new rocket engine had failed to ignite because of a flaw in the fuel-feed system, and Kosberg probably recommended several design changes to cure this problem. (Over the next two years the engine-failure rate would be reduced from 100 percent to 75 percent; a decade later it would be pushed down to 20 percent.)

The implication of the engine flaw was chilling: Nedelin's tragic order to inspect the rocket had been a completely useless gamble. The rocket would not have worked anyway. Even if it had been launched, even if the ground crew had safely found and fixed the problem which had stopped the original lift-off, the mission would have failed a few minutes later, since the new upper stage had the same built-in flaw which had caused failures on the first two launches.

Had Korolev been able to pay enough attention to Kosberg's original work (so *many* projects had to be personally supervised by Korolev), he might have spotted the flaw and fixed it before launch, thus forestalling the desperation caused by the first two failures and eliminating the very need for such a life-or-death decision. Or at least he might have been able to recognize the causes of the first two failures in time to call off the third launch. But he hadn't, and dozens of his people had died horrible deaths because of it.

Such a disaster would, of course, have had profound effects upon the Khrushchev-Korolev relationship. Perhaps Khrushchev was also stunned—but it seems impossible that he could ever admit that any of it was his fault. However, despite the continued Kremlin pressure for more and more space spectaculars, many years were to pass before there was anything at all similar to the mass slaughter on the pad at Tyuratam in the autumn of 1960. Korolev, for his own part, probably would have been torn with feelings of guilt: he had allowed Nedelin to order the people out to the rocket, a serious safety violation; he had, indeed, apparently chosen in the first place to ride the crest of political pressure in order to finance his plans for space exploration. Sometime, someday, someone was bound to have been pushed too fast, too far, too soon. But even in his worst nightmares, Korolev could not have imagined the cost would be so high. He had repeatedly shown (and would continue to show) his willingness to pay a terrible price to fulfill his dream of space exploration—but the currency in which that price had been exacted in October 1960 may not have allowed him much peaceful sleep.

4
☆

Man and Woman
in Space

For several weeks every spring, the steppes of central Asia are covered with flowers. They burst forth soon after the snows have melted, to thrive in the brief period before the sun scorches the ground to a yellowish brick-hard glaze. Only the hardy grass survives through the summer.

These prairie flowers were blooming on April 12, 1961, when Yuriy Gagarin became the first human being to venture into space. For Korolev and his team it must have been a glorious day, the best since Sputnik. Disasters, deaths and political deceptions were momentarily forgotten in the celebration of an epochal event whose significance even Moscow's propaganda machine could not exaggerate.

Russians love flowers, and there was an additional need for them that spring: wreaths were needed for dozens of fresh graves near the settlement of Tyuratam, graves less than six months old. The flowers were blooming, but the hot, parching summer still lay ahead.

During the year leading up to the voyage of the spaceship Vostok, a series of unmanned test flights had paved the way. The first flight, in May 1960, had been a test of the Vostok attitude-control system (an orientation system), with a mannequin seated in the cosmonaut's couch; but instead of returning to earth, the vehicle went into a higher orbit when the retrorockets were fired in the wrong direction. The next attempt, in July, failed when the carrier rocket exploded in midair (of course, no public announcement was ever made), but the following month a successful mission was flown: a canister containing two dogs was returned safely to earth after twenty-four hours in space.

Two major setbacks occurred in December: one ship was destroyed during reentry, incinerating its canine crew, and a second ship fell back to earth after a launching mishap. Following three months of redesign work, two more unmanned test flights were made, in which test animals made a single pass around the earth. Both shots were successful and the way was then clear for a man to follow.

Expectations and excitement mounted among informed circles in Moscow during the first week in April, since it was obvious that the first manned space flight was imminent. (The American plans for a short suborbital Mercury flight were at least a month away.) Then on April 10 came electrifying news from London (!) that the space shot had already occurred, but that the pilot—identified as Lieutenant Colonel Vladimir Ilyushin, son of a leading aircraft designer—had been badly injured. This story was written by Dennis Ogden, the Moscow correspondent of the British Communist party newspaper *Daily Worker*—who presumably had good contacts in Moscow. But the story was quickly denied by official Soviet spokesmen.

Even today, the origin of this report is obscure. The most reasonable explanation is that Ogden leaped to a wrong but plausible conclusion when he learned that Ilyushin, a neighbor of his who also was a test pilot, was in the hospital after an "auto accident." Ogden reported the flight had made three orbits around earth, which was really the plan for the American Mercury program. He also claimed that the spaceship was named Rossiya. Radar sites in the United States and Europe confirmed that no rocket had been launched, so the entire affair was imaginary. Ogden had picked up a random collection of pieces and had woven them into a logical but totally fallacious picture—a pitfall which is all too easy to fall into when dealing with sensitive subjects in the Soviet Union.

The actual flight of the spaceship Vostok on April 12 was almost anticlimactic. At 9:07 A.M. Moscow time, the rocket was launched, and the first official announcement came out at 10:00 A.M.—while Gagarin was still in flight. By 10:55 he was back on earth, and the successful landing was announced over *Radio Moscow* at noon.

During the 108 minutes of the flight, Gagarin experienced a sequence of sensations. At lift-off, he excitedly shouted, *"Poyekhali!"* ("Let's go"), and then kept assuring flight controllers that "the machine is working normally." As the rockets' fuel burned off, the acceleration forces built up (less mass, constant thrust—ergo, higher acceleration), finally reaching 6 Gs about nine minutes into the flight. Then as the rockets shut down, the capsule entered a free-fall orbit around earth. He flew across Siberia, Japan, southeastward to the tip of South America, then northeastward across west Africa. The course of the spacecraft gave Gagarin an excuse to relay revolutionary greetings to many third-world countries. Then the retrofire forced the capsule back down into the atmosphere, where the deceleration forces exceeded 8 to 10 Gs. Moments later, as the capsule descended under a series of parachutes, the flight ended.

The space scientists had not known what to expect from the flight. On earlier flights dogs had come back alive and their heartbeat rates showed they had adjusted to weightlessness. But many doctors feared that the psychological stresses of the mission would render the human pilot senseless, totally incapable of controlling the spacecraft.

So prior to blast-off the decision had been made to conduct the entire flight on automatic pilot. As a precautionary move that made some sense, but the space doctors carried it to an extreme: they were not simply concerned that the cosmonaut would be somehow unable to control the spacecraft; they feared that the man would actually interfere with the guidance system. Hence, the manual controls were deactivated. The pilot was effectively disconnected from his own ship.

Naturally, the pilots objected. They wanted to be more than experimental animals, particularly since the Vostok autopilots had broken down twice already.

The space doctors made a slight concession about a month before the first flight. A combination lock was installed in the cockpit, and the doctors at the control center promised to radio up the correct sequence in the event of the failure of the autopilot. But at this point Korolev intervened: since a radio failure seemed more probable than an autopilot failure, the doctors' plan didn't make much sense. Instead, the secret combination would be placed in an envelope which would be fastened to the inside wall of the cockpit.

Gagarin never needed the combination (it was 1-4-5, by the way), since the autopilot performed perfectly. From launch to landing, he never touched the controls.

Gagarin's flight grabbed headlines around the world. But outside of the simple fact that the event had taken place, the world knew very little about the round-the-world flight. It would be at least five years, for instance, before photographs of the spacecraft and rocket booster would be released. And what little was known was usually misinterpreted: for example, the spaceship's name, Vostok, became translated as "East," with all the concomitant political and geographic connotations; however, the word also means "an upward flow," as in a sunrise or as in the original meaning of "orient." The symbolism was quite appropriately connected with the upward flow of humanity into the universe. No doubt it was Korolev's idea (and he may have had the name in mind for decades).

Meanwhile, the Ogden report of the "Ilyushin flight"

helped confuse Western observers—eliciting strong skepticism in some commentators. And Soviet newsmen themselves obscured even the most basic details of Gagarin's flight, in particular one aspect which very quickly assumed a great significance: the method of the final landing. How was it done?

The earliest published Soviet descriptions of the landing told of Gagarin swinging from a personal parachute, singing hymns to the motherland. But suddenly the official accounts became vague. At the post-flight press conference, a Western newsman asked the question directly: At touchdown, was Gagarin inside or outside his ship? After a moment's consultation with the political official in charge of the conference (who had already approved the script of questions and answers for the Soviet journalists), Gagarin delivered a hymn of praise to the brilliance of the "chief designer" of the spaceship (Korolev, of course—but it was forbidden to reveal his name, so his job title was used instead), who had made *both* modes of descent possible. But he would not answer the question: *Which* mode had been used?

This uncertainty came to a head in Paris three months later, when the International Astronautical Federation, or FAI (the acronym for the French name), convened a meeting to certify the world records being claimed for the flight. A longstanding FAI rule could have meant an embarrassing propaganda defeat: to qualify for any new world flying records, a pilot must take off *and land* in his aircraft or spacecraft. The rule book was quite explicit on this point.

As it turned out, the Vostok capsule was equipped with an ejection seat, which served to catapult the pilot clear of the booster in the event of a launch failure. The same system was to be used during the final descent to earth, since the three-ton spherical landing capsule did not pack a parachute large enough to ensure a gentle (or even a survivable) landing. The pilot was supposed to fire the ejection seat at about 20,000 feet and come down separately. Gagarin had almost certainly used this method.

In Paris, the FAI director-general confronted the Soviet delegate with the crucial question: "Where was the pilot on return in relation to the space vehicle?" Perhaps sensing a plot to deny the Soviet Union its rightful recognition, the Soviet spokesman loudly protested: "Ask the Americans if the U.S.A. believes that these records claimed for Gagarin were actually made. All the people of the world have already endorsed Gagarin's flight and have accepted it as fact." The wrangling went on for five hours, with the FAI officials demanding documentation that Gagarin had landed inside the ship and the Soviet delegates denouncing such requirements as obstructionist and insulting. Finally, as dinnertime approached, the FAI officials gave in and agreed to certify the Soviet version of the flight that Gagarin had been inside the capsule.

Subsequently, when foreign newsmen asked for evidence that Gagarin had landed inside the ship, Soviet officials would point to the FAI certification as independent proof of their claims. But as the proverb goes, nobody has a good enough memory to be a successful liar. A year later cosmonaut Popovich was asked how he landed, and without checking he blurted out, "Like Titov and Gagarin, I landed outside the ship"; in 1964 the three-man Voskhod capsule would include a small retrorocket to cushion the final landing, and boastful Soviet space officials would point to it as "the first time that a crew could land in its ship." Ten years later a book by chief Soviet space correspondent Evgeny Riabchikov would describe how the Vostok came down in a plowed field while Gagarin himself came down in a pasture near a deep ravine.

If the landing-method deception has evaporated with time, the launch-site hoax has grown stronger. Another piece of information required by the FAI for certification was the precise point of takeoff and of landing. Since the field where the Vostok landed (without Gagarin) had no strategic significance, its exact location could be released without any harm (and the Russians even generously offered to take FAI officials to that site!). However, it was inconceivable that the true location of the space center could ever be officially revealed to the outside world. That was an inviolable state secret.

So another space fiction was invented: the Baikonur Cosmodrome. Official Soviet documents gave the location of the launch site as 47°3'N, 65°6'E, near the town of "Baikonur" on a rail spur southwestward from Karaganda. However, an analysis of Soviet satellite trajectories soon showed that the actual launch site was more than two hundred miles to the southwest of Baikonyr (the fiction was so clumsy that somebody had even mispelled the name of the town). Western intelligence agencies of course knew the correct location from U-2 pictures and, later, spy satellite pictures. The Western public's first view of the real Soviet space center didn't come until 1974, when some photographs from LANDSAT-1, NASA's first earth resources satellite, showed a sprawling missile row right in the middle of what the Soviet maps showed to be empty desert.

This space center is just north of the town of Tyuratam, on the main rail line from Russia to Tashkent. To this day, twenty years after Gagarin's flight, all Soviet space stories are datelined "Baikonur Cosmodrome" and all world space-flight records filed with (and approved by) the FAI in Paris contain this geographical deception—while the name "Tyuratam" has vanished from the latest editions of official maps and gazetteers. The people in Baikonyr, who have never seen a space rocket, probably get some measure of amusement out of the deception—but they know enough about the KGB's security regulations to keep their amusement to themselves.

Behind this curtain of Soviet misinformation, cover-up,

and outright deception, and hampered by anti-Soviet wishful thinking and rumor-mongering, many Western observers tried to formulate rational theories about the techniques, tools and motivations of Soviet space officials. They had precious few real clues to go on, and the literature of the first few years is stocked full of fantastic stories about the "truth" behind the Soviet space program. Perhaps the program was being run by "smarter Germans" (it wasn't); perhaps Russian missiles were launched on long ramps up mountainsides (they weren't); perhaps the cosmonauts in orbit were only tape recorders (they weren't!). In the absence of hard information, many similar stories were believable—or at least could be made to appear so.

Probably the most interesting popular notion about the Soviet man-in-space program back in the early 1960s was that the announced flights were only the successful ones, and that a whole string of manned space shots had ended in failures which had killed the cosmonaut crews. These secret dead Russian spacemen have achieved near-mythic status, since reports about them are so widespread. The deaths of dozens of rocket technicians in the Nedelin catastrophe in October 1960 is now well documented—but how about the in-flight deaths of several space pilots?

As a memorial to Russian and American space pilots who lost their lives in the course of their training or on actual space flights, the crew of the Apollo-15 moon expedition in 1971 left a plaque on the lunar surface, together with a small metal figurine representing a "fallen astronaut." Eight Americans and six Russians are listed. But if one were to give any credence to the stories which circulated so widely in the early 1960s, that list of Russians would be considered incomplete. Additional names would have to be added, names such as Ledovskiy, Grachev, Belokonev and Dolgov. These and others allegedly were the names of Soviet cosmonauts who had perished on secret space missions whose fatal results were never revealed to the outside world.

Some were supposed to have lost their lives on suborbital flights in 1959. Others were trapped in orbit between May 1960 and February 1961, or were incinerated during rocket explosions. Even after Gagarin's flight, rumors continued about other unsuccessful attempts: in May 1961 a man and a woman were reported to have died in orbit; the following October a manned capsule was supposed to have been knocked off course by solar flares, whereupon it vanished into interplanetary space. Up to twenty such space disasters were described in the Western press.

With hindsight, it's easy to see how such stories came about (and stories they were—there has never been the slightest indication that any of them were accurate). In the face of one Soviet space spectacular after another, juxtaposed with the humiliating explosions of American rockets, many people were eager to believe that the Soviets were suffering even worse disasters but were covering up. So whenever a mystery payload was launched (such as the first unmanned Vostok flight in May 1960, or an aborted Venus shot in February 1961), "reliable Western observers" began hinting that there were dead Russians on board, because the absence of official propaganda boasts was taken to prove the presence of some embarrassing malfunction. Sometimes mysterious radio signals were picked up on frequencies used by Soviet space vehicles. (This was the strategy used by a pair of over-eager Italian amateur radio listeners, the Judica-Cordeglia brothers, who singlehandedly wiped out an entire squadron of cosmonauts in the early 1960s.) Sometimes *any* signals from space would do. (In October 1961 a rumor was set off by the radio beacon of an American Discoverer satellite.) Sometimes an official Soviet news item would be misinterpreted, such as a magazine article in *Ogonyok* in October 1959 which portrayed men testing high-altitude aircraft equipment. When the men, who were incorrectly thought to be cosmonauts, failed to show up during the Vostok series, observers decided they had perished secretly. Sometimes the stories came from presumably reputable sources, men such as Dr. Hermann Oberth, who claims he heard such stories while working for Wernher von Braun in America soon after Sputnik-1, and Oleg Penkovskiy, who reported in his journal that several "highly trained cosmonauts" had been launched into the stratosphere and were never heard from again.

The official Moscow space spokesmen repeatedly issued vehement denials. Aleksey Adzhubei, editor in chief of *Pravda* by virtue of being Khrushchev's son-in-law, denounced the reports in no uncertain terms in 1963: "These stories are concocted by American yellow journalists eager to outdo each other in defaming the Soviet Union." General Nikolay Kamanin, director of cosmonaut training, also publicly denied the rumors—a sure sign of Soviet sensitivity on the question. But the louder the Russians denied the stories, the more convincing the stories appeared.

The discomfiture of the Soviets is particularly ironic because they probably were really telling the truth. But by this point they had been caught in so many distortions and cover-ups regarding their space program that nobody doubted that they would try to lie their way out of any potential embarrassment about "secret dead cosmonauts"—if there ever were any.

These dead-cosmonaut stories have been repeated and embellished for so long that there seems little hope of ever stamping them out. Columnist Drew Pearson endorsed them in 1962. Publications as diverse as *Fate, Reader's Digest, U.S. News and World Report* and *Saga* magazine's *UFO Report* have chronicled these deaths as established facts. Bob Considine's news column on the secret space fatalities was read into the Congressional Record. A week after the Apollo fire which killed three astronauts in 1967, Washington political columnists Robert Allen and Paul Scott disclosed a "secret CIA report" which described five fatal Soviet flights and six fatal ground accidents; the report would soon be released, the newsmen expected, "to demonstrate that the U.S. space program is still by far the safest." These uncontrolled recyclings of the same old rumors underscore the point that people accept what they like to believe and that believing in these space fatalities was comforting to many people in the West —the stories "felt" true.

Today, none of these indications bears much weight. Just the opposite is true: a very convincing circumstantial case can be made that there were *no* Soviet in-flight fatalities in this period. As Dr. Charles Sheldon II, the Library of Congress's leading authority on the Soviet space program, has put it: "We are asked to believe that in parallel with a public success program, which always brought its pilots back alive, the Soviets were also conducting a secret failure program, which always killed its pilots. That is hardly credible."

This is not to say that some of the early cosmonaut candidates have not mysteriously disappeared. In fact, I've discovered evidence which clearly demonstrates that many of the original members of the Soviet cosmonaut cadre have become nonpersons due to injury, indiscretion or character flaw (or perhaps death—in training, not in flight).

My discovery was made possible when, in their typical way, the Soviet space-news censors blundered badly. They had somehow authorized the publication of two different versions of the same group photograph. In one, the top six cosmonauts of the class of 1960 were shown smiling with leading space-training officials at Sochi, a resort on the Black Sea; in the other version, there are only *five* cosmonauts— one man had been airbrushed out of the middle of the back row. In his place was a shadowed rose bush.

And that was just the beginning. Other before-and-after photo pairs showed up after I made a careful search of Soviet books and magazines. Sometimes I found a sequence of retouching stages: a backup cosmonaut stood behind Gagarin in one photo, but in the subsequent edition his face had been smudged away. This clumsy job was cleaned up in the final version of the scene when the entire background was blacked out.

Soon after the publication of the before-and-after cosmonaut photos in space magazines in the mid-1970s, the Soviets released an official explanation for the missing men. In the autobiography of Georgiy Shonin, one of the first cosmonauts (the book was entitled *The Very First*), some remarkable revelations were made: the original cosmonaut class had had twenty members, of whom only twelve "graduated" to space flight. The eight dropouts left the program for various reasons, some medical, some academic. No other information about these men was published, except their first names: Ivan, Anatoliy, Dmitriy, Grigoriy, Mars (a Tatar) and three Valentins (distinguished as "Number One," "Junior" and "Gramps").

The first casualty occurred late in the summer of 1960, when the cosmonaut corps had been in existence only six months. Valentin "Number One," the most promising cosmonaut candidate, injured his back while swimming in a shallow lake near the training camp. He spent a month in a hospital and recovered sufficiently to return to air force flying duty—but his space career was aborted. This was particularly tragic since he was the only one of the group who had no trouble at all with the theoretical schooling given to the future cosmonauts. He was considered one of the best pilots and unquestionably the most intellectually brilliant of the group.

A second man, Anatoliy (who may be the erased face in the Sochi group photograph), was in training for the Vostok-3 flight in mid-1962 when he failed a 12-G centrifuge test. Shonin's book says it was because of hemorrhages throughout his body; another cosmonaut attributed it to heart trouble. In any case, Anatoliy was grounded and replaced by his backup cosmonaut.

In mid-1962 there was also a purge of sorts. The "junior" Valentin faced a review board for "difficulty in adapting himself to the severe discipline which governed both work and leisure" of the cosmonaut corps. His expulsion evidently led to further unrest and a few months later he was followed by three more comrades, Ivan, Mars and Grigoriy. These four cosmonaut casualties seem to have left for a variety of academic and disciplinary reasons, but ideological unreliability may also have been part of it.

The third Valentin, nicknamed "Gramps" because of his relatively advanced age of thirty-eight, also failed a review board in 1962—but for medical reasons connected with his age. According to Shonin's book, he was extremely well liked by the other cosmonauts and they were sorry to see him go.

The last casualty did not leave the group until 1969, nine years after selection. Dmitriy, who had served on several backup crews and was about to command a Soyuz mission, failed a medical review board and was grounded.

"Yes, the road into space is difficult and thorny," wrote Shonin (or, more likely, the political adviser to his ghost writer). "On this road there are not only victories but also defeats and even tragedies. Of the twenty people of the 'Gagarin selection' only eight still remain in our center. One died in space, another in the air, and still another on earth. Some nerves broke down; their health failed others. Such are the facts, such is life." And such is the Soviet fetish for secrecy that these admissions came out only after the publication of the missing-cosmonaut retouched photos in Western magazines—but Shonin's book didn't comment on that.

Still, the Shonin revelation may not be the whole truth, since it claimed that all eight men were still alive. Privately, Soviet cosmonauts have admitted that "six or eight" candidate cosmonauts had died in training between 1960 and 1975, and it would be surprising if they had all been from later groups. No, the Soviet response to the publication of the missing-cosmonaut photographs was intended only to save face, not to set the record straight. If that record showed that some of these young men were dead, we have no reason to assume that we are ever going to be told. The list of space casualties on the memorial moon plaque is still incomplete.

In 1961 Gagarin's flight, despite the surrounding confusion and suspicions, had been all that Khrushchev and Korolev could have hoped for. It had reasserted Soviet space supremacy and had upstaged the much shorter American Mercury space hop a few weeks later. The new American President, John Kennedy, in office only three months, had been given a stunning demonstration of Soviet technological virtuosity.

So what should come next? For Korolev, the answer was simple: longer and longer flights, testing human reactions to extended periods of weightlessness. The second cosmonaut would spend a full day in space, followed by a trip of several days. Eventually, men could spend ten to twelve days in orbit. Such cosmonauts need not even be jet pilots, but could be doctors or scientists.

For Khrushchev, however, this just wouldn't do. Breaking one space record after another would soon lose its public appeal, especially at a time when U.S. astronauts would begin orbiting earth inside Mercury capsules. No, something more impressive, something spectacular, would have to be produced—if Korolev's budget was to be approved.

By the time the second cosmonaut was launched in August 1961 (evidently timed to coincide with the building of the Berlin Wall), follow-on plans had been completed. Korolev would get his desired three-day flight in 1962, as long as he launched a *second* Vostok into a nearby orbit—as Khrushchev demanded. Korolev would also get his week-long flight in 1963, but only if it was part of a sensational space extravaganza involving the launching of a woman into space. It was something Korolev had never considered, but Khrushchev demanded it be done—and he signed the checks.

The problem was, what sort of woman? There had not been any women jet pilots considered for the 1960 class, since there were very few women pilots. But there were some highly qualified women doctors and engineers in the space program, and they seemed likely choices. However, the woman-in-space project was Khrushchev's idea from the very beginning, and he set the standards: she must be an *ordinary* Russian girl, a factory or farm worker, whose flight would demonstrate that anybody at all could go into space under socialism. No elitist intellectual here: she must have the common touch to fulfill plans Khrushchev had for her.

The selection process, under the direction of veteran cosmonaut Gagarin, began in the summer of 1961. Thousands of letters had poured in after the first Vostok flight from would-be space-farers, and many of them were from women. At first, these letters had been stashed away; now that women cosmonauts were needed, the sacks of mail were dug out of storage and the letters were screened for likely candidates. Eventually, after extensive investigations and interviews, four were chosen.

The one named Valentina Tereshkova is the only one we know about, although the first names of two others, Tanya and Irina, were published many years later. Of the fourth young woman, not even her name is known, although one foreign journalist claimed it was Ludmilla—and that will have to do.

Tereshkova was twenty-four years old when the call to Moscow came. She had been born on a collective farm near the ancient Russian town of Yaroslavl in 1937, soon after the worst famines of the forced collectivization of the peasants had eased, to be replaced by political purges. Her family survived (there was no hint of political pathology in her pedigree), but her father was killed fighting Germans when Valentina was six years old. With her mother and older sisters she moved into Yaroslavl, and after high school she took a job as a spindler in a textile factory.

Tereshkova was active in the Young Communist League at her factory, and eventually became the chapter secretary.

She also took up skydiving and made several dozen jumps between 1958 and 1961.

When her letter to Moscow had been answered by a series of interviews and medical exams, and ultimately by a trip to Moscow for the final screening, she carried out her first space duty: to maintain secrecy. In November 1961 she moved to a training camp after telling her friends, her colleagues and even her mother that it was for special studies connected with a women's precision sky-diving team which would soon enter international competition. (Her mother learned that Valentina was a cosmonaut when the flight was announced over *Radio Moscow*.)

The four young women received mixed reactions from the male cosmonauts. (The reactions from the cosmonauts' wives have never been documented.) Some thought the idea was wonderful. Others were paternalistic: "Space flight is no picnic," one told a journalist. "It will be hard on them."

The training was arduous since the planned flight was less than a year and a half away. There were months of classroom work, physical training and parachute jumps. The women were commissioned second lieutenants in the Soviet air force and went through an extensive jet aerobatic program in two-seater Mig trainers (they never soloed). In one respect their training differed from that of the men, although no mention has ever been made of it in Soviet sources: the men knew they competed for each flight assignment, but that barring any medical disability or behavior slips, they would *all* eventually fly in space; for the women's program, created by Khrushchev's edict for Khrushchev's purposes, there was never any intention of making more than one flight—so the competition must have been keen and the pressures intense.

And as the months went by, the male cosmonauts came to understand the purpose of the female detachment. The piloting skills which had earned for the men their chances of a ticket into space had been set aside for the women. It soon became apparent that the women had been selected precisely for their *lack* of "elitist" qualifications. And although the medical and psychological standards were comparable, the criteria of ideological purity and correct class origin had even more stringently been applied. The women had been picked not with the space mission but with the post-mission ceremonial duties foremost in mind.

Years later, during the brief Apollo-Soyuz cosmic camaraderie in the mid-1970s, some cosmonauts talked freely with their American colleagues about the blend of amusement and condescension they had come to feel toward those women. What, the men had feared, would become of their macho reputations when it was realized that *anybody* could fly into space inside an automatic remote-controlled Vostok? The cosmonauts had soon recognized the woman-in-space project as the political price Korolev had to pay in order to receive Khrushchev's backing; their mistake may have been in thinking it was a temporary aberration, a necessary chore to be gotten out of the way so the *real* space program could carry on. As it turned out, their concept of an aberration was Khrushchev's idea of normality: the cosmonaut program existed to provide him with politically exploitable space spectaculars, and that was why he signed the checks.

Throughout 1962 and early 1963, public statements by touring cosmonauts and private news leaks to Western journalists alerted the world to the coming flight: "We will pave the road into space together," cosmonaut Popovich told one women's club in early 1963. The women of the world were ready.

But who was it they were waiting for? Which of the four would be the one to go? As the launch date approached, the time came to pick the primary pilot and her backup (or "double"). According to the official version of the story, Tereshkova had been the obvious choice all along—even though a strict training rule had been that the actual pilot was not to be notified until shortly before the flight, to keep *all* the candidates at their peak readiness.

Several unofficial sources both inside and outside the Soviet Union have claimed that the leading candidate for the flight had actually been the girl "Ludmilla." Valentina, according to these unconfirmed but consistent accounts, had been the second choice, the double. Shortly before the launching on June 16, 1963, "Ludmilla" is supposed to have been medically disqualified, and Valentina stepped in. (I can personally testify to Tereshkova's sensitivity regarding *her* backup pilot. In 1976 at a press conference at the NASA Space Center in Houston, I asked her who and where the other three woman cosmonaut trainees were; immediately she demanded that I be expelled from the meeting room— and I was.)

Whatever the truth of these suspicions and rumors, the other three women have vanished almost without a trace. In a series of Soviet space publicity movies, the whole quartet, three brunettes and a blonde, appears in the distance or from behind. Beyond those views, and the first names of two of them, nothing more is known about these losers in the first Miss Outer Space contest.

On June 16, 1963, Tereshkova was launched aboard Vostok-6. Her launch was part of a second group-flight of two separate Vostok capsules. The first, the previous August, had seen cosmonauts Andrian Nikolayev and Pavel Popovich ride their spacecraft in parallel orbits a few miles apart. Two days before Tereshkova's blast-off, the Vostok-5 (with Valeriy Bykovskiy) had been put into orbit, but her Vostok-6 was later sent up on an entirely different orbital path, not in the same plane at all. At one point the ships passed each other at a range of three miles, but they then drifted apart and soon there were thousands of miles between them. This odd flight path perplexed Western observers at the time and has never been explained.

But the navigation details were unimportant. A *woman* was now in space! And what a fine, typically Russian girl, too! Like the earlier cosmonauts, Tereshkova was allowed to choose a bird's name as a radio call sign. She chose *Chaika,* or Sea Gull. Cheers and excitement circled the globe almost as quickly as Sea Gull's spaceship. Whatever their national or political leanings, women around the world reacted with pride and exuberance when Sea Gull, a simple everyday Russian girl, broke into the male preserve of "manned" space flight.

An important part of the flight plan was to send greetings to the nations she flew over and to underscore the reasons she was able to make the flight. "Warm greetings from space to the glorious Leninist Young Communist League which reared me," she broadcast. "Everything that is good in me I owe to our Communist party and the Young Communist League."

Tereshkova soared on. Originally a flight lasting a single day had been scheduled, with two possible day-long extensions if all went well. These extensions were allowed after she seemed to make a good adjustment to weightlessness. Years later, there were malicious rumors about how she had fainted, or had become delirious, or had vomited all over the cabin as she screamed in terror. Such ugly accounts sound like exaggerations, but it is entirely possible she did throw up her dinner once or twice. (Many of the male astronauts and cosmonauts did so too during the first few hours of their flights.) Whether or not she panicked momentarily remains a state secret, but she did complete her three-day flight in reasonably good shape.

To return to earth, Tereshkova allowed the Vostok autopilot to line up the spacecraft and fire the braking rocket engine. After passing through the flames and deceleration of atmospheric entry, the capsule stabilized under a small parachute, and Tereshkova was ejected through the side hatch. She completed the descent on a personal backpack parachute. In the few moments of that silent final descent, she must have felt very proud of herself—as she had every right to. She had earned a new place for herself in world history, a place which was to ever more deny her the ordinary right to make any more parachute jumps or to do anything else which seemed too risky.

The mission was the propaganda triumph Khrushchev had planned. He crowed the loudest: "Bourgeois society always emphasizes that woman is the weaker sex. That is not so. Our Russian woman showed the American astronauts a thing or two. Her mission was longer than that of all the Americans put together." Other broadcasts stressed that last theme, as for example *Radio Berlin* (East): "This single fact [seventy hours for Sea Gull versus fifty-five hours for six Mercury flights] is evidence of the great superiority of Soviet science and technology compared with the United States, and of the ever-growing superiority of the socialist order of society over capitalism altogether."

The women's angle was embellished by Tereshkova herself: "Since 1917 Soviet women have had the same prerogatives and rights as men. They share the same tasks. They are workers, navigators, chemists, aviators, engineers. And now the nation has selected me for the honor of being a cosmonaut. As you can see, on earth, at sea and in the sky, Soviet women are the equal of men."

And in the United States, a lot of people agreed. The wife of Senator Philip A. Hart (Democrat–Michigan), herself a qualified pilot, was quoted by UPI as saying, "All it shows is that Russia is giving women a chance and we're not. [The United States] is one hundred years behind in using the full abilities of women." Senator Ernest Gruening (Democrat–Alaska) criticized NASA on the Senate floor for its indifference to the use of women as astronauts; he read an article by Clare Boothe Luce, former congresswoman and wife of the publisher of *Life* magazine, which claimed that "the Soviet Union has given its women unmistakable proof that it be-

lieves them to possess the same virtues [as men]. The flight
of Valentina Tereshkova is, consequently, symbolic of the
emancipation of the Communist woman. It symbolizes to
Russian women that they actively share (not passively bask,
like American women) in the glory of conquering space."

Such complimentary comments measure up poorly against
later Soviet actions and Soviet statements. One would be
tempted to say that once the gimmickry of Tereshkova's
flight had been accomplished, the Soviets reverted to a male
chauvinism which should have made such Western spokes-
persons choke on their fatuous praises. Cosmonaut Leonov,
for example, expressed it this way in an interview in 1975:
"When we analyzed the results of her flight afterward, we
discovered that for women, flying in space is a hard job and
that they can do other things down here [laughs] . . . [After
training, she will be twenty-eight or twenty-nine], and if she
is a good woman she will have a family by then. Now, you
don't subject a mother to such severe physical loads that go
with the training, aside from physical tensions." The following year, Tereshkova's husband elaborated: there never were
any more spacewomen "because this kind of work is tough.
The mission program makes big demands on her, especially
if she is married. So nowadays we keep our women here on
earth. We love our women very much; we spare them as
much as possible. However, in the future, they will surely
work on board space stations, but as specialists—as doctors,
as geologists, as astronomers and, of course, as stewardesses." Cosmonaut chief Shatalov told Russian newsmen in
1980 that space flight was too demanding for women: "In
such conditions we just had no moral right to subject the
'better half' of mankind to such loads."

Tereshkova herself would eventually proclaim much the
same thing: "I believe that a woman should always remain
a woman and nothing feminine should be alien to her," she
wrote in 1970. "At the same time, I strongly feel that no work
done by a woman in the field of science or culture or what-

ever, however vigorous or demanding, can enter into conflict with her ancient 'wonderful mission'—to love, to be loved— and with her craving for the bliss of motherhood."

But all these comments would come later. In 1963 the only things that were important were the image of the brave young woman and the uses to which such an image could be put.

The eighteen months of training and three days of flight had been arduous enough, but now Tereshkova began the work she had been intended for. Soon after landing, she flew back to Moscow just in time to address a Soviet-sponsored international women's peace congress, and then began a world tour through India, Pakistan, Mexico, the United States, Cuba, Poland, Bulgaria and points between. While the three other women space trainees were shuffled out of the space program forever (presumably with appropriate cover stories so that they could explain where they had been for a year and a half), Tereshkova rocketed from glory to glory. She assumed dozens of ceremonial posts and moved into the office of the president of the Committee of Soviet Women on Pushkin Square in Moscow. She parroted the official Moscow line with a degree of charm and grace which had never been seen before in Russian diplomacy. She did her job very, very well.

There was one more task to perform, and Khrushchev probably had a hand in it as well. During the final months of training, the Vostok-3 pilot Nikolayev had been assigned to help coach the women's group. He was the only bachelor; all the women were single (had that also been a selection factor?). As later recounted, a cosmic romance sprang up during the training period—and lo! it was Nikolayev's girl friend who was picked to make the flight.

Their wedding the following November was the Moscow social event of the year. The Soviets have always treated their cosmonauts like royalty or Hollywood stars, and this time they outdid themselves in the lavish pageantry. Khrushchev gave the bride away and grinned uncontrollably all day.

Now, some things about all this still seem strange. The odds were three to one against the single cosmonaut bachelor falling in love with the future spacewoman. Their only child, a daughter named Yelena, was born seven months after the wedding; since Khrushchev's overthrow, they have reportedly not even lived together, and in official Soviet cosmonaut group portraits they are nowhere near each other.

There's no way to tell if this was just a love match that went sour or some callous Khrushchevian ploy arranged to capitalize on cosmonaut popularity—which cannot be undone for fear of embarrassing the Soviet Union, at whatever personal cost to the three people involved.

Ceremonial duties were sufficient for Tereshkova, but by 1963 Gagarin was fed up with ribbon cutting, speech making and smiling into cameras. He kept insisting that he was a space pilot, not a diplomat, and that he wanted a chance to control a spacecraft, not just ride in one. Once there were additional cosmonaut heroes available for public display, Gagarin could be spared—and he soon was assigned to a new space mission as a backup cosmonaut.

Early one morning in March 1968, Gagarin took off with a flight instructor for a routine jet proficiency flight. Other pilots gathered at the airfield awaiting their turn with the two-seater training jet—but Gagarin's flight became overdue. Search planes were sent out and soon spotted a column of smoke coming from a birch forest. Wreckage littered the trees; there were no survivors.

Since there had never been any call for help, investigators concluded that a mechanical failure had probably not been involved. The men had been flying at very high speed near the treetops and had suddenly nosed over and hit the ground. The accident report listed "pilot error." Less charitable gossip claimed that Gagarin had been drinking all night and was hot-rodding dangerously near the ground, but he was so close to flying again in space that it's hard to imagine him being so careless. He had been backup pilot on the disastrous Soyuz-1 mission a year earlier and had made brave speeches at that cosmonaut's funeral. He was young enough to be patient but old enough to be cautious. Neither helped.

Gagarin's remains were cremated and the ashes were placed in an urn which was to be inserted into a niche in the Kremlin Wall during a televised state funeral. Tereshkova and three other cosmonauts carried the flower-decked catafalque on which the urn rested. It was the second public cosmonaut funeral in less than a year. There were many more ahead.

5

☆

The Voskhod Follies

Fighting off wolves at midnight while freezing half to death was not what Aleksey Leonov had expected when he enrolled in the cosmonaut program. But here he was with Pavel Belyayev, another equally uncomfortable space pilot, sitting under the stars inside their downed space capsule in a snow-filled birch forest somewhere in northern Russia. They were sitting in the dark, since Leonov was saving his emergency flashlight to signal rescuers (if they ever showed up), and they listened to the snaps and growls of a pack of hungry wolves as they prowled outside the partially open hatch.

Still, Leonov could consider himself lucky to be alive at all. He had cheated death twice during training—once when his parachute tangled and once when his car went off a lake-side road one night and broke through the ice into deep water. But he had untangled his chute by hand only a few hundred feet off the ground, and he had swum to safety in the dark. He had also cheated death twice already on this space flight, once when he managed to struggle back into the spacecraft's air lock after a harrowing spacewalk, and once when the spacecraft's autopilot had broken down, forcing Belyayev to perform an untested manual backup procedure that had led to this two-thousand-mile miss during landing.

In order to get the flight off before the first American Gemini manned flight, all the corners had been cut and all the safety measures sacrificed. It had all been planned in order to present Nikita Khrushchev with another space spectacular to use in yet another ideological offensive. The irony was that Khrushchev had been overthrown five months before, but the new regime had ordered the risky mission to proceed—a space success presumably would legitimize their own new order (and the launch did upstage Gemini-3 by just five days).

Leonov didn't even know where they had sent Khrushchev in retirement. Maybe they were still looking for a suitable spot. The cosmonaut shivered in the dark, his skin rubbing raw against loose wires and pinching joints in his spacesuit, and listened to the animals moving around just a few feet outside. If he were bitter enough, Leonov could have easily thought of *one* place he wished Khrushchev could be sent: right next to his favorite toys, the glorious cosmonauts, right there in the cold, dark capsule. But if such thoughts occurred to Leonov, he never told.

Both the Mercury program and the manned Vostok program had ended in the spring of 1963. The United States looked next toward the two-man Gemini capsule, with the first manned launchings set for late 1964, involving space rendezvous, space dockings and spacewalking. The logical next step in the Soviet program was the development of a versatile multipurpose spacecraft called the Soyuz, but Chief Designer Korolev did not expect it to be available until 1965 at the earliest.

In 1963 the Soviet space budget again came up for review, and once more Khrushchev's needs prevailed over logical development. According to the account of the defecting science writer Vladimirov (which is entirely consistent with external evidence), Khrushchev demanded that Korolev find some way to counteract the Gemini program and keep the initiative in Soviet hands. If the Americans were planning on sending two men up in one ship, well then, the Soviets would send three men into orbit aboard one ship! Such was the order which Korolev received in mid-1963.

Since the Soyuz would simply not be ready in time to upstage the Gemini, its development was suspended. The only manned spacecraft available to satisfy Khrushchev's demand was the one-man Vostok, so Korolev set his engineering teams to work upgrading it. Through ingenuity and daring, Korolev was able to accommodate this requirement —but at a terrible risk, and with a total sacrifice of any semblance of scientific or engineering research.

Here's how it was done: the Vostok ejection seat was removed and the reserve parachute eliminated. This provided room for three men squeezed in sideways, without spacesuits. Enough food, water and oxygen was crammed in for a single day in space (two days in an emergency). A small solid-fuel rocket, fused to ignite just prior to touchdown, would make the landing survivable. A reserve retrorocket was added, since it was no longer possible (as on Vostok) to pack sufficient supplies to allow the pilot to survive long enough (a week or so) for natural air drag to bring the ship back to earth if the main retrorocket failed. Two slightly different models of the ship were produced: one simply supported three men for a short space flight, and the other added a collapsible air-lock unit, which—together with the equipment needed to pressurize the crewmen's spacesuits— squeezed out the room for the third cosmonaut couch, making the ship a two-man vehicle.

To signify these changes, the ship received a new name, Voskhod, which means about the same as Vostok in Russian: a "trip upward," or "rising" (as in "sunrise").

It took about a year to make the changes and build several capsules. In September 1964 one of them was launched for a one-day unmanned test, clearing the way for the manned shot. Once again, there was a flurry of "inside reports" and "high-level leaks" from "usually reliable sources" in Moscow: the story was that a major new Soviet manned space mission involving three cosmonauts was about to blast off. Once again, the Soviet manned space program was going to upstage the Americans, whose two-man Gemini was six months away and whose three-man Apollo was at least two years away.

When the three-man spaceship Voskhod blasted off on October 11, 1964, the Soviets exulted. SORRY, APOLLO! was the mocking headline in *Pravda*. Predictions that the United States might ever catch up were discounted in a prominent article: "Now such prophecies from the Americans can bring forth only an ironic smile. The gap is not closing, but increasing. This is natural . . . the so-called system of free enterprise is turning out to be powerless in competition with socialism in such a complex and modern area as space research." Many people in the West—including otherwise well-informed specialists—believed these claims of an ever-widening space gap.

Particularly impressive was the fact that two of the three men aboard the Voskhod were non-pilots: an engineer named Konstantin Feoktistov (whose bureau was responsible for the Vostok-to-Voskhod conversion work) and a young doctor named Boris Yegorov (who had been involved with the earlier dogs-in-space tests). Feoktistov later became a leading project manager for the Salyut space-station program in the 1970s, and Yegorov came to head a large space-medicine institute. Their prestigious (and courageous) space flights certainly may have contributed to their promotions, but they were evidently highly qualified space scientists already. It later turned out that they, and their anonymous backups, had received only four months of flight training—and returned to their former jobs immediately after their safe return.

Voskhod-1's landing was only twenty-four hours after its launching, and this brevity puzzled Western observers: a mission of at least six days had been forecast. (Why take a doctor except for a flight longer than any previous one?) To explain the shortness of the mission, various theories were suggested by observers: the non-pilots had gotten sick (pilots liked this suggestion); the orbit had not been stable; the ship had experienced control problems; the space program had encountered political problems.

That last theory deserves elaboration. The stunning news that Khrushchev had been overthrown by the Brezhnev faction came out shortly after the announcement of the cosmonauts' return to earth. Several political observers suggested that as a slap at Khrushchev's space-spectacle approach, the crew had been peremptorily ordered back to earth, thus signifying the establishment of a new order of priorities. Moreover, when the cosmonauts had asked for a one-day extension of the flight, Korolev had quoted *Hamlet* to them: "There are more things in heaven and earth, Horatio, than are dreamed of in your philosophies." That quotation appeared to be an oblique reference to outside political pressures.

But the schedule of events in Moscow does not support speculation that the flight was aborted for political reasons. During the early hours of the flight, Khrushchev had chatted exuberantly with the cosmonauts over a telephone link from his vacation retreat on the Black Sea. When the conspirators made their move, Khrushchev flew to Moscow—and there probably was considerable and prolonged doubt over who was really in control for many hours. By that time the cosmonauts had already landed. They remained in the recovery zone for several days until the situation stabilized, instead of returning immediately to Moscow for the customary ceremonial greetings. When they eventually got off their plane and marched to the Moscow airport reviewing stand, the leaders who greeted them were not the leaders who had talked to them while they were in flight. But if they thought anything amiss (or ironic), they gave no sign.

Probably the most convincing piece of evidence regarding the science-and-safety sacrifices made in order to carry out the manned Voskhod flights concerns the debate over the Voskhod's launch escape system. No rescue system was apparent: the Vostok ejection seat had been thrown away; an escape tower (such as on Mercury, Apollo and Soyuz) was not visible in any of the illustrations eventually released; the spacecraft's own retrorockets were nowhere near powerful enough. Following these eliminations, there was nothing left; yet when some analysts (such as myself) suggested in the early 1970s that the Soviets had been forced, under political pressure, to send up Voskhod space crews *without* any escape in the event of booster malfunction, this idea was widely ridiculed. The Soviets would never have any reason to do such a reckless thing!

Finally one of the former Voskhod cosmonauts was cornered during a press conference on a West European tour in 1975 and was asked to "set the record straight" so all these nasty insinuations could be dissipated. He characteristically did not give a straight answer, but he did clear up any doubts when he replied, "The chance to escape is very small. What really counts is the reliability of the booster spacecraft system. The Voskhod booster was very reliable."

So no launch escape system *had* been installed. The cosmonaut's rationalization, of course, was nonsense. As soon as the Soyuz program came along, an escape system *was* built into the spacecraft—even though it used the same "very reliable" booster as had the Voskhod. The risks had been accepted on the Voskhod shots in order to reap the political gains of scoring a few more space firsts.

What turned out to be the last big manned space spectacular, Khrushchev style, was the spacewalk of Aleksey Leonov in March 1965—five months after Khrushchev's overthrow. It was done by the usual modus operandi—with complete surprise, with disregard for the crew's safety and with a public disinformation campaign that later came close to having a serious impact on the U.S. astronaut program.

The spaceship Voskhod-2 was launched on March 18, 1965 (just *five days* prior to the first manned Gemini flight). An unmanned precursor test vehicle had apparently disintegrated on orbit the previous month, but the manned follow-on proceeded anyway; either the cause of the February failure was understood and easily fixed (not likely, considering the minimal amount of data sent back by radiotelemetry), or the political pressure to beat the Americans remained as decisive as ever. In any event, cosmonauts Pavel Belyayev and Aleksey Leonov blasted off from the Baikonur Cosmodrome at ten in the morning local time amid light snow flurries. The two cosmonauts began their preparations for the world's first spacewalk as soon as they reached orbit. While Leonov unstrapped himself from his couch and attached his backpack oxygen system, Belyayev activated the air lock, an inflatable section attached to a special door on one side of the cabin. Less than an hour after launch, all was ready.

Leonov then closed his visor, turned on his oxygen unit and crawled into the air lock. The air pressure in this chamber was reduced from 15 psi to 6 psi, the level chosen for use inside the suit (full air pressure would have ballooned the suit into immobility), and then was dropped to zero. The suit held its own air pressure, so Leonov proceeded to open the outer hatch and float headfirst out, drifting away from the spacecraft until reaching the end of his safety line.

After several minutes floating around in open space, Leonov returned to the hatch: his orders had been to simply get out and get back in. But at first he could not get his legs into the chamber. Holding on to a handrail next to the hatch, he was unable to bend at the waist far enough to slip his feet through the opening.

At this point, he nearly panicked, and his pulse and breathing rates zoomed. Although he had air for an hour, his exertions threatened to accelerate the onset of the dreaded bends, the depressurization malady caused by dissolved nitrogen suddenly fizzing in the blood. So Leonov resorted to an emergency gambit: he reduced the suit's air pressure still further (from 6 psi to less than 4 psi), virtually assuring the imminent onset of the bends but also offering the only apparent means of providing the spacesuit flexibility he needed to get back into the ship.

It worked. On the next try he managed to catch his toes on the far edge of the opening, and from there was able to slip feetfirst into the chamber. Partway in, he struggled to release a clasp on a movie camera and succeeded in retrieving it. Once he was all the way in, he fought with the air lock's outer hatch, pulling it closed behind him. By the time he repressurized the air lock (twelve minutes had elapsed since depressurization), he was soaked in sweat, his eyes were stinging from the salt in his perspiration and he was panting so hard he had fogged his visor.

He later made a candid appraisal of the experience: "It was much more difficult to go back in . . . it's very difficult to work. Of course, I was tired by then. And the way we had done during the training sessions—of course, it didn't work at all, so I really had to strain and put all my efforts in order to complete this return into the spacecraft. And it did not go at all like the way we prepared."

But that admission was not made until ten years later, while discussing his experiences with astronauts in Houston prior to the Apollo-Soyuz linkup. The account published immediately after the spacewalk was much different:

"It is no wonder," Leonov wrote in June 1965, "that in making the actual space flight we were essentially doing only what we had already done many times on earth. We were not called upon to do anything unusual, since the system of training on the ground was well thought out. [Return] into the ship did not present any particular difficulties. Pulse rate during the extravehicular activity coincided to a great degree with the data obtained during the ground studies in the spacecraft mock-up."

This public image of the spacewalk was more than deceptive—it was dangerous because it encouraged overambitious spacewalk plans at the NASA center in Houston. The following year, astronaut Eugene Cernan, on a spacewalk in June 1966, found himself in a desperate predicament, his heart racing, his lungs aching, his body soaked in sweat, his helmet fogged over; he eventually made it back into the capsule, temporarily blinded. Had anyone in the United States been aware of the serious difficulties which Leonov had actually experienced, Cernan's life would never have been placed in such jeopardy.

On Voskhod-2, Leonov had survived the spacewalk— barely. A new danger loomed a day later when it came time to return to earth: the autopilot failed and the cosmonauts canceled the rocket burn which was meant to divert their course back into the atmosphere. Belyayev took over manual control, the first Russian to do so, and on the next pass around earth was able to make the necessary maneuver.

Far off course and behind schedule, the Voskhod-2 plunged back to earth. The entry and landing sequences went normally and the cosmonauts landed gently in deep snow. When they crawled out of their capsule, they were dismayed to see not the flat, treeless steppes of Kazakhstan, but a thick birch forest amid mountains. They were somewhere in Russia, true, but far, far away from their would-be rescue teams. (It turned out they were in the Urals, two thousand miles off course.)

They had landed about noon, and the rest of the day passed without a single aircraft appearing in the sky. Still dressed in their spacesuits (whose scanty hygienic facilities soon were overloaded), since that was the only way to keep warm, the men built a small fire shortly before nightfall. The slight comfort which the flames afforded, both physical and psychological, was fleeting: Leonov caught sight of moving shadows amid the trees, which turned out to be wolves, who quickly displayed a late-winter hunger that overcame any fear of fire. The cosmonauts abandoned their campfire and fled back into the Voskhod capsule, where they spent the night in extreme discomfort, their misery and anxiety only increased by frantic wolves trying to force their way into the capsule.

Before midnight, the cosmonauts heard a search plane and determined by its sound that it was circling—their capsule distress radio beacon had been picked up. A few hours later, a helicopter came low overhead but could not land in the thick forest and soon went away. The wolves also left about this time. Just at dawn, a ski patrol arrived at the campsite: the helicopter had landed in a clearing only a few miles away. The cosmonauts changed clothes, ate and warmed themselves by a new fire for an hour before skiing out to the helicopter.

That was the end of the Voskhod program, although Western observers spent the next two years wondering when Voskhod-3 would be launched. It seemed logical that two men would spend several weeks aboard such a spacecraft, and when amateur radio observers in Europe detected brief Voskhod-like radio signals on July 3, 1965, some people assumed that a manned launch had failed.

But that's extremely unlikely, knowing what we now do about the Voskhod. The Soviets could count themselves lucky to have gotten two crews back alive from one-day flights. Longer manned missions were not feasible, nor were they part of the purpose of the Voskhod program. It had succeeded in doing the spectaculars *first:* it could do no more.

In the balance sheet of history, the Soviet cosmonaut spectaculars of the 1961–1965 period must be judged by several often contradictory standards. The web of secrecy surrounding the missions allowed and encouraged most people in the West to grossly overestimate the actual levels of Soviet space technology, although it also led to the equally erroneous conclusions that there were dozens of secret space disasters, or even that the whole program was actually a charade. While this secrecy may have been useful to the Soviet Union in the short run, it also contributed to a vigorous reaction from the United States. John Kennedy's commitment to the moon landing came in direct response to the Gagarin flight and the Bay of Pigs humiliation. Additionally, euphoria over space successes may have contributed to Khrushchev's bold —even reckless—power plays over Berlin in 1961, Cuba in late 1962 and Southeast Asia in 1963–1964, moves which led to direct eyeball-to-eyeball superpower confrontations.

In engineering terms the Khrushchev approach practically crippled the rational development of the Soviet manned space program by demanding an unending series of frantic "beat-the-Americans" projects, each one more risky than the last and none of them justifiable on other than propaganda grounds: the 1962 two-ships-at-once, the 1963 woman-in-space, the 1964 three-men-in-one-ship and the 1965 space-walk were each dead-end detours (none were repeated) which absorbed nearly the entire attention of the whole Soviet space industry—an attention which otherwise could well have been devoted to more productive developments.

Without this Khrushchevian approach, which sidetracked advanced programs in favor of immediate sensational space shots, the first successful Soyuz flight might have come as early as 1966, two years sooner than it really did; the first successful Salyut space station might have come in 1969, five years sooner; and the first man to the moon might have been a Russian. But such a rational space program would not have impelled the United States to a response. If the truth be told —the Apollo program would probably not have been started or sustained.

The responsibilities forced on Korolev had continued to

increase after the Gagarin triumph in the spring of 1961, which had temporarily, at least, eased the pain of the October 1960 tragedy. Korolev continued to walk a precariously balanced path, fulfilling Khrushchev's demands with minimum possible risk—all the while trying to accomplish meaningful space exploration.

In the last year of his life, 1965, Korolev sought to redirect Soviet space efforts and to manipulate the new Brezhnev-Kosygin regime into allowing him to rebuild the cosmonaut program. Work on the Soyuz spacecraft and on the giant Proton space booster continued. He personally directed the recruitment of Russia's first professional civilian cosmonauts, expert space engineers from his own design bureau. A series of robot lunar probes came closer and closer to making a successful soft landing on the moon. A new generation of applications satellites—some for communications, some for navigation and others for military reconnaissance—was ready to appear.

But every day seemed harder. Korolev was only fifty-nine, but the privation and beatings during his slave-labor-camp and prison years had wrecked his health even before the pressures of the last ten years of space shots had taken their toll.

He would come home after a twelve-hour day to his apartment in Moscow (now a private museum) by chauffeured limousine, walk past the KGB guards, whose uniforms were still the same color they had been at Kolyma (but now they were there to protect him, of course) and greet his wife. They would sit inside at the foot of the stairs, discussing the day's events, while he gathered the strength to ascend to his bedroom. There he worked on his memoirs, we are told—but that document, even if it still exists today, has never been published.

For a while, it might have seemed that his colossal willpower would continue, almost unaided, to allow him to overcome the never-ending obstacles before him: the budgetary battles, the equipment failures, the scarcity of resources, the low quality of the resources which were available. The web of secrecy and anonymity must have chafed, but that, too, would pass.

What more did he need? That question was posed by a visiting journalist in mid-1965. Korolev's answer was simple: "Time and health." He was to have neither.

6

☆

Death and Disaster

Korolev died in early 1966. The next seven years were all downhill for the Soviet space program.

It is hard to overestimate Korolev's uniqueness and the essential spark which he seems to have provided. With him gone, the soul seems to have gone out of the Soviet space drive. The ensuing chronicle of failures, death and disaster is a tribute to Korolev, if only we can read it correctly.

The irony is that the early loss of Korolev need not have happened. True, his health had not been good and his heart was not strong. He suffered from the aftereffects of the GULag death camps. But the best interpretation of the reports of his death is that Korolev was the victim of a botched operation, of medical malpractice brought on by the defects of Soviet science bureaucracy.

The official obituary in *Pravda* on January 16, 1966, reported that Korolev had died two days earlier of "cardiac insufficiency" after an operation. A medical report described his problems with a malignancy in the large intestine, arteriosclerosis, emphysema and a generally disturbed metabolism. The operation had been for removal of the colon tumors, and the surgery itself had been a success—except that the patient died because his heart gave out.

There also was a different version of his death. At first it was whispered among friends, then mentioned obliquely in letters, then printed openly in underground newsletters. The first public revelation came in 1970, when the memoirs of a long-time close friend of Korolev's, professor Georgiy A. Ozerov, were published in Yugoslavia. Ozerov reported that the operation had been for hemorrhoids, not for cancer—and that Korolev had died because of mistakes by the Kremlin doctors who performed the operation.

Additional details continued to leak out as the years passed. When the Russian biologist Zhores Medvedev emigrated in the mid-1970s, he brought with him a manuscript, subsequently published in 1978 as *Soviet Science.* Medvedev identified the surgeon in charge as Dr. Boris Petrovskiy, the Minister of Health of the Soviet Union. Petrovskiy, despite his lack of recent surgical practice, took command of the operation, which had been planned as a simple removal of hemorrhoids. However, cancerous tumors were discovered and Petrovskiy decided to continue the operation despite the absence of proper equipment or sufficient blood supplies. Complications ensued, which led to Korolev's death on the table.

In 1979 an eminent Moscow surgeon named Vladimir Golyakhovskiy emigrated to the West. When asked about Korolev's death, he corroborated Medvedev's account but added an extra dimension concerning Health Minister Petrovskiy's character. According to Dr. Golyakhovskiy, the Soviet Health Minister had done his best to impress Korolev with his own expertise, to the extent of making a quick (and wrong) diagnosis of Korolev's colon problem, while refusing to consult any other specialists. But midway through the operation, Petrovskiy had realized his error when he discovered the more serious tumor. Rather than admit the error of his diagnosis, he had continued the surgery far beyond the safe limits of the anesthesia. While his assistants looked on in astonishment, the Health Minister had begun a complicated surgical procedure for which neither his fingers and eyesight nor his recent practice made him at all capable. "Soon a large blood vessel ruptured and severe hemorrhaging began," recalled the exiled Dr. Golyakhovskiy. "The situation became critical."

Swallowing his pride in the panic of realization of what he had done, Petrovskiy had sent for the best surgeon on his staff—who was also a personal rival for status in the hospital. The man, Dr. Aleksandr Vishnevskiy, could not be located at his home or office; eventually he was found by police as he was driving through Moscow. Vishnevskiy was rushed to the operating room, but one glance at the unconscious Korolev was all he needed. "I do not operate on dead men," he solemnly announced, and walked out of the room.

"With proper diagnosis and competent surgery," the emigrant Dr. Golyakhovskiy told an interviewer in 1979, "his condition could most probably have been corrected." The Soviet system finally caught up with Korolev, it seems.

Korolev was cremated and his ashes were interred in the Kremlin Wall, the place of highest honor in the U.S.S.R. mausoleum hierarchy. Soon, year by year, he would be joined by the ashes of his best cosmonauts. But for a few months, Korolev's magic continued to cast its spell of good luck on Soviet space launches. Three weeks after his funeral, a robot probe (the ninth attempt) made a hard, but survivable landing on the moon and sent back television pictures. The following month, a surplus Voskhod capsule was launched with two dogs on board; after three weeks in space they were brought back to earth for medical examination.

Next, another giant Proton rocket was launched, the third in a series that had started with two successes the year before. But this time the hardware broke down, and the rocket fell back in flames from the edge of space. It was the first Proton failure ever. It was a bad omen. Korolev had been dead only two months.

As 1967 began, the glamour had worn off the space race in the United States. John Kennedy had been dead for three years; Khrushchev was stashed away somewhere on the Black Sea coast; the cost of war in Southeast Asia continued to soar.

Since the time of the last Soviet manned space flight in early 1965, there had been ten consecutive American launches in the two-man Gemini series. It seemed that the United States had finally pulled ahead in the space race, and many people called for a reduction in space expenditures, for a redirection of technology. Then came the catastrophic Apollo fire on January 27, which claimed the lives of three astronauts. Suddenly, the whole future of the astronaut program seemed in doubt.

At the annual conference of the International Astronautical Federation in Madrid a few months earlier, American space experts had confided some of their anxieties over budget cutbacks to their Soviet counterparts. "Don't worry," they were told, "we'll help you out with that shortly after the first of the year." These private assurances came at a time when rumors had once more started to be heard: a major new Soviet space advance was in preparation, one which would eclipse the entire Gemini program in a single mission.

In March, while the United States was still reeling from the Apollo fire, the Soviets began to openly discuss the impending flight. The director of cosmonaut training, General Nikolay Kamanin, was quite explicit: "When the crews are ready for the flight, then we will give the orders to take off. This might take place in the spring or the summer."

Kamanin continued, with what turned out later to be unintentional irony: "We must be fully convinced, however, that the flight will be a success. The flights we are preparing will be more complicated than the previous ones, and thus the preparation for them will have to be appropriately longer. . . . We do not intend to speed up our program. Excessive haste leads to fatal accidents, as in the case of the three American astronauts last January." (Kamanin was ultimately forced to eat his words when he was unceremoniously retired in 1971, following the second manned-space-flight fatality in four years.)

Soviet officials were so confident and proud of the impending mission that they were uncharacteristically open in their discussions with Westerners. By the middle of April, the Western press community in Moscow was hearing many extremely specific forecasts. An Associated Press dispatch on April 20 described the coming "spectacular and significant" mission as "imminent." On April 22, the United Press International reported further that the flight would come within forty-eight hours and "will include the most spectacular Soviet space venture in history—an attempted in-flight hookup between the two ships and a transfer of crews."

The following morning, the spaceship Soyuz-1 was launched. It was the first Soviet manned space shot since the death of Korolev, and the first cosmonaut flight in more than two years. The pilot, Colonel Vladimir Komarov, had been the commander of the Voskhod-1 spaceship, and this was the first time a Soviet cosmonaut was making a second flight. At forty years of age, he was the oldest cosmonaut yet to fly.

But the grandiose forecasts were not to come true. After twenty-four hours of remarkably low-key publicity, Moscow announced that Komarov was returning to earth. An ominous twelve-hour silence then followed. Finally came the shocking news: Colonel Komarov was dead.

From the official point of view, things were quite straightforward. Komarov had taken off on a simple one-day test flight, had completed it successfully and had headed back to earth. Just prior to landing, a freak accident caused the parachute lines to tangle, leading to a fatal crash landing. Komarov's body was cremated and the ashes were placed in a niche in the Kremlin Wall.

At the funeral for Komarov in Red Square, Gagarin delivered the eulogy. "We will not be deterred by temporary setbacks," he affirmed. "We will continue with our program for exploring space, at whatever cost."

A few weeks after Komarov's funeral, Gagarin expressed his thoughts in carefully considered words in a long newspaper interview. "Mankind never gains anything without cost," he wrote. "There never has been a bloodless victory over nature."

"Nothing will stop us," he continued. "The road to the stars is steep and dangerous. But we're not afraid. Every one of us cosmonauts is ready to carry on the work of Vladimir Komarov—our good friend and a remarkable man."

Later in the article he described the future of Soviet manned space flight, which would go on despite the tragedy: "How long is this dramatic list of explorers of our planet! Men have perished. But new ships have left their moorings, new aircraft have taxied to the takeoff strip and new teams have gone off into the forest and the desert.

"Space flights can't be stopped. This isn't the work of any one man or even a group of men. It is a historical process which mankind is carrying out in accordance with the natural laws of human development.

"Both new cosmonauts and those who already have been in space will fly again . . ."

But for Western observers, there were baffling questions. Had the predictions of the planned second launch been correct? If so, what could have gone wrong? Why had Komarov landed so far from the normal recovery zone? What had really caused his death? And would the disaster have as serious an impact on the Soyuz program as the Apollo fire had on the American program?

Weighty speculations and fanciful suppositions proliferated. The flight had been rushed, one commentator said, to occur in time for May Day and to help dispel the bad publicity caused by the recent scandalous defection of Stalin's daughter. Other theorists speculated about the significance of the ship's name: a second flight must have been planned because the ship was called Soyuz-1, although no previous first flights had ever used an ordinal digit, thus implying that a Soyuz-2 was already in existence. The Soyuz-1 had been tumbling; the pilot had become sick; the life-support system had failed, killing Komarov while still in space; there actually had been other cosmonauts on board, but they had been injured or killed during the launching; the ship had been totally incinerated on return; another rocket had exploded on the pad, killing more Soviet cosmonauts; Komarov was not even dead.

The gossip, like good wine, improved with age. The incident eventually became so well wrapped in myth and hearsay that people were convinced that "anything could have happened." According to an account published in 1973 by a pseudonymous ex-National Security Agency technician who claimed to have monitored the radio transmissions from Soyuz-1 at a listening post in Turkey, the doomed cosmonaut tried repeatedly to bring his ship under control. A few hours before landing, Komarov sobbed a last farewell to his wife, who had been rushed to the control center; then he was praised by a tearful Soviet Premier Aleksey Kosygin.

That whole story can probably be safely dismissed as exaggerated hearsay or pure fabrication, since there has never been any reason to suspect that Komarov believed he would not survive the landing. But in an attempt to stick to the few known facts, Western space analysts (myself included) went overboard and gave the Soviets "the benefit of the doubt" on the flight. They generally concluded, based on consideration of the modest flight plans of two unmanned Soyuz capsules launched earlier in the winter of 1966–1967, that the Soyuz-1 mission probably had really been intended only as a short solo hop. (The more complex two-ship docking and space-walk was probably to follow later.)

Meanwhile, the theories and facts about Soyuz-1 remained unanswered. There was nothing new for almost ten years. Then in 1977, the Soviet space censorship apparatus approved the release of some old cosmonaut photographs of Yuriy Gagarin. One showed Gagarin, who was the backup pilot to Komarov on the Soyuz-1, posing with a group of cosmonauts. When this innocuous photograph (for so it must have seemed to the censors) reached Western observers, it overturned all of their former ideas about the goal of the Soyuz-1 flight.

In the photo, Gagarin was seen talking with four cosmonauts who were preparing for a space mission. Two wore spacesuits (they were Khrunov and Yeliseyev, who were eventually to walk in space from Soyuz-5 to Soyuz-4 in 1969); two were dressed in flight coveralls, as befitted the non-spacewalking ship commanders. One of the spaceship commanders was Komarov, who had his arms draped over the shoulders of the spacesuited figures.

The implication was obvious and startling. Since Komarov was in the picture, it had to have been taken prior to April 1967. The picture, then, must have been a group portrait of the men who were *supposed* to have been the crew on Soyuz-1 and Soyuz-2, if everything had gone as planned. The double linkup and spacewalk rumors had been accurate and authentic; the subsequent Moscow denials had been deceptions; the conclusions of Western observers had been too generous.

Now, these deductions, while interesting, were not particularly earthshaking. (Although, of course, it's nice to see such a big cover-up fall to pieces.) What is significant is that in early 1967, two and a half years after Khrushchev's overthrow because of, among many other things, mismanagement and political demands on the space program, the Kremlin pressure to produce space spectaculars had not relented. The safe, reasonable approach into the Soyuz program would have seen a year-long series of each more complex flights leading to the two-ship linkup and spacewalk transfer. This was abandoned in favor of an overambitious gamble that would indeed have been a sensation—had it worked.

It did not work, and Colonel Vladimir Komarov paid with his life. That was bad enough, but it also demonstrated that Korolev's successors (who, after all, must have expected the mission to be safe, if not successful) had made an incredible blunder in judgment regarding their actual chances of success.

And we still don't really know what killed cosmonaut Komarov. Normally reliable sources, both in Europe and in Washington, D.C., have recently independently corroborated that the Soyuz-1 had an electrical power shortage and one of the two solar power wings failed to unfold immediately after reaching orbit. Later, once Colonel Komarov had decided to return to earth, he missed two perfect landing passes and only caught the third and last. But what any of this has to do with the fatal parachute failure is still unclear.

There is one hint: the Soyuz-1 fell short of its landing point by six hundred miles. Because of the shape of the command module (which, like the Gemini and Apollo capsules, could provide a small amount of gliding power), space engineers have calculated that the actual undershoot could have been caused by the capsule's spinning during the reentry. Such a maneuver would have been useful if the spaceship's guidance system had failed, since it would balance out all aerodynamic lift forces.

Thus, an equipment failure could have forced Colonel Komarov to choose an emergency backup guidance program, in which the command module would be deliberately put into a controlled roll. There is one drawback: such a landing procedure imposes double the normal G forces associated with the reentry, 8 to 10 Gs instead of 4 or 5. Komarov may have blacked out momentarily from this overload, and consequently may have not been able to manually halt the capsule's spin. If the capsule was still spinning when the parachutes popped out automatically, the shroud lines could have twisted up or tangled. The impact speed would have been about five hundred miles per hour.

We may never know the true drama of those final moments prior to the crash. As the Soyuz-1 descended, the pilot probably tried desperately to straighten out the parachute by shaking the capsule. Radio communications with Mission Control would have been bad because the ship was so far off course. Even after Komarov's ship had hit the ground, there would have been reasons for hoping that the pilot had survived due to a last-minute parachute opening or to impact in deep snow. Many hours probably elapsed before the wreckage of the Soyuz-1 was located (its directional radio beacons, of course, would have been smashed). At long last the hopes would have been dashed as word finally came from the would-be rescuers: no survivors.

It is hard to say what shape Komarov's body would have been in when rescuers reached the crash site. The Soyuz itself would probably have remained in one piece, although the hatch in the nose could have sprung open or even torn loose to smash onto Komarov's head. The impact itself would, of course, have killed him: it would have broken his hips, back and neck while rupturing nearly every blood vessel and organ in his torso. His couch was probably torn loose from its moorings, with support struts piercing his body from below. Any kind of cabin fire would have been unlikely, so searchers would have found him lying amid the wreckage of the command module—recognizable but quite dead.

His fellow cosmonauts engaged in a program of public reassurance. A few weeks after the crash, Gagarin denounced the people who refused to believe the official version of events: "It is very annoying to hear all these cock-and-bull stories. I frequently heard Komarov's reports from orbit. There wasn't even a shadow of alarm. Everything conformed completely with calculations."

Image once again triumphed over reality, at least for a while. Gagarin's image, too, was to become bigger than life. Nine months after proclaiming that Komarov's death had been a minor glitch on the road to glory, Gagarin lost his own life in a jet crash, and like Komarov's, his body was cremated and his ashes were placed in a niche in the Kremlin Wall.

There seems to have been one additional casualty of the Soyuz-1 disaster: cosmonaut Valeriy Bykovskiy, a veteran of the Vostok-5 flight four years earlier. Photographs and informed sources provide evidence that he was supposed to have been the command pilot of Soyuz-2, the spacecraft on which the two ship-to-ship spacewalkers would have been launched in April 1967. Yet when the ship-to-ship stunt was ultimately carried out in January 1969, Bykovskiy had been removed from the flight crew. Years passed and dozens of cosmonauts blasted off—but Bykovskiy did not fly until Soyuz-22 in 1976, nine years after he should have flown Soyuz-2.

No official explanation has ever been offered. That is odd because in those other cases where medical complications temporarily removed cosmonauts from flight status, such information was quickly released (as in the cases of Komarov, Belyayev, Grechko, Gorbatko, Kubasov and others). So apparently Bykovskiy didn't get sick. One clue may be that Bykovskiy's return to cosmonaut activities began in 1972, when he became the training director for the Soviet side of the Apollo-Soyuz orbital linkup; that was soon after the major cosmonaut shake-up which saw General Nikolay Kamanin, aging war hero and authoritarian space tsar, replaced as cosmonaut corps commander by three-time space veteran Vladimir Shatalov. Perhaps, just perhaps, Bykovskiy's reaction to Komarov's death on Soyuz-1 made him lose favor with the martinet Kamanin. Did he accuse somebody of pushing the launch prematurely, thus killing his friend? Did he express reservations about his own willingness to fly a new Soyuz craft? Whatever it was, it led to many years of disgrace.

Twenty-one months after Komarov's death, following three more unmanned test missions, including two automatic orbital linkups and one simple manned flight, the time came to fulfill the Soyuz-1 predictions and make the linkup/spacewalk. On January 14, 1969, Soyuz-4 was sent up with a single pilot and two empty seats; Soyuz-5, with three cosmonauts, blasted off the next day. They linked up nose-to-nose. Two of the men donned spacesuits, exited through a side hatch in their ship and proceeded along handrails to a waiting open hatch on the other ship. Five hours later the ships unlatched; they each landed separately.

It was a neat trick, and soon afterward the Soviet press heralded the mission as a precursor to space rescue and space assembly. The docked ships were billed as having formed "the world's first space station"—which they hadn't. American-manned spacecraft had performed orbital rendezvous and docking operations three years before, and the Soviets had twice linked up unmanned Soyuz craft (without ever disclosing the vehicles had been of the Soyuz type)—so the new manned linkup was not really a breakthrough. (Even the ship-to-ship spacewalk had been practiced by American astronauts in 1966, when they inspected the Agena satellites with which their Gemini spacecraft had docked.) Nevertheless, the Soviet news media hailed the mission as the most important space event since Gagarin's pioneering flight in 1961.

The cosmonauts themselves were exuberant—it was their most sensational space success in more than five years, and it helped erase the bitter memories of Komarov's and Gagarin's deaths. Their excitement was so boundless that their human sides showed through: as the two ships had approached each other and one slipped its docking probe into the latching mechanism of the other, a crewman on the second ship shouted out in mock alarm over the radio, "We're being raped! We're being raped!" Laughter and cheers followed as the ships linked firmly together. Moscow TV viewers saw and heard the whole sequence when the videotapes were first played over the air a few hours after the linkup, but all subsequent replays of the docking deleted the audio portion of the historic moment.

The Soviet publicity verged on hysteria and it was not hard to see why. The Apollo-8 astronauts had just returned from a trip around the moon, and some counterbalance was needed. One central fact took awhile to sink in: the much-vaunted linkup and spacewalk were in reality a technological dead end. They were obsolete. The efforts served no useful engineering or scientific purpose, but clearly were supposed to have propaganda value. And that was all they turned out to be good for.

Still, it was something to celebrate. A parade through Moscow was to be followed by a televised awards ceremony in the Kremlin, and despite the January cold, the public turned out to cheer the motorcade.

One man had other intentions. As the cars passed slowly through the Borovitskiy Gate into the walled Kremlin compound, a young army lieutenant named Ilyin stepped from the crowd, produced two pistols and fired them into one of the cars. He may have been aiming for Brezhnev, but the car he hit was full of cosmonauts (one of whom had eyebrows as bushy as Brezhnev's, possibly leading to the mistake).

The car's driver was hit several times and died soon after; in the back seat, cosmonauts Nikolayev, Beregovoy and Leonov pushed Valentina Tereshkova down to the floor and crouched over her as they were showered with flying glass. None of them was hit by bullets, but Beregovoy's face was covered with blood from cuts from the glass fragments. Ilyin, meanwhile, had been grabbed by security guards and taken to an insane asylum. The awards ceremony proceeded as scheduled. A brief *Tass* dispatch denounced the "provocation" and life went on normally.

In October 1969, three separate manned ships were launched on consecutive days for a week-long space spectacular. As in the January linkup, the event was boldly proclaimed as another space breakthrough; but as with the January linkup, the purpose was public relations. Apollo-11 had landed the first men on the moon only three months before, and new Soviet political directives had evidently been issued: come up with something, anything, to take the edge off the American triumph. And so space continued to serve politics —in the form of a three-ring space circus, three manned ships in space simultaneously.

The direction which space officials themselves were urging was connected with preparations for the launching of the first space station, a habitable module which would be repeatedly visited by cosmonauts. The twenty-ton space station would be lifted into space atop a Proton rocket, and cosmonauts would follow soon afterward inside a seven-ton Soyuz. The technologies which needed developing included rendezvous and docking (which had succeeded in January) and the opening of a transfer tunnel between two spacecraft (which had probably been planned for the October triple flight but had been abandoned when the linkup failed). Since the space station would host cosmonauts for many weeks, Soviet space doctors wanted some medical information from longer flights—and this was the purpose of an eighteen-day solo Soyuz marathon in mid-1970. Due to factors in the ship's control and environmental systems, the cosmonauts' health deteriorated alarmingly, and after landing they were carried from their capsule on stretchers. The doctors diagnosed vertigo and overall weakness, conditions which had to be counteracted if long-duration space-station missions were ever to succeed.

The first Salyut space station was launched in April 1971,

slightly more than ten years after Gagarin's flight—and two years before the American Skylab. The vehicle was named in honor of the decennial: a "salute" to Gagarin.

Once a three-man cosmonaut crew was able to board the station in early June (the first attempt late in April had failed), Moscow spokesmen began acclaiming the mission as better than the American moon flights. The Apollo program was a dramatic and technologically impressive stunt, but it had long been criticized as being expensive and dangerous, and lacking in staying power and true scientific value. In contrast, the Salyut space-station program was touted as being equally dramatic, equally difficult, but far more valuable to science, medicine and the national economy.

Throughout the month of June, there were nightly reports from Salyut broadcast over Soviet television. Live telecasts were made of the three cosmonauts: Lieutenant Colonel Georgiy Dobrovolskiy, forty-three, the commander; civilian engineer Vladislav "Vadim" Volkov, thirty-five, a veteran cosmonaut; and civilian Viktor Patsayev, thirty-eight, another flight-test engineer. The men joked, somersaulted and showed off their home in space. Two decided to grow beards; Patsayev celebrated a birthday in flight and his comrades toasted him—on camera—with fruit juice in tubes.

The Soviet space station was a genuine first, flying long before Skylab, the U.S. equivalent. So for more than three weeks, the entire Soviet population was treated to the glorious spectacle of Russian spacemen setting new space records in an arena of the space race which the Americans had not even dared enter. The tremendous public exposure of the mission excited the public's imagination, and the three "space colonists" overnight became the most beloved space heroes since Gagarin and Tereshkova. It was the Sputnik and Lunik and Vostok and Voskhod days all over again, and the Soviet propaganda machine made the most of it. Moon flights were a detour; space stations were the wave of the future, and the Soviet Union was leading the wave.

As week followed week that June in 1971, the excitement and exultation mounted. A glorious welcome home was in store for the cosmic heroes. The humiliation of the Apollo moon triumphs had been exorcised. Soviet space supremacy had been restored by three personable, heroic cosmonauts.

Then, on the twenty-fourth day of the mission, it all came to an end. Although there never had been any official indication of how long the flight was intended to last, Western observers had speculated that Dobrovolskiy, Volkov and Patsayev were going to spend about a month in space—so the sudden radio announcement of their return to earth caught everyone by surprise. And the final few sentences of the official bulletin, tagged onto the end almost as an afterthought, wiped out the public euphoria in an instant: "When recovery forces reached the Soyuz, the men were found in their seats without signs of life. An investigation has been ordered."

Those dry words conceal the drama behind them. Imagine the scene: the capsule lands gently in a wheat field and rescue helicopters touch down nearby. There's some puzzlement—the crew's radio doesn't seem to be working—but it's forgotten in the overall excitement. People run over to the capsule, which is lying on its side, and quickly unfasten the hatch. It swings open and sunlight streams inside. The first man there —probably a doctor—shouts a greeting and thrusts his hand inside for a hearty welcoming handshake. There is no answer —the men hang from their seat straps. Momentary puzzlement turns to horror as the doctor, now inside, checks for a pulse three times—and three times finds none.

Imagine again: how does the news work its way up the chain of command? What, all dead? Check again, there must be some mistake! The momentum of the jubilation already in motion must have been switched off in an instant. Some must have asked, "How?", thinking of the sudden deaths. Others must also have asked, "How?", thinking of how to tell the Kremlin, how to tell the families, how to tell the world.

The most worrisome possibility facing space officials was that the flight itself had killed them, that three weeks of weightlessness had so weakened their bodies that the shock of reentry had overloaded their hearts. Or perhaps they had been poisoned by the fumes of an electrical fire. The future of the entire manned space program was in doubt.

The deaths of these three cheerful, competent young men hit the Soviet people devastatingly hard. Westerners in Russia at the time compared the national grief there to the American public's trauma over the assassination of President John Kennedy in 1963. It was more than just unexpected death: for the Soviets, it was the crushing of a dream. The flight had been seen as a return to glory for the Soviet space program, as a riposte to American space successes.

There were no triumphal parades. While the nation mourned, the bodies of the three cosmonauts were openly displayed on biers in a hall in Moscow. Hundreds of thousands of Russians filed by, leaving mountains of midsummer flowers. Then the bodies were cremated, and in a televised state funeral, the ashes were interred in niches in the Kremlin Wall.

An American astronaut, Tom Stafford, was one of the pallbearers. When astronauts had volunteered to attend the funerals of Komarov in 1967 and Gagarin in 1968, they had been told it was an internal affair. But détente—in space and on earth—was now in the air, and the scale of worldwide expressions of sympathy surprised Soviet officials.

What had gone wrong *this* time? For foreign observers, there were several unanswered questions. They asked what the significance was of the now almost forgotten *first* linkup attempt, and why *that* crew had so precipitously returned to earth. What had been the intended mission duration of the doomed Soyuz crew, which did board the station in June, and had they been called down early for some reason? What was the exact cause of death for the cosmonauts? And how would this disaster affect future Soviet space-station efforts, especially with the impending launch of the American Sky-lab?

It soon turned out that they had suffocated. The air had leaked out of the capsule through a valve which had failed right after the de-orbit rocket burn, and the men had not been wearing spacesuits—their ship did not even carry any. The pressure drop would have led to a painful attack of the bends, but the men lost consciousness first, due to anoxia. As the ship entered the atmosphere, air would have leaked back in—but too late to save the cosmonauts. They had become the first human beings to die *in space.*

As usual, there were plenty of rumors in the absence of official candor. According to one Moscow story, there had been a near-disastrous electrical fire on board the Salyut, which had taken several hours to put out and which had nearly suffocated the crew—and the exhausted and shaken cosmonauts had rushed back to earth as soon as they could. Another piece of gossip related how the cosmonauts had cast off for home when suddenly they had an alarm which signified an air leak. They redocked with the Salyut and could find nothing wrong with their spaceship. As a precaution, flight controllers advised them to stay up another day so the alarm could be checked out, but the crew wanted to come home, and General Nikolay Kamanin, head of cosmonaut training, overruled the control center and ordered them back. When they cast off once more, the alarm sounded again, but Kamanin advised them to ignore it and proceed with the landing. (Kamanin *was* sacked soon after the disaster.) And several sources came up with a consistent account of how the men had been ordered back to earth prematurely after they had succumbed to exhaustion due to lack of sleep —they had been running two shifts with at least one crewman awake around the clock.

American space experts were given a briefing on the disaster in 1973 as part of negotiations for the Apollo-Soyuz linkup. They were told how the valve, designed to open near touchdown in order to equalize cabin pressure and outside pressure, had been jarred open when the command module had jettisoned the service module and the orbital module soon after firing the engine to head back to earth. The crew was momentarily distracted because the outrushing air spun the capsule around, leading to the automatic firing of small guidance rockets. When the men realized what was happening, they tried to crank the malfunctioning valve closed manually, but while struggling with it they lost consciousness. (It was here that one of them picked up the massive facial bruise that was visible while he lay in state.) Subsequent tests on the ground revealed a shocking oversight: although the air would leak out in less than a minute, the valve—even in optimal circumstances—took almost two minutes to close manually. Somebody had overlooked this basic incompatibility.

The first thing to do was to give spacesuits to all future cosmonauts. This was easier said than done, since the equipment needed to pump air into these spacesuits had to be added to the already cramped cabin. Room was finally made by removing one of the three cosmonaut couches—and for the next ten years, the Soyuz became a two-man spacecraft. In the meantime, the abandoned Salyut space station fell back into the atmosphere in October and disintegrated.

The modifications to the Soyuz design took about a year, and when an unmanned Soyuz went on a week-long orbital shakedown cruise late in June 1972, observers suspected that a new Salyut space-station launching would soon follow. Western newsmen in the Soviet Union began asking questions and soon had confirmation of their expectations. Among the most specific was the report on July 27 from a UPI correspondent: "The Soviet Union probably will launch a new Salyut space laboratory and a two- or three-man Soyuz spacecraft in the next few days, qualified communist sources said."

But nothing happened. Weeks passed, then months. There

was no doubt that the lack of space activity was suspicious. It took a year for Western observers to announce what they claimed to have learned later from intelligence sources: a Salyut *had* been launched on July 29, only two days after the UPI report had been filed. But the Proton booster rocket had malfunctioned and the space station had been destroyed. The subsequent manned launchings aboard the smaller Soyuz ships thus never took place.

By late 1972, after the secret Salyut launch failure, Soviet space officials must have been apprehensive about the approaching Skylab launch (which eventually took place on May 14, 1973). Spokesmen let it be known that Russia "deserved" to make the first successful space-station flight, in recognition of past Russian sacrifices. They were less explicit about the growing pressure which must have been coming from government agencies: unlike the moon race, the space-station race could not be sidestepped or dropped out of. Moscow had already publicly announced that it was going to win it, and had already tried once and failed.

On April 3, 1973, just six weeks before Skylab, it looked like the Soviets were going to succeed. The unmanned Salyut-2 was put into orbit, and all observers expected cosmonauts to follow shortly aboard Soyuz-12. But once again, the expectations were not fulfilled: after three weeks, Moscow announced that the mission had "ended successfully." There never had been any plan to send cosmonauts to visit *this* Salyut, according to Moscow spokesmen: the Salyut program was intended to include variants which would operate entirely in the automatic mode, or so went the official claims.

Western observers were extremely skeptical but had no hard evidence with which they could dispute what they suspected was another attempted cover-up of a major Soviet space failure. And suddenly a new complication appeared: a mystery spacecraft bearing the name Kosmos-557 was launched on May 11, only *four days* prior to the Skylab.

Kosmos-557 was put into an orbit very similar to that of Salyut-1 and Salyut-2. According to the terse official announcement, it was just another in a series of scientific satellites. But significant data soon became available: the radio signals from Kosmos-557 were very similar to those from Salyut-1 and other Soviet manned space vehicles; furthermore, the space vehicle was seen by visual space-trackers as very bright (and large), apparently about the size of earlier Salyut satellites. But again, no cosmonauts were ever launched, and as the weeks passed, the spacecraft drew nearer and nearer to earth as its orbit decayed without any counteraction from on-board rocket engines. Something was wrong with the satellite.

The ultimate fate of these twenty-ton spacecraft, Salyut-2 and Kosmos-557, was a foretaste of the Skylab scare of 1979, with one big difference: whereas NASA would warn the world of the out-of-control terminal descent of its space laboratory, the Soviets simply said nothing about where or when their two space labs would hit. The derelict Soviet space stations inexorably fell back toward the atmosphere, where both eventually burned up late in May. One showered burning fragments into the Pacific just east of the Phillipines, while the other just barely missed hitting Australia a few days later. Yet since the world was at that time busy watching the dramatic Skylab space-station repair effort (space-walking astronauts had to fix the crippled solar power wings), nobody paid attention. But it certainly was ironic how, six years later, the Soviets maintained a prim, holier-than-thou public stance about NASA's troubles with Skylab's uncontrolled return to earth.

While Americans were setting space records on Skylab in 1973, where were the Russians? The clues available at that time were not sufficient to figure out the true meaning of the Salyut-2 and Kosmos-557 debacles, but over the next two years additional information came in from radio amateurs, from leaks of U.S. intelligence data and from the Soviet

Red Star in Orbit

Union itself—mostly in the form of successful follow-on missions. A pattern emerged.

It now appears that the Soviet Union had intended to operate not one but two independent space stations in the weeks just prior to Skylab's launch in May 1973. The political pressure to upstage the expected American space spectacular must have been overwhelming, because a rational approach would never have involved dual missions, nor would the Soviet cosmonaut program have been in such a "rush" posture devoted to beating the public Skylab schedule at any cost. Under such a frantic pace, all risks were multiplied enormously, and it must be considered a stroke of luck that the space-station-control failures occurred prior to the on-orbit arrival of each station's cosmonaut visitors: fatalities would have been sure to follow had anyone been on board when the space stations broke down.

The exact technical problems that crippled Salyut-2 and Salyut–Kosmos-557 (as the May 11 launch might more accurately be designated) remain unknown, and we'll probably never get the full details without help from some Soviet defector or disclosure of Western intelligence reports. The best speculations center around a sudden loss of attitude control for Salyut-2, resulting in a violent tumble which ripped off its solar panels, and some sort of remote-control-radio failure on Salyut–Kosmos-557 that made the spacecraft unable to respond to ground command.

This string of failures did not pose insurmountable difficulties to official Soviet space historians. The 1972 launch failure, of course, was never mentioned. Salyut-2 was a "success," and the Kosmos-557 was only a small scientific satellite with no relation to the manned space program. (This line was maintained by high-ranking Soviet space officials and cosmonauts all through the Apollo-Soyuz program.) As for the tragic deaths of Dobrovolskiy, Volkov and Patsayev in 1971, they, too, became more proof of Soviet space superiority: as recounted in the documentary film *Steep Road into*

Space (1972), sudden death has always been a close companion to explorers pushing back the unknown, whether it be in the Atlantic, the Antarctic, Siberia or space. The deaths of the three cosmonauts became a testimonial to their equally pioneering expedition, which cleared the way for (and implicitly deserved much of the credit for) the American Skylab successes. In the Soviet movie the actual chronicle of the flight itself makes no explicit mention of the fatal ending; it is all upbeat, praising the scientific results of Salyut-1. Other propaganda publications were even more devious, as exemplified by a foreign-language pamphlet distributed around the world in 1974. In it, not only is there no mention of the cosmonauts' deaths, but there is a photograph at the end of the Salyut-1 section showing smiling, waving cosmonauts. The photo is captioned "A Successful Return to Earth," and only a handful of people would be able to recognize the individuals involved and identify them as the Soyuz-6 crew of 1969, two years earlier. (I once asked a Soviet diplomat why such tactics were becoming so typical, and he replied that since everybody knew the men had died, there was no reason to dwell on that fact morbidly.) Image was triumphing over reality once again.

For one group of people, the reality would never be forgotten, but it would never be mentioned, either. A few weeks after the Soviet's double pre-Skylab debacle in the spring of 1973, the cosmonaut crews for the planned 1975 Apollo-Soyuz linkup were announced. The prime crew would be the Voskhod-2 spacewalker Aleksey Leonov, along with veteran civilian cosmonaut Valeriy Kubasov; the backup crew, which would also make a shakedown test flight of the Apollo-Soyuz Test Project modifications, was Anatoliy Filipchenko and Nikolay Rukavishnikov. It soon became apparent that these men had been transferred from the Salyut program, and that they had been training for space-station visits in 1971, 1972 and 1973—without success. One report even claimed that Leonov and Kubasov had (with a third, unidentified cosmonaut) been the prime crew for the Soyuz-11 visit to Salyut-1, and were replaced at the last moment by their backup crew, due to some illness or training injury. If so, they never mentioned this close brush with death during their two-year joint training program with their American colleagues. But that rumor has a ring of truth to it, since Leonov and Kubasov frequently appear in *Steep Road into Space,* the movie about the Salyut-1 mission.

This period of 1967–1973 is one which official Soviet histories treat with exaggerated bravado, dwelling on the sensational successes and passing over in silence the heartbreaking setbacks. Korolev's successors did not have an easy time of it. (Mikhail Yangel, the first man who took Korolev's place, died himself in 1971.) The Kremlin demands for headline-grabbing space spectaculars had repeatedly led to disaster and death, and the professional space propagandists in Moscow had to work overtime to twist the resulting setbacks into successes.

Later, with the Apollo and Skylab successes on the record book, the pressure to beat the Americans was gone. At this point, some fundamental shifts seem to have been made in space policy, but the particulars and participants in this decision remain hidden. A long-range, unhurried development plan was drawn up, and secure levels of resource allocation were guaranteed.

The United States relaxed; with Apollo and Skylab, the space race was won. Space funding plummeted and massive layoffs took place in the space industry. Surplus spaceships were set outside to rust.

Yet if the space race was over, nobody told the Soviets. They studied their mistakes, cataloged their capabilities and set to work. But this time they refrained from the Khrushchev-style bluster which had ignited such a massive response in America. If the American manned space program wanted to sleep (or even fall into a coma), the Soviets had no desire to hasten its reawakening.

7
☆
The Moon-Race Cover-up

John Kennedy's decision in 1961 to gamble America's prestige on getting to the moon ahead of the Russians was not widely opposed at first, when the psychic wounds of the early Soviet space spectaculars were still smarting. But as the 1960s went on, the budget of the moon race mounted and the manifold costs of Vietnam began to hurt. Soon John Kennedy and Camelot were gone. And by the middle of the decade a string of Gemini manned flights, Surveyor robot moon landings, Orbiter moon mappers and Mariner planetary probes had helped assuage the wounded pride of Washington politicians. Doubts arose about the wisdom of a precipitous man-to-the-moon race.

Suppose it had all been a trick? Those sly Russians, suggested right-wing politicians, were trying to snooker us into a side show on the moon while they forged ahead and seized control of strategic orbital regions much closer to earth. The Russians, suggested left-wing politicians, were too clever to waste money on an empty "moon-doggle" stunt; but even if they were, the American people had desperate social needs from which funds had been diverted for cosmic flag-waving. The Russians, suggested much of the scientific community, were developing a rational unmanned deep-space exploration program without the costs or risks of sensational manned space flights, and we should do the same.

Later, in the aftermath of Apollo-11's successful landing, when the histories of the space race were written, it became "obvious" that these suspicions had been correct. The Soviets, after all, never did send men to the moon, and the official Soviet spokesmen later confirmed that they never had intended to. (If they had, of course, they would have won—that was the implication.) Admittedly, the Apollo program was exciting and inspirational, but the verdict of the 1970s seemed to be that it was not relevant to its original purpose, which had been to demonstrate the superiority of American science and technology over Soviet science and technology.

This question—Did the Soviet Union ever really want or try to send men to the moon?—is probably the knottiest problem in a quarter century of space history. The answer I have come to (and it is shared by most specialists in the field, but apparently not by the authors of the popular books on the subject or by the news media) is that, yes, the Soviets did indeed have a very ambitious man-to-the-moon program, which came very close to upstaging Apollo's lunar circumnavigation late in 1968. Further, I think the evidence now available also strongly suggests that, yes, in fact the Soviets were serious about landing their cosmonauts on the moon in the early 1970s.

This contrasts with the present-day official Soviet position: the Soviet Union never meant to send men to the moon because it would have been too risky, too wasteful and not nearly as productive as robot probes. This superficially attractive assertion is probably the biggest about-face of the space age, although we have seen that such propaganda is completely in character. Further, this disclaimer was remarkably successful in convincing even Western observers, and this resulted in the effective neutralization of the political implications of the Apollo project.

It's not hard to document the widespread acceptance of the Soviet assertion that they had never bothered with the moon race. Walter Cronkite, during an Apollo-11 fifth-anniversary memorial TV news special report in 1974, reviewed the history of the 1960s and intoned: "It turned out that the Russians were never in the race at all." (Cronkite's researchers had actually reported that there was considerable controversy over this issue and that the best-informed specialists in Washington, D.C., thought the Russians had been in the race —but that was not the way the script wound up.) Such confidence was probably based on a brief perusal of popular books on the moon landing. A typical one was *Journey to Tranquillity* (Doubleday, 1969), whose book-jacket blurb proclaimed the self-styled "startling fact" that "the struggle to get an American on the Moon by 1970 thrived on an overwhelming fear of Russian space superiority, a fear which NASA still fosters as a challenge to American security and prestige. But by 1963 it had become clear that the Russians had little immediate interest in the Moon and that the race for space did not, in fact, exist."

Post-Apollo revelations by defecting Soviet science journalist Leonid Vladimirov supported this attitude. Discussing Vladimirov's report, the London *Sunday Times* wrote in 1971: "It became obvious long before the Americans landed on the Moon that they were winning the space race hands down . . . There was never the remotest chance that the Russians would get to the Moon first." London's *Guardian* quoted the defector as saying that "Russia knew a long time ago that she cannot build a moon rocket," but the *Guardian* went even further by stating that "this is an argument which tilts at a shadow, for five years ago, some Western observers were arguing that the 'Moon race' was a myth. . . . This has turned out to be the case."

Revelations from American experts connected with the

1975 U.S.A.-U.S.S.R. joint Apollo-Soyuz project also provided supportive evidence. Howard Benedict, the Associated Press aerospace writer, filed a story from Washington in June 1974 that began: "During the 1960s, the United States conducted a crash program to beat the Russians in putting a man on the Moon. Now American space officials have evidence that the Soviets never were in the race . . ." The Soviet manned ship, the Soyuz, "could not make a lunar trip," Benedict asserted, quoting an unnamed NASA official.

What, then, is the hard evidence that can stand against such remarkable public unanimity? The evidence divides into two classes: first is the proof that the Soviets were serious about sending men out to the moon on simple "fly-by" circumnavigations, with quick returns to earth; second is the evidence that suggests strongly that their lunar ambitions included the same ultimate prize as did the American Apollo program, the actual manned lunar landing itself. In both of these goals, the Soviets expected—indeed, planned, as the very justification of the project—to beat the Americans. Analysis of the evidence, which consists of actual unmanned and manned space tests, of photographs, of public and private statements by Soviet space officials and of leaks from Western military intelligence agencies, has revealed a consistent and persuasive picture of a massive Soviet effort to upstage the Apollo lunar missions.

The Soviet manned lunar circumnavigation plans are easy to document. The actual moon ship for the first lunar mission can be identified. In hindsight the often strident moon-race warnings in the late 1960s were absolutely correct: the race to send men to the moon was neck-and-neck up until the last moment.

In 1968–1970 the Russians sent four unmanned space capsules around the moon and back to earth. Called Zond probes, these vehicles were, in hindsight, merely modified Soyuz spaceships, launched without the front "orbital module" and with more powerful heat shields, radio systems and heat-control systems. They were entirely capable of carrying at least one pilot out to the moon and back to earth—and Soviet statements strongly indicated that such flights were planned.

This Zond program is compatible with a picture of a serious and significant Soviet man-around-the-moon program. Such an effort was in accord with their main space-program philosophy of the 1960s: beat the Americans to all major space targets even if the technology to be used is not nearly as sophisticated. The Soviets seemed to want to maintain the public image of their space superiority, while leaving the real science and engineering research to the United States.

The first test launchings in the Soyuz-Zond lunar program had been made in early 1967. With luck (or with the presence of Korolev's firm hand), a three- or four-flight program might have led up to a manned lunar circumnavigation just prior to the November 7 celebration of the fiftieth anniversary of the Bolshevik seizure of power in Russia. Plans for such a space spectacular were widely rumored in Moscow and Washington at the time, and would obviously have had great appeal to the Soviet government—but it was not to be.

The first two launch attempts, in March and April 1967, apparently failed in their purposes of rocketing out to and around the moon. Instead, both probes fell far short of the moon and soon slipped back into the atmosphere, where they burned up. The failures were probably attributable to problems with the new upper stage for the Proton rocket; these problems would continue off and on for another four years as one would-be moon probe after another tumbled back from the edge of space at an altitude of barely one hundred miles.

Further launchings planned in 1967 were probably hindered by the diversion of manpower to the investigation and repair of the Soyuz-1 disaster in April (when cosmonaut Komarov died), and a third lunar attempt was not made until late November. This time it was the first stage of the powerful Proton booster which broke down, sending the rest of the vehicle tumbling back onto the icy steppes of Kazakhstan barely five minutes after blast-off.

The first successful launching came the following April, when Zond-4 headed off on a deep-space trajectory. It was headed directly away from the moon, but that course had evidently been chosen to simplify navigation for the probe. Something else may have gone wrong, since the planned recovery of the capsule after its six-day space flight was evidently not successful. A new launch the following month ended in another debacle when the still balky Proton booster rocket exploded shortly after takeoff.

By now it was mid-1968, and more than a year had passed since the Apollo and Soyuz tragedies. The moon race had resumed its forward momentum. In August NASA announced plans to "consider" sending the manned Apollo-8 around the moon in December if the October earth-orbital test flight of Apollo-7 (the first manned flight) went perfectly. It was a daring plan, and it depended on a lot of things going right if the mission was to succeed (or even if the men were to survive). The Soviets may not have felt it was likely to occur quite so soon, but they did take notice that an American man-to-the-moon flight might be less than a year away.

In the light of this new urgency, and with more than two years to work out the management problems following Korolev's death, Soviet space officials committed themselves to their own bold plan: they would make two more unmanned test flights, which, if successful, would be followed by a cosmonaut's lunar fly-by. The first probe, Zond-5, was launched successfully on September 15, and six days later it had made a safe splashdown in the Indian Ocean after circumnavigating the moon. It was a major technological achievement in its own right, but it promised to be followed by even more stunning flights.

The unmanned Zond-6 went up in November and made a similarly successful fly-by of the moon. However, this time it did not splash down in the Indian Ocean but instead made a highly sophisticated "double-dip" return, skipping off the upper atmosphere over the Southern Hemisphere and then plopping down gently right inside the standard Soviet space recovery zone in central Asia. The way was clear for a Soviet manned flight to the moon; the next lunar launch window for a simple fly-by was December 9. Meanwhile, since Apollo-7 had also been a complete success, NASA decided to push for its own manned lunar orbit—but because of differences in trajectories, the Apollo window would not open until December 20.

December 9 came and went, and nothing happened. There was no Soviet launch. The world's attention returned to Cape Kennedy, where Apollo-8 was in its final stages of preparation. On December 21, 1968, it blasted off atop a giant Saturn-5 booster. The three astronauts were circling the moon by Christmas Eve, where they were entertained by a poem from Mission Control, which started, " 'Twas the night before Christmas, and way out in space, the Apollo Eight crew had just won the moon race . . . " And they really had—but even they didn't know how close it had been.

The Soviets sent the obligatory congratulations on the success of the circumlunar expedition. But they insisted that the American flight had not been a victory in any U.S.–U.S.S.R. moon race, because there never had been any such race.

However, prior to the success of Apollo-8, the Soviets had explicitly asserted just the opposite about their intentions. The *Soviet Encyclopedia of Space Flight,* published in late 1968, unequivocally stated that the Zond flights "were launched for flight testing and further development of an automatic version of a manned lunar spaceship." Cosmonaut Vladimir Komarov, before his death in 1967, had told newsmen that "I can positively state that the Soviet Union will not be beaten by the United States in the race for a human being to go to the moon . . . The U.S. has a timetable for 1969 plus 'X' but our timetable is 1969 plus 'X' minus one" (that is, a year before the Americans, no matter when they landed). Cosmonaut Gherman Titov had written: "As for myself, I dream of flying around the moon . . . Cosmonauts have a good chance of getting a close view of the moon." Aleksey Leonov had stated that "man will visit the moon in the nearest future. I dream of this being accomplished by men of our detachment. If I am very lucky, I will get the assignment."

Although it's possible to think of such statements as merely propaganda boasts, they were more than that. Soviet cosmonauts rarely ad-libbed in public: if they didn't have an approved script which reflected official policy, they remained silent.

But even more convincing is an account from Apollo-11 astronaut Michael Collins concerning a private, off-the-record meeting he and fellow-astronaut David Scott had with cosmonaut Pavel Belyayev at an air show in Paris in early 1968. The men were discussing their own future flight plans, and Collins later noted that "we found that Belyayev himself expected to make a circumlunar flight in the not too distant future." Since Belyayev's statements had not been made for public consumption, the astronauts felt that he had been telling the truth.

Nikita Khrushchev also referred to the man-to-the-moon program (which would have been just the kind of space shot he would have demanded) in his own memoirs when he paid homage to Sergey Korolev. "I'm only sorry," Khrushchev recalled, "that we didn't manage to send a man to the moon during Korolev's lifetime." Korolev's premature death, as we have seen, may have been the single most important contributing factor which prevented this cosmonaut lunar flight from occurring.

Aside from such authoritative personal testimony, additional evidence from the unmanned Zond vehicles themselves confirms that they were built to carry pilots. Drawings published in the early 1970s show that the Zond was identical in shape to a stripped-down Soyuz manned spacecraft; photographs of the crated Zond-5 command module being transferred off a Soviet recovery ship in Bombay harbor in 1968 show that the shipping canister is equal in size to the canister used to send a Soyuz command module to the National Air and Space Museum in 1976. Furthermore, on manned Soyuz orbital flights, most of the air supplies are packed in the forward ("orbital") module, but six man-days' worth are installed in the command module—which is precisely enough to get one pilot out to the moon and back alive, relying solely on the command module's oxygen supplies. (The Zond had no orbital module, to save weight.) The distinctive and sophisticated "double-dip" reentry trajectory used by the Zond was obviously designed to lighten the G loads for the sake of frail human passengers, since later unmanned Soviet capsules bringing soil samples from the moon followed less complex routes which subjected them to hundreds of Gs during reentry into earth's atmosphere. A photograph released by the Soviets in 1973 was immediately recognized by Soviet space expert Charles Vick as showing a Zond spacecraft being tested with a launch escape system —an extra piece of gear the use of which has always been reserved only for manned space vehicles.

It seems certain beyond a reasonable doubt that the Soviets were, until late 1968, trying very hard to beat America to the moon, at least with regard to a manned circumlunar flight. Unfortunately, we still do not know why they did not launch in December, the last date available for several months because of complex constraints in orbital navigation. There were hints in Moscow that the booster had been ready and that the pilot, presumably Belyayev, had been at the space center awaiting final approval for blast-off. Whether the approval never came, based on a computation of risks, or whether the approval did come but the space vehicle broke down during the final countdown is still unknown. All we do know is that a year later Belyayev was dead, succumbing to an operation for peritonitis brought on by "a severe bleeding ulcer"; he was the first cosmonaut *not* to be buried in the Kremlin Wall, but was given a minor funeral and interred in Novodevichy Cemetery, not far from where Khrushchev would be buried one year later.

Leaving aside the mystery of why Belyayev's moon flight had not been launched two weeks ahead of Apollo-8, a bigger question is why the Soviets never went on later to send manned Zond ships around the moon. They had spent all the budget money and had nearly completed the test program successfully. Why should they now leave the moon entirely to American astronauts?

Considering the patterns of space-mission planning exhibited by the Soviet Union throughout the 1960s, the answer to that question should by now be obvious. The entire purpose of the Zond program had been to beat the Americans to the moon: that could have been the only value of the feat. When Apollo-8 circled the moon in December 1968, it should have become clear that the Soviets would never consider coming in a poor second in a race they had promised they would win. It was better to drop out in silence and to claim they never had been in the race so then they could appear not to have lost. The billions of rubles and hundreds of thousand of man-hours spent on the Zond gamble were a total loss and were wiped from the slate of history.

But there was still another possibility in the spring of 1969. Although the man-to-the-moon race was over, a man-on-the-moon race was probably still on. In a top-level Kremlin policy study made early in 1969, Russian experts concluded that an American moon landing was out of the question before mid-1970 at the earliest and was unlikely until well into 1972 because of continuing technical problems with the Saturn-5 rocket and with the lunar module that was intended to make the actual touchdown on the moon. In the meantime, any repetition of the astronaut deaths in the Apollo-1 tragedy might be expected to give the new Nixon administration an excuse to scuttle the lunar landing project (Nixon allegedly saw the whole project as contributing to the posthumous glory of his arch-rival John Kennedy, anyway) and turn the space program over to the Air Force generals and their "Manned Orbiting Laboratory" space-station project. So Moscow continued work on its manned lunar landing effort.

The existence of a Soviet man-on-the-moon program is still problematical even with years of hindsight; but there is good circumstantial evidence to suggest that it was a reality. This evidence consists of actual hardware, of strange Soviet space tests and of additional human testimony.

The biggest piece of relevant evidence is the Soviet "super booster," also called (without affection) "Webb's giant" because NASA administrator James Webb continually referred to it during NASA budget hearings on Capitol Hill in the late 1960s. The monster rocket, allegedly almost four hundred feet tall, was supposed to be twice the size of the American Saturn-5 but, because it used less efficient propellants, reportedly had a payload slightly smaller than that of the American moon-ship. There were many reports of its existence throughout the late 1960s, although skeptics saw it as just another NASA budget ploy. Eventually, when it never actually appeared on space missions, some experts suggested that it had repeatedly failed in flight—while others saw this absence as proof it had never existed.

But the vehicle was real. In 1976 a CIA briefing official for the first time publicly confirmed that the Soviets had such a vehicle. Three of them were built: the first was destroyed in a fueling accident in June 1969 (possibly involving casualties among rocket engineers working at the pad) and two others disintegrated early in flight in June 1971 and November 1972. Afterward, the launch pads were mothballed and the project was written off as a bad try.

What purpose could such a vehicle serve? It had no military significance. It had no application to earth-orbiting space stations, since more than ten years have now elapsed and the Soviets are still working out the potentials of their medium-size Proton booster. There remains only one conceivable use for the super booster: manned flight to and landing on the moon.

An additional piece of space hardware would have been needed for such a flight to the lunar surface: a lunar module, or at least a lunar descent stage (if the entire command module was to have been landed). In the American program, this type of hardware was tested in earth orbit, first on unmanned flights in 1968 and then during a manned trial run in early 1969 (the Apollo-9 mission). The Soviets followed a pattern with intriguing similarities: after one reported launch failure in late 1969, they put a heavy payload in orbit late in 1970 which exhibited characteristic man-related telemetry signals and which then proceeded to go through a series of orbital course changes. These maneuvers duplicated in many respects a lunar landing and subsequent ascent. Additionally, three other unmanned orbital space tests in 1970–1971 also carried out similar maneuvers. In mid-1981 one of them —Kosmos 434 (see appendix page 251)—burned up over Australia, and the Soviet Foreign Ministry in Moscow tried to allay fears of nuclear contamination by identifying the payload as only "an experimental lunar module"!

Based on an analysis of Soviet statements, it's possible to reconstruct how they planned to land men on the moon in the early 1970s. The Soviet lunar expedition (which in early 1969 was still competitive with the Soviet's belief in a mid-1972 Apollo landing) would have involved the launching of the major pieces of lunar hardware atop the giant booster, along with the separate launching of the manned spacecraft atop a more reliable Soyuz-type rocket. The two vehicles would link up in orbit a hundred miles above earth, and then head out for the moon, propelled by an extra stage of the super booster.

Another aspect of Soviet space procedures in 1967–1969 also testifies to the plausibility of this scenario. During the space rendezvous and docking maneuvers carried out five times in those years, the Soviets would launch the active "chase" ship *first* and then the passive target ship a day or two later. Such a sequence made absolutely no sense at all in the light of later applications of orbital rendezvous, in which a manned ship would blast off and link up with an already orbiting space station. And the Soviets did eventually adopt this sequence: starting in 1971, they switched to this passive-first-and-active-second sequence, and have never reverted to the opposite technique they used originally.

Now, consider that original maneuver in light of the assembly of a man-on-the-moon spaceship from two parts, a small manned ship and a larger spacecraft complex launched by a less than totally reliable giant booster. Since the large spacecraft complex would include a fully fueled upper stage needed for the final boost from earth's orbit out toward the moon, it would not be able to endure a long flight: the propellants could become unstable or could leak away. However, if the manned ship was launched *first,* the large spacecraft complex could follow the next day, after which the linkup could be accomplished on the very first orbit of the unmanned complex. Ignition of the upper stage, and injection onto a moon-bound trajectory, could follow within an hour or two.

Such a scenario is a good justification for the bizarre Soviet space maneuvers in that period—which are otherwise totally unexplained. And this supposition is compatible with the other information we have assembled from other sources.

For instance, Soviet cosmonauts spent the late 1960s engaged in helicopter training. (Since then, they have eliminated such training.) In the Apollo program, such activities were devoted solely to familiarizing astronauts with the controlled vertical descents and ascents associated with lunar landings. Neither program had any training time to waste,

so the Russians were not doing it just for recreational purposes. Astronaut Michael Collins correctly perceived the
significance of the Soviet activities when he wrote in 1974: "If
the Russians weren't interested in a manned lunar landing,
if—as they subsequently said—they were not racing us to the
Moon, then why were they training cosmonauts to fly helicopters?" That is still an excellent question—and the best
answer is that they were indeed planning on making manned
lunar landings.

This hypothetical Soviet man-on-the-moon program remained alive at least through late 1970, as flight tests showed.
Perhaps the Soviets would have been encouraged to proceed
with manned lunar landings if the Americans had abandoned
moon flights (the Soviets doubtlessly were hoping that this
would be one result of the early 1970 Apollo-13 failure),
particularly if the Soviet expeditions were demonstrably su-
perior to the American ones in terms of stay times or some
other highly visible factor. But when it became clear Apollo
was going to continue into the 1971–1972 period with even
more advanced lunar missions, and that the Soviet giant
booster was not going to become available until several years'
more effort, the Soviet man-on-the-moon program was ter-
minated.

The Soviets seem to have had another backup plan for
upstaging Apollo. Only days before the blast-off of Arm-
strong, Collins and Aldrin on their moon-landing expedition
in July 1969, the Soviets shot Luna-15 into space. The unmanned probe reached the moon and went into orbit around
it.

Speculation about its mission was rife: could it be an attempt to return soil samples using only remote-controlled
equipment, thus stealing the thunder from Apollo-11? Or
could it be an attempt to interfere with the American landing
by jamming radio channels?

When the American astronauts reached the moon, the
Russian probe was still circling. Soviet space officials had

assured American experts that there would be no interference, and there was none. Instead, Luna-15 maneuvered toward a soft landing on the Mare Crisium—and crashed. The Soviet failure on the Sea of Crises, and the subsequent American success on the Sea of Tranquillity, seemed almost too metaphorical to be real.

From 1970 to 1976 the Soviets ran an unmanned lunar probe program, with orbital reconnaissance, with robot "scooper ships" (which brought back a few ounces of moon soil) and with remote-controlled "moon buggies," the Lunokhods. They advertised this program as their alternative to manned lunar flights, and boasted about how cheap and safe that approach was.

But even in scientific results alone, the Apollo manned landings showed themselves to be far cheaper in terms of total results than the Soviet robots. A single Apollo expedition collected hundreds of soil and rock samples over a wide area, emplaced long-lived scientific instruments, surveyed the lunar surface from orbit and launched exploratory subsatellites. To carry out an equivalent program would have required a dozen or more robot flights, each costing perhaps a quarter of a manned flight—with a total cost many times that of the manned flight. And the Soviets continued to run into problems with reliability of their equipment: half of their scooper-sample return probes failed, and the total weight of samples was about a thousand times less than the weight of the Apollo samples. The Lunokhod moon buggies were cute (working models were being sold in Moscow toy stores within a year of the first flight), but they were so expensive in terms of scientific return that they were quietly scrapped in 1972.

It now seems clear that the Soviet unmanned lunar program was only a stopgap measure to show the flag on the moon while the Americans were making Apollo landings. When the Apollo program ended, the Soviet robot lunar program's funding was also cut off. Luna-15 and its successors may even have been thrown together from equipment originally built to support the abortive man-on-the-moon program. In that light, the Luna-15 flight in mid-1969 may have been a test of a manned moon landing craft; more than a year would follow before the design was refitted for purely robot operations.

Moscow's desire to rewrite old space history—once it had lost for a time the ability to write new space history—is completely understandable, since knowledge of the existence of their manned lunar flight programs would have been a glaring advertisement of their inferiority in an arena in which they had long boasted of their inevitable preeminence. Rather than face such propaganda bankruptcy, the Soviets tried to lie their way out of the impasse—not for the first time, as we have seen, but on a scale far grander than before.

And as usual, they had trouble keeping their cover story straight. According to official Soviet accounts in the 1970s, their manned space program of the 1960s had always been aimed at the establishment of space stations—manned lunar flight had never been even considered. But in the background profile of one engineer-cosmonaut who visited a space station in 1979, the biographer mentioned offhandedly that the cosmonaut had been working on the space-station project since it had been officially approved—on January 1, 1969. Since that was only a week after the landing of the U.S. manned around-the-moon Apollo-8 expedition, something else had been on the minds of Soviet space officials in the late 1960s, some other goal which they turned away from only after the success of America's Apollo-8 flight.

The eagerness with which this no-moon-race claim was accepted in the West is remarkable, since those involved were in no way dupes or Soviet sympathizers—indeed, most of them had had long experience in penetrating other Soviet deceptions. But whether by accident or crafty design, this particular Soviet claim reinforced prevailing prejudices among these disparate Western groups. The left gained support for the oft-expressed complaints about the wastefulness of Apollo expenditures. The right found confirmation of beliefs that the Soviets were too backward to ever dream of competing head-on with American know-how. The scientific community found ammunition for its general condemnation of wasteful astronaut jaunts rather than allegedly more productive unmanned exploration. The net result was the political neutralization of the implications of the Apollo program and the frustration of the original political motivations for initiating it.

But the race was real, and the Soviets were in it to win. They failed because their technological and management skills were not sufficient to the task. But at least they learned the correct lessons from their defeat. The West, meanwhile, achieved victory, but has been left with the wrong lessons—and the irony is that we helped write them ourselves.

8

☆

The Long Climb
Back

The recovery helicopters were circling over the landing zone, their crews scanning the sky for an orange parachute. Even more important, they were listening by radio for a greeting from the returning cosmonauts of Soyuz-12.

These helicopter pilots had seen Soyuz-11's parachute two years before—but there had been no reply to their radio calls. The crew had been dead. Now, suddenly, the pilots spotted the parachute and flew toward it.

"Ural, how do you read?" demanded the chief rescue pilot, addressing the cosmonauts by their call sign. "Ural, come in!"

"Hello, Earth. This is Ural!" crackled the voice on the radio. "I just saw a helicopter flash by. Don't hit us!"

Relief swept through the listeners. After two years of jinxed space shots, a modest but crucial two-day test had ended successfully. For the cosmonauts—Vasiliy Lazarev and Oleg Makarov—this September 1973 flight was to be just a warm-up for a promised space-station mission in 1975. Everything had worked well at last—and a second two-man test flight twelve weeks later confirmed the correctness of the hardware modifications.

Between mid-1974 and mid-1975 the Soviet space-station program was resurrected. Two new Salyuts, 3 and 4, were put into separate orbits, and five Soyuz spaceships were sent up with visiting crews. For the Soviets, it seemed as if the nightmare years had ended; for Western observers, these missions cleared up some earlier enigmas and revealed a hitherto unknown aspect of the Soviet space-station effort.

The Salyut program had a split personality. That is to say, it turned out that there were two distinct types of space stations, with two distinct operating modes and purposes, both included under one cover name—Salyut.

For convenience, the two types came to be known (among Western experts—the Soviets have never acknowledged any difference) as the "civilian" Salyut and the "military" Salyut. The latter designation should not be taken literally, since those Salyuts also carried out a considerable amount of genuine scientific research—but the designation is based on activities which the Soviets have never officially admitted: reconnaisance from space, or in the idiom of newspaper headlines, "space spying."

The first major difference between these two breeds had been noticed by radio amateurs in Europe in 1973, when Salyut-2 and Salyut–Kosmos-557 were launched on their aborted missions; however, the significance of the observations was not appreciated at that time. Salyut-2 had transmitted radio signals at a frequency of 19.944 megahertz (MHz) with a coding system called frequency shift keying. Kosmos-557 had been heard at both 15.008 MHz with a "CW [continuous wave] pulse-duration modulation" and at 922.75 MHz, the same as Salyut-1. The question arose: Why launch a "new, improved Salyut" (2) to be followed by a step backward to the radio systems of the old design?

It all became clear in 1974 when Salyut-3 was launched on

June 24 and sent signals just like those of Salyut-2, followed six months later by Salyut-4 in December, sending signals like those of Salyut–Kosmos-557 and Salyut-1. Neither type was an improvement over the other: they were *parallel* developments.

More differences between the two Salyut programs showed up when cosmonaut crews visited both Salyut-3 and Salyut-4 in 1974–1975: although a military pilot was always the mission commander, the second man was always a civilian research engineer on the "civilian" version but was always a military officer on the "military" version. The civilian version operated at an altitude of 220 miles, while the military version orbited 50 miles lower, which provided a significantly better view of the earth while involving a penalty in total lifetime in orbit. The civilian flights were extensively publicized and volumes of details were released on mission activities, while the military flights were scarcely mentioned and the announced activities were far too meager to account for any large fraction of the cosmonauts' time. (The military crews were clearly performing activities which the Soviets did not want to advertise.)

We don't even know what the military Salyuts look like. All published Salyut drawings, photographs and schematics refer to the civilian version; for the military version, only a few fuzzy on-board television images have ever been released. There have been suggestions from some sources (such as the aerospace magazine *Aviation Week,* sometimes known as *"Aviation Leak"*) that the military Salyuts had their docking ports at the end opposite that of the civilian Salyuts. And one additional military Salyut feature has never been explained: the design and true function of a "recoverable module," which is jettisoned at the end of the space station's lifetime. The presumption is that such a small capsule, ejected automatically from some unknown hatch on the military Salyuts, carried exposed film from a large reconnaissance camera.

The 1974–1975 Salyuts, for all their differences, shared one feature: each had one attempted Soyuz linkup fail. The first launch to Salyut-3 (Soyuz-14, July 3–19, 1974) was successful, but the second launch (Soyuz-15 on August 26) was followed by the crew canceling the planned linkup and hastily returning to earth. The first launch to Salyut-4 (Soyuz-17 on January 10, 1975) was also successful, and its thirty-day mission doubled the Soyuz-14 record, but the second attempt on April 5 ended when the rocket went off course, dumping the cosmonauts onto the snow-clad Altai Mountains. A third attempt (Soyuz-18 on May 24) succeeded, however, and that crew doubled the previous Soviet mark, spending sixty-three days in space.

On each successful mission, the Soviets followed a routine procedure. First, the orbit of the space station was adjusted slightly, using small on-board rocket engines. (Western observers could detect these changes and forecast an impending launch.) This was done to place the target Salyut on a proper heading across the launch site so that the Soyuz chase ship could follow a standard preset ascent trajectory. Once launched, the Soyuz found itself several thousand miles behind and below the Salyut, but its lower, faster orbit allowed it to gradually overtake the space station. Over the course of a twenty-four-hour chase, during which both spacecraft circled the world sixteen times, the Soyuz was able to make a series of midcourse corrections to compensate for the inevitable inaccuracy of the launching and to gradually raise its altitude. The men slept their first night in space in their couches in the Soyuz.

At a range of about ten miles, the Soyuz radar detected the Salyut, and the cosmonauts were able to see it as a bright star just above the horizon ahead of them. Additional rocket impulses slowed the rate of approach until at a range of about a hundred yards, the Soyuz pilot took over manual control for the final docking maneuver. The nose of the Soyuz was inserted into a special docking berth at one end of the space station. After checking the pressure integrity of the tunnel

formed between the nose of the Soyuz and the special compartment on the Salyut, the cosmonauts opened the hatch
and crossed into the space station. After a few hours more
of switching on some essential equipment, the crewmen were
allowed to get some well-deserved sleep.

The return to earth was less complicated. Once the exposed film, biological and medical samples, logbooks and
other materials were loaded into the Soyuz, the cosmonauts
let the pressure out of the transfer tunnel and checked that
all the Soyuz hatches were airtight. Satisfied, they cast off
from the Salyut and spent the next few hours checking out
their spacecraft and moving off to a safe distance from the
space station. A five-minute firing of their small rocket motor
was enough to slow them sufficiently for earth's gravity to
pull them back toward the atmosphere, where air resistance
slowed them down to subsonic speeds. A parachute and a
pre-touchdown solid-fuel rocket pack finished the voyage.

That was the way it was for Soyuz-14 cosmonauts Pavel
Popovich and Yuriy Artyukhin in July 1974. During their
two weeks on the Salyut-3, they photographed earth's surface and atmospheric phenomena, and ran a few experiments
on the effects of space conditions on biological samples. They
also tested out some new design features of the Salyut, including a trash air lock for the disposal of bags of waste and
a water purifier to collect cabin air moisture for use as wash
water; both systems became standard on subsequent Salyuts.
To control the orientation of the vehicle, an "inertia sphere"
(a sort of spherical gyroscope) was spun up within a magnetic chamber; spinning the sphere along any axis twisted the
entire station in the opposite direction without the use of
rocket fuel. Another new device was a boom-mounted television camera for inspecting the exterior of the station—but it
must not have worked out, since no other Salyut ever carried
one. Popovich and Artyukhin completed these and many
other unspecified tasks and then became the first cosmonauts
to complete a Salyut mission alive.

Six weeks later, on August 26, two more cosmonauts were launched toward Salyut-3. But instead of linking up with the orbiting station, they flew past it and then turned back to earth. Two days after blast-off, they were back on the ground.

The Soviets were quick to claim that the two-day flight was a "complete success." The cosmonauts were supposed to be testing emergency night landing procedures and the psychological compatibility of crewmen of vastly different ages (the commander was thirty-two and the flight engineer was forty-eight). A new docking-control system was being tested, and even though some officials admitted there had been some minor glitches with it, others insisted that the men would have landed immediately even if the docking had been successful. So the mission of Soyuz-15 was not a failure after all, according to official Soviet spokesmen.

But nobody in the West believed them. They had good reasons. The flight had been launched at an hour which would have opened up normal midafternoon landing opportunities after several weeks in space, but which required a midnight (and highly undesirable) emergency landing if the linkup failed. The only planned Soyuz two-day flight (Soyuz-12, the year before) had been announced as such right after blast-off to avoid adverse speculation about a mission abort. And a strange story appeared in a weekly Moscow newspaper, written by a reporter who had been briefed about the flight and who tried to compensate for a long printing delay (the story was written during the first day of the flight but would not hit the streets until a few days later) by writing as if the flight had been a success: "All is going well in the latest Soviet manned space flight" went the article entitled "New Visitors for Space Station," adding that "like its predecessor Soyuz-14, [Soyuz-15] is a ferry, intended as a transport rather than a research vehicle." By the time the failure occurred, it was too late to recall the story.

So the Soyuz-15 was a failure, despite the official attempt

to portray it as a success. It didn't matter: the first mission had gone well, the second had been survivable. Some confidence began to return to Soviet space specialists. Perhaps the worst was over.

A new space station, named Salyut-4, launched late in December 1974, reinforced that optimistic point of view. Over the next six months, two long missions were successfully carried out on which visiting cosmonauts conducted an impressive program of scientific research. The two-man space teams used a powerful solar telescope for studies of the sun's energy; they had several smaller specialized telescopes for other branches of astrophysics. They tested Salyut improvements, such as a "Delta" autopilot and a bicycle ergometer, or "exercycle," for physical fitness. In a space garden called Oasis they grew green peas and other vegetables; they carried biological specimens, including bacterial cultures and the inevitable fruit flies. And each day in space increased the skill and confidence of Russian cosmonauts and flight controllers.

There was one setback in the Salyut-4 success story: the world's first known manned launch abort. On April 5, 1975, cosmonauts Lazarev and Makarov blasted off on their second space trip for what would have been Soyuz-18, on what was supposed to be a two-month space sojourn. Instead, they set new space-flight records of bad luck.

The trouble began at an altitude of ninety miles and a speed of about 10,000 miles per hour. When the third stage of the rocket tried to drop the spent lower stage, the Soyuz began a violent tumble (evidently caused by a problem with the explosive bolts designed to cut the two sections apart). The cosmonauts called the control center and advised them of the problem, but at first nobody there believed them: telemetry showed that the engines were normal, and the tumble rate was so high it was off the scale, leading to the conclusion at the Moscow Mission Control Center that the reading was defective. It took a string of earthy Russian curses from Lazarev to convince ground specialists that the cosmonauts were in real trouble. The Soyuz was blasted free of the errant rocket on ground command and began falling back to earth.

The cosmonauts were immediately worried about coming down across the Chinese border: their flight path just skirted the northwest corner of Sinkiang, and now that they were off course, they might well be descending on the wrong side of the mountains. The cosmonauts knew that two Russian helicopter pilots had recently touched down by mistake near this area and had been captured by a Chinese patrol; they eventually would spend three years in a Peking prison. This might have been on the cosmonauts' minds as they urgently asked ground control, "Are we going to land in China?" There was no answer, but the cosmonauts were insistent. Their final question before losing radio contact was a plaintive "We have a treaty with China, don't we?"

The cosmonauts faced a particularly severe reentry. Normally, returning spaceships shed their tremendous velocities along a lengthy near-horizontal path; but this spaceship was now plunging back down at a steep angle which would subject it to a short, vicious deceleration—if it survived at all. The G forces quickly surpassed 4, the standard level; they surpassed 8, the emergency level; they surpassed 15, the design level of the spacecraft; somewhere above 18, all measurements went off the high end of the scale, and the G meter "pegged," bent over and jammed.

After twenty or thirty seconds, during which their bodies weighed more than a ton and a half, the cosmonauts (if they were still conscious) would have noticed a reduction in the deceleration forces. Having survived reentry, the capsule was now falling like a rock, straight downward toward the Altai Mountains, where, to make rescue even harder, the sun had just set.

A series of parachutes opened properly, slowing the capsule's fall. Reportedly, the actual touchdown on a snow-covered slope was very gentle—but almost immediately the capsule began rolling down the mountainside. Just before the edge of a precipice, the capsule's parachute lines snagged on some scrub pines, and the Soyuz was pulled up short. The voyage of Lazarev and Makarov was over, fifteen minutes after their hopeful blast-off two thousand miles to the west.

The cosmonauts' luck turned good. They had come down near a village and their parachute had been seen in the twilight sky. A search party had located and reached the capsule within an hour. When Lazarev and Makarov heard voices outside the capsule, they realized they had come down on the safe side of the border: their rescuers were speaking Russian, not Chinese.

Neither cosmonaut was in any shape to fly again soon, due to injuries sustained in the reentry and the crash landing. These were never specified but could have ranged from broken ribs to concussions and serious internal bleeding. Makarov, who was forty-two at the time, did get another chance during the Salyut-6 mission in 1978. Lazarev, at forty-seven, had come to the end of his space-flight career—his advanced age and unspecified injuries forced his removal from flight status and assignment to a desk at the cosmonaut training center. (He was put in charge of training the East European "guest cosmonauts" who began to show up in late 1976.)

Embarrassment aside, the failure of the Soyuz-18 launching meant trouble for Soviet space operations, since an overlap of the Salyut-4 mission with the Apollo-Soyuz linkup now seemed unavoidable—and this would cause staffing problems. A successful April 5 launch would have allowed a landing (after about sixty days) on or about June 4, leaving another six weeks before the July 15 blast-off of the long-scheduled international mission. But now the second attempt at the planned two-month Salyut-4 second visit could not start until late in May, thus guaranteeing an overlap of flights and requiring that two independent mission control centers be in operation simultaneously. Many observers in the West did not think the Soviets had enough trained people to provide sufficient depth in the event of trouble on either flight. There were demands in Congress to delay the international linkup a few months, since the Salyut two-month visit itself probably could not be postponed because of the limited shelf life of food and film supplies already in orbit. But the Soviets assured American space experts that the overlap would be no problem; they did not want to admit that their setback could be responsible for delaying the long-scheduled Apollo-Soyuz mission.

So both missions went ahead in parallel, doubtlessly with frantic training programs in Moscow (at the new control center being inaugurated for the mission) and in the Crimea (at the old control center, which was being gradually phased out). The experiments planned for the Salyut's sixty-day mission were scaled down to reduce risks. For example, plans for Russia's first extravehicular activity (spacewalks) in more than six years were dropped to lighten the training load on the cosmonauts and the flight controllers.

On May 24, cosmonauts Pyotr Klimuk and Vitaliy Sevastyanov blasted off to visit the Salyut-4. They had been the backup crew of the abortive Soyuz-18 launch on April 5, which, because of its failure, never received an official designation. (In conversations with American space engineers, the Soviets disingenuously called it "the April fifth anomaly.") So the spaceship which carried Klimuk, a veteran of Soyuz-13 in 1973, and Sevastyanov, a veteran of Soyuz-9 in 1970, was given the designation of Soyuz-18 as well.

The second try at a second visit to the Salyut-4 went perfectly at first. Cosmonauts Klimuk and Sevastyanov kept busy with a wide range of experiments as they tried to double the previous Soviet space endurance mark.

But the flight was even harder on the crewmen than Moscow was willing to admit at the time. A few years later, a Soviet book did disclose that the Salyut-4 had encountered "difficulties" with its humidity control system—but this was not mentioned during the flight, nor were the resulting problems for the cosmonauts even hinted at while they were in orbit in 1975. Some Western radio eavesdroppers, however, had been well aware of the situation as it was happening, but their reports were classified, since they were working for the U.S. government listening post in Istanbul.

"The windows are still fogged over," one of the cosmonauts reportedly complained halfway through the mission, "and the green mold—it's halfway up the wall now." The space pilot's report on the situation aboard the Salyut-4 space station ended with the plea, "Can't we come home now?" The answer from Mission Control was consistently curt: "No! You must complete the scheduled flight and not interfere with the plans for the Apollo-Soyuz linkup."

Weeks passed and the high cabin humidity kept the windows nearly opaque. The cosmonauts periodically reported on the progress of their struggle against the green mold spreading through the station, and they regularly repeated their plaintive request to come home. But after forty-five days the answer was still "No!"; after fifty-two days, at the time of the historic international linkup of Soyuz-19 and Apollo-18, the answer was still "No!"; only on the sixty-first day of the mission, as the planned flight duration was reached, did the cosmonauts receive the welcome permission: "Proceed with plans to land the day after tomorrow."

After touchdown, they walked easily from their ship, the rigors of the flight having been withstood. Not all of the rigors were publicly disclosed—so the full scope of the men's courage was hidden.

The total lifetime of Salyut-4 was impressive. It continued to circle the earth for another year and a half, its orbit slipping lower and lower under the influence of air drag. Finally in February 1977, only hours from a meteoric plunge to destruction, the Salyut's rocket engine made one last spurt, dropping the vehicle harmlessly into the empty northern Pacific. It had been in space for 770 days, nearly the equivalent of a round trip to Mars.

The controversy over the Apollo-Soyuz Test Project (or ASTP), the 1975 linkup of the last Apollo with a modified Soyuz, has faded only because it now seems irrelevant. For many, the mission symbolized political détente at its best or at its worst: either it was a symbol of what could be accomplished if only the United States and the Soviet Union would set aside their ideological idiosyncrasies and join forces, or it was a symbol of how Russia suckered America for all the scientific secrets it could steal. Conceived in the enthusiasm of Nixonian détente in the early 1970s, the linkup was a political anachronism by the time it took place, with the caretaker Ford administration struggling to deal with the reverberations of Watergate and the fall of Saigon. By the time it took place, it had become a "wheat deal in the sky," a "quarter-billion-dollar space handshake"—or, as one American space official put it, a fitting metaphor of the posture of U.S.-U.S.S.R. space brotherhood: "Our arms around their shoulders and their hands in our pockets."

The personal relationships among the astronauts and cosmonauts were excellent, especially after they began learning phrases in each other's language. The men endured countless ceremonial functions together; they relaxed by hunting, water skiing and auto racing together; they engaged in heroic drinking bouts, especially in Moscow; they told space stories. It was good that the human element went so smoothly, since other aspects of the program coordination never got off on the right foot. The orientation visits, for example, were scheduled at exactly the worst times of the year: the Americans went to Moscow during the dead of winter and had a hard time rounding up the needed warm clothing in Houston; the Russians came to Texas every year in midsummer, as Houston took on the climate of a steam bath.

One thing the Americans had to get used to in Moscow

was the constant surveillance. They presumed that their rooms were bugged and their luggage searched—and acted accordingly. One astronaut, arriving at his Moscow hotel, griped to his American roommate that there weren't any coat hangers—and upon retiring from dinner found about a hundred of them, in the closet, on doorknobs and hanging from the arms of chairs. He piped out a loud "Thank you!" to the walls. Standing in line at the hotel cafeteria one day, a space engineer idly remarked to his roommate that it would be nice if they had little American flags at their tables—and the very next day, the flags were there. Another time, at the Soviet Mission Control Center near Moscow, an astronaut was passing through a waiting room outside the American control room when he saw some Russians watching a soccer game on television. Joining them, he pulled a large easy chair from its position in the corner and slid it toward the television for a better view. There was a loud rip, and the astronaut noticed a broken wire protruding from the carpet where the chair had been located. The most amusing thing, he later recalled, was how studiously the Russians stared at the television—nobody acknowledged seeing anything.

The original plans for the joint flight, as projected in 1972, called for a U.S. docking to a Soviet Salyut space station. However, the Soviets balked. Some observers thought the Russians were just being over-secretive in refusing to allow outsiders to participate in a Salyut mission. But it turned out that they were only trying to hide their schedule slips: the two-port Salyut originally scheduled for 1975 had been put off at least two years, and the available one-port models could not support joint activities. This left only the option of a direct Soyuz-to-Apollo linkup.

Since the Apollo and Soyuz spacecraft used different atmospheric systems, an intermediate air-lock chamber was needed to allow spacemen to pass from one ship to the other. This was built by the American side. In their turn, the Soviets modified the atmosphere-control system of their own

Soyuz spacecraft and made a manned orbital dress-rehearsal flight in December 1974 to test these and other modifications. (The Soviets had offered to give NASA advance warning of the launching of the dress-rehearsal mission so the Americans could practice space tracking—but they insisted that NASA keep the date secret, a stipulation which the Americans rejected.)

There's some truth to the observation that Apollo did most of the work during the actual rendezvous and docking, while the Russians, of course, shared half the credit. The Soyuz was launched into its standard parking orbit, 120 miles high at the typical inclination of 52°. As earth's rotation carried Cape Canaveral into the plane of the Soviet spaceship's orbit, the American spaceship was completing its countdown. Following blast-off on a northeastward azimuth, the Apollo wound up, as desired, in the same vertical plane as the Soyuz (otherwise, any precise rendezvous would have been physically impossible), but several thousand miles behind and below. More than a day would have to pass before the Apollo would overtake the waiting Soyuz.

The astronauts were impressed by the view—it was the lowest orbit ever flown by American spacemen. "The thunderheads seemed to reach a quarter way up to us," Deke Slayton recalled. (It was closer to one tenth.) Tom Stafford, a veteran of three earlier space flights, remarked on how fast the ground was zipping by on this flight. Such low orbits had been avoided by Americans before because of the high air drag and poor communication associated with the low altitude—but it was as high as the Russian ship could fly, so it would have to do.

The docking was the responsibility of the U.S. side. The Apollo homed in on an American radio unit installed on the Soyuz, while the Soyuz held steady. Stafford took over manual control and lined his ship up for the nose-to-nose linkup. The two docking units touched and locked.

A few hours later, as the spacemen equalized air pressure

and opened the hatch, the historic space handshake took place. A series of mutual visits and activities filled the next two days.

Perhaps ASTP should best be viewed as the pinnacle of space image-manship. The Soviets wanted it in order to make up for their loss of face in the space race, to portray themselves as equal space partners with the United States, even though they were not. The United States had still not grasped the mechanics of space imagery and may have felt that play-acting in orbit could lead to fundamental changes in Kremlin thought patterns.

This basic American misunderstanding of what factors motivated Soviet space projects led to further confusion. When ASTP was not followed up by additional joint ventures (by 1978, the United States and Soviet Union were not even *talking* about future joint manned programs), it appeared that somehow an opportunity had been flubbed. In fact, the Soviet restrictions on ASTP had forestalled the existence of any such further opportunity in the first place.

Disregarding the pomp and pageantry of the actual space handshake, both sides still got practical and psychological benefits from the project. Confusion over what (if anything) the flight symbolized should not be construed to imply the project wasn't worth doing. The Soviets, after all, were using the project as an exercise in which they could develop capabilities which would later be integrated with their mainstream manned space efforts: the ASTP missions marked the inauguration of a new Mission Control Center in Moscow to replace the old one in the Crimea, and the Soviet ASTP spacecraft introduced some new technological systems (such as improved solar panels), which later showed up during the Salyut-6 mission. For the United States, the project was a technological dead end, employing the last Apollo spacecraft, the last Saturn rocket and the first and last use of a special docking module as interface between the two vehicles.

The Soviet cosmonauts had come right out of the mainline civilian Salyut program and had, in all probability, been the prime flight crews for the Salyuts which blew up or broke down in 1972–1973. After ASTP they returned to the real Soviet manned space program and flew again during the Salyut-6 project in 1977–1980. The American spacecraft was commanded by a veteran astronaut called out of retirement, Tom Stafford, and included in its crew a leftover Mercury astronaut, Deke Slayton, who had only recently overcome a medical disqualification which had barred him from space missions for twelve years. At fifty-one, he was (and remains) the oldest man ever to be sent into space.

The alleged technology transfer from the United States to the Soviet Union during ASTP has probably been exaggerated. Most of what the Soviets could have learned about American space techniques was already available to them through the open literature. They may have wished to confirm it: since they were so accustomed to creating deliberate space disinformation campaigns, they may have been suspicious of what they had found in the open U.S. literature. And the Apollo-Saturn technology was more than a decade old, practically obsolete. Learning how space operations were planned and executed in America was only the first step, anyway: the exploitation of such information was limited by some essential Soviet bureaucratic practices, the most important being a severe restriction on the free flow of information between different organizations. So it's unlikely that the United States "gave away the farm," as many critics alleged.

In fact, the Soviets suffered from a perceptual gap caused by their own basic misperceptions of the U.S. space program. Their space officials took a long time in realizing that the Americans weren't lying to them about there being no more Skylab flights: the Russians, extrapolating from their own experience, were convinced that a super-secret all-military spy Skylab was being prepared and that American space officials were deliberately trying to deceive them when they denied it.

On the other hand, American space officials received a remarkably candid and complete view of Soviet manned space capabilities, which was presumably of some value in assessing overall Soviet technological levels. There were some definite limits: Soviet officials declined to discuss the Salyut program much and vigorously insisted that the 1972 and 1973 Salyut debacles had never occurred. But within the narrow technological bounds of the project itself, cooperation was genuine.

The practical benefits of ASTP to the American program were twofold. First, the Apollo flight went on for a week after the Russians landed, during which the astronauts conducted extensive experiments similar to those done on the Skylab space station in 1973. For example, a materials processing furnace had been installed in the docking module, which now became a sort of mini–space station. Second, the three-year program (1972–1975) came between the tail end of Apollo-Skylab activities and the pickup of Space Shuttle efforts, so it enabled NASA to retain a cadre of experienced space specialists through what otherwise would have been a serious space-flight activities gap—during which most of them would have been laid off (and subsequent rehirings and re-trainings would have been very expensive) and most of the valuable experience of the personnel would have been lost for good. When all is said and done, the flight would have been worth it even as a solo mission; the Russian connection was useful for getting it financed.

Salyut-5 was put into orbit in late June 1976, almost a year after ASTP. It's hard to tell what this next Salyut space station, officially the fifth but actually at least the seventh, really accomplished. For Western observers, it nicely confirmed the civilian/military dichotomy of the entire Salyut program, since although it followed the civilian Salyut-4 by a year and a half, it was obviously an outgrowth of the military Salyut-3 two whole years before. For the Soviets, the mission held a lot of frustrations and unpleasant surprises and probably was considered a disappointment . . . but a learning experience nonetheless.

The Salyut-5 spent two weeks in space empty and then was visited by Soyuz-21 cosmonauts Boris Volynov and Vitaliy Zholobov on July 7. As week followed week, the two men conducted observations of the atmosphere and surface of earth, carried out a series of materials-processing and biology experiments and tested new on-board equipment. But most of their activities probably dealt with military reconnaissance: late in July they were in a position with the right lighting conditions to monitor Soviet military maneuvers in eastern Siberia and the northern Pacific. Observations over China and the United States were also possible.

The best available guess, backed up by informed sources in Moscow, was that the flight would extend the sixty-three-day record of the year before. But without warning, on August 24, after seven weeks in space, Moscow announced that the flight of Soyuz-21 was ending; the men were back on earth by nine-thirty that very evening, Moscow time.

Normally, Soviet space spokesmen would give up to a week's advance notice of the impending return of a Salyut crew, so the suddenness in this case was suspicious. Absent, too, had been descriptions of any special pre-landing exercises and medical preparations which had characterized earlier Salyut missions. Last, the nighttime landing was clear evidence for the prematurity of the cosmonauts' return: it would have been at least three weeks before the Salyut space station's orbit would have allowed a landing during the preferred midafternoon pass over the recovery zone, and Soviet practice has always been to choose the original launch hour so as to provide enough time (depending on planned mission duration) for the orbit to shift to a path which allowed a convenient midafternoon landing hour. All of these factors added up to the conclusion that the decision to call the men back had been a precipitous one.

But why? Moscow's official statements were of little help: it was just another "totally successful" space triumph. Yet one hint was that the "general condition" of the cosmonauts was characterized as "satisfactory," a far cry from the usual "excellent." Also, the landing notice was downplayed on *Radio Moscow,* earning an inconspicuous place at the end of the evening news broadcast. And then there were the earlier Soviet news items about the problems of psychological isolation and sensory deprivation faced by space crews; space medicine reports released a year later revealed that the copilot's health showed a marked deterioration during the last ten days of the flight. So there seems to be some justification in presuming some sort of medical motivation for cutting the flight short.

A different reason for the premature return was proposed by *Aviation Week* magazine a few months later. According to its sources, the spacemen had been complaining about an "acrid odor" which was coming out of the cabin air-regeneration system. Repeated attempts to repair the unit were fruitless, and finally (so wrote the aerospace weekly) the men told Mission Control that they couldn't stand it any longer.

Whatever it was that caused the early termination of the flight, it must have looked fixable, because a new visit to the Salyut-5 was launched on October 14. But an electronics failure in the Soyuz-23 guidance system frustrated the planned linkup, and rookie cosmonauts Zudov and Rozhdestvenskiy headed back to earth—the fourth Salyut linkup failure out of nine tries in five years. (The Soyuz-22 was a week-long photographic mission in September which was never meant to visit Salyut-5.)

Soyuz emergency landings can be tricky, since they have only a handful of safe landing passes and since—as in this case—they usually have to be at night. The weather in the recovery zone was extremely bad: snowstorms with practically zero visibility, with temperatures of about −15°C (5°F). But there was no way to wait for them to clear: the Soyuz

EARLY PERSONALITIES

The architect of initial Soviet space program successes was Sergey Korolev (1906–1966), who survived Stalinist slave labor camps to single-handedly organize rocket development in the mid-1950s.

Field Marshal Mitrofan Nedelin (1902–1960), Khrushchev's hand-picked rocket chief, often had to sacrifice scientific development in order to serve Khrushchev's purposes. In the end, his life, too, was sacrificed.

Nikolay Kamenin (b. 1908), first commandant of the cosmonaut detachment, conducted frequent purges of trainees thought to have ideological or motivational weaknesses. He himself was purged in 1971 following several years of flight disasters and space-crew fatalities.

THE SECRET SPACE CENTER

The rocket launch pad at Korolev's central Asian test center was emplaced at the edge of a deep flame pit. One of the greatest tragedies of the space age apparently occurred here on the night of October 23, 1960, when several dozen technicians were killed by the sudden explosion of a balky space booster. Khrushchev had ordered that the launch take place while he was at the UN; his missile chief, Nedelin, forced to ignore some safety precautions in order to keep to the schedule, was among the dead.

The Soviet missile test center has been under surveillance by American intelligence organizations (via radar and radio eavesdropping as well as direct overflights by reconnaissance aircraft) since about 1957. This is a U2 spy-plane photo made in 1959 but not released until 1979.

Moscow datelines all of its space news from the "Baikonur Cosmodrome," which is a geographical fiction named after an obscure mining town hundreds of miles from the site of the actual missile base. This NASA photo was taken by Landsat-1 in 1973 and covers an area about a hundred miles from side to side. The real space center stretches across the middle of the picture, and is quite close to the town of Tyuratam (Tyu-rah-tom, arrow), which is the name by which Western observers refer to the Soviet spaceport.

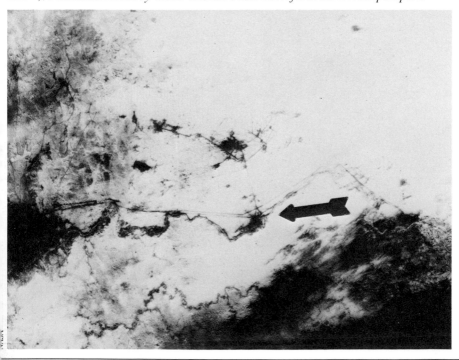

PHOTO FORGERIES

The notorious "Sochi forgery" photograph (below) shows Korolev surrounded by his leading cosmonauts and training officials a few weeks after the success of the first manned space flight in 1961. The pilot Gagarin sits with a tie at front row, left. The entire manned space-flight team was taking a month's holiday at Sochi, the famed Black Sea resort. Note the change in composition of the back row: one of the cosmonaut candidates has vanished via some very artful retouching of the original image.

The first photo shows a busload of cosmonauts on their way to the launching of Voskhod-2 in March 1965—but in the later version of the scene, one man's head has rolled. The missing man was identified years later by a colleague as a cosmonaut named "Dmitriy" who subsequently had "medical problems" after serving on the backup crew for the flight in question.

Some Soviet photographic forgeries seem to deal with purely aesthetic problems. In 1975, a photograph of two cosmonauts emerging from their space capsule was apparently too crowded with extra figures—so while one version went out over the international wire, another neater (and less populated) version was used on the front page of Pravda ("Truth," in Russian). Cosmonaut Pyotr Klimuk (in black sweater, left) is the star of a new generation of young Soviet spacemen; cosmonaut Vitaliy Sevastyanov (in spacesuit, right) is a talented engineer and popular radio commentator on space exploration.

TERESHKOVA

The world's first—and so far only—woman in space was Valentina Tereshkova, a Russian textile factory worker. Her three-day flight in 1963 was widely accepted as proof of the equality of women under socialism.

Khrushchev used the cosmonaut program to enhance his own prestige and for international diplomatic advantages. The "woman-in-space" program had been his idea from the start, and space chief Korolev had carried it out only to insure further funding for the real Soviet space program—which did not include women.

NASA

Another idea of Khrushchev's was to have Tereshkova marry the only bachelor cosmonaut, Andrian Nikolayev. It was the U.S.S.R. social event of the year, and marked the end of Tereshkova's space career. The other women cosmonauts were expelled from the program. Tereshkova's husband remarked years later that more women might someday fly as specialists "and, of course, as stewardesses."

SPACEWALK

Some Western skeptics have claimed that films of the 1965 Russian spacewalk were faked, since the cosmonaut's visor is reflecting a triple light source, more like a studio light than the sun. The film could well be a fake, but the walk was real. Although the cosmonaut nearly died at the end of the ten-minute stunt, he later publicly boasted about how easy it had been, encouraging NASA to take some dangerous cuts in its own spacewalk program.

The Voskhod-2 "spacewalk" cosmonauts missed their intended touchdown point by more than two thousand miles, and came down in a snowy birch forest in the Ural Mountains. They spent the night inside their capsule fighting off hungry wolves who tried to force their way past the partially open hatch.

DISASTERS AND FUNERALS

An overambitious two-ship linkup and crew-transfer mission ended tragically in 1967 when the pilot of the first ship (Colonel Vladimir Komarov, center) *died during an emergency landing. The two spacesuited figures in this photograph later took part in a successful attempt to conduct the maneuver in 1969. Moscow's desire to cover up the full scope of the 1967 disaster was frustrated by the accidental release of this official group portrait in 1978: it clearly shows that Komarov had been involved in training for the two-ship linkup and spacewalk.*

Komarov's crushed body was cremated and the urn with his ashes inside was placed in a niche in the Kremlin Wall, the place of highest honor for Soviet heroes. Here his widow pays last respects. (Due to Soviet space secrecy regulations, Komarov had not been allowed to tell her he was going to make a flight when he left for the spaceport.)

Between 1967 and 1971, the Soviet public watched three nationally televised cosmonaut funerals in Red Square, Moscow: (top to bottom) *Komarov (killed aboard Soyuz-1 in 1967), Gagarin (killed in a plane crash in 1968) and the three Salyut-1 cosmonauts (suffocated aboard Soyuz-11 in 1971). Top Soviet space officials have admitted privately that "six or eight" trainee cosmonauts have also lost their lives in various accidents, but they were buried in secret.*

MOON FLIGHT

When this cover appeared in late 1968, both the United States and the Soviet Union were only weeks away from sending men around the moon. But following the success of the unexpectedly rapid Apollo schedule, Moscow canceled all further man-to-the-moon plans and publicly proclaimed it had never been in the race after all—a deceptive propaganda ploy widely accepted by the Western news media.

Russian cosmonauts look wistfully at moon photos sent back by a robot scout ship in 1967. Until the Apollo flights, Russian spokesmen (including cosmonauts such as Gagarin, seen here at left) had made it clear they expected Soviet spacemen to reach the moon ahead of Americans.

The Soviet man-around-the-moon mission planned for 1968 would have carried a single pilot making a single pass around the moon before returning to earth. The flight path had been followed twice successfully by unmanned versions of the Soyuz spacecraft (as illustrated in this collage by the author).

PERSONALITIES

Yuriy Gagarin (1934–1968), first man to travel in space, was a perfect role model for Soviet youth and is now revered as the official communist "patron saint of space travel."

Pavel Belyayev (1925–1970), apparently selected to be the first man to fly around the moon, lost his chance when the Soviet moonshot program was delayed and finally canceled. Less than a year after the termination of the program, he died of surgical complications during an operation for a severe bleeding ulcer.

Vladimir Shatalov (b. 1927), three-time space veteran and, since 1971, commander of the cosmonaut detachment, has surprised nearly everyone by turning out to be a competent administrator during a crucial period.

Vasiliy Lazarev (b. 1927) is a physician and test pilot who has experienced the most frustrating space career ever: at first rejected several times for the program, he was later thrice scheduled for a space station mission that was repeatedly canceled due to equipment failures or budgetary constraints. He was also the commander of the only known manned-space-launch abort ever, leading to a near-fatal crash landing on a mountaintop in Siberia.

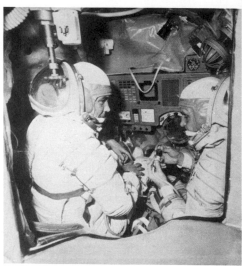

The cramped Soyuz command module offers little elbow room, but a more spacious "orbital module" attached to the front end of the spacecraft does provide additional room for work or storage.

More than eighty Soyuz-type space vehicles were launched between 1966 and 1980; thirty have gone up in the last three years alone. The Soviet booster is based on the original Korolev missile design, from 1956; no larger vehicle has yet been successfully "man-rated" for sufficient reliability to carry cosmonauts.

*Unlike ocean splashdowns of American manned space flights, the Soviet flights termi-
nate over dry land when a small solid rocket engine ignites just prior to impact. The
landing zone is usually in some wheat field in Kazakhstan.*

*Traditional cosmonaut ceremonies following "thump-down" include crew's autographing
spacecraft side with chalk.*

SALYUT!

Pilot's eye view of Salyut space station just before docking at the forward hatch. Panels generate electricity from sunlight. Near the docking port is a side hatch used for spacewalks.

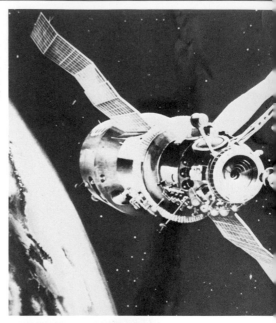

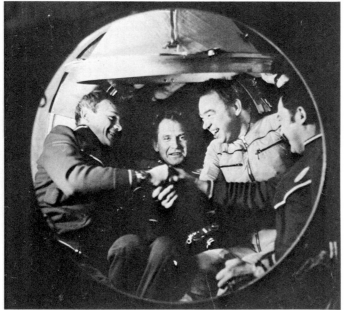

World's first double docking occurred during the record-breaking Salyut-6 expedition early in 1978. Two visiting Soyuz-27 cosmonauts (left) greet their orbital hosts Georgiy Grechko and Yuriy Romanenko. They also knew that Grechko's father had just died back on earth, but they decided not to tell him, since he had months left before he could return.

In December 1977, during an emergency spacewalk to check for possible external damage, cosmonaut Grechko saved the life of his shipmate Romanenko (shown here in the air lock prior to the spacewalk) when he fell out the hatch without a safety line. Grechko managed to grab him just before he drifted out of reach. The cosmonauts withheld news of the incident even from Soviet space officials until their postflight news conference.

The interior of the two-room Salyut space station shows attempts to utilize every available corner for storage or for mounting equipment. The main hall is about six by eight by eighteen feet, with a small air-lock room visible through the round hatch.

TRIUMPHANT LANDINGS

The Russian crews on the long-duration Salyut-6 expeditions in 1977–1980 also hosted week-long visits of "guest cosmonauts" from Soviet-bloc nations. The first was Czechoslovakian pilot Vladimir Remek (arrow), selected for his political reliability rather than his physical fitness or flying skills. (His father was also the Czech Deputy Defense Minister.) The foreigners were given crash courses in space flight, even though a Russian pilot would be along on each flight to do the actual work. Remek was retired from flight duties and assigned to ceremonial and political tasks in Prague.

The cosmonauts returning from the months-long visits to Salyut-6 showed that the medical problems of long-duration space flights had been, for the most part, overcome. Here, Valeriy Ryumin (left) and Vladimir Lyakhov celebrate their landing after six months in space; the following year, Ryumin was launched on a new expedition and spent another six months in orbit.

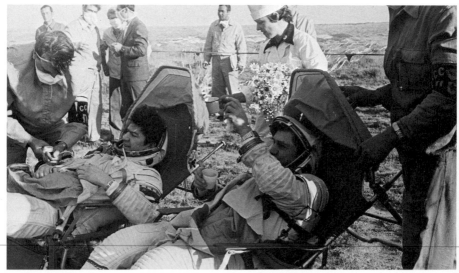

was quickly running out of air and electrical power.

Although the landing zone in Soviet central Asia is mostly level prairie, there are some salt lakes near the northern edge, and twenty-mile-wide Lake Tengiz is the largest of these. That's where Soyuz-23 came down, about a mile from the southern shore. Since it was only autumn, the surface of the lake was still ice-free—but bitter cold. It was a terribly unlucky landing, right into the lake: Russia's first (and so far only) manned space splashdown.

The first sign of trouble the cosmonauts probably got was when their touchdown impact shock was followed by rocking back and forth. Within minutes, the temperature inside the capsule plunged toward freezing, as the men scrambled out of their spacesuits and into their cold-weather survival suits. The copilot, a navy engineer and former deep-sea diver, had ironically suggested before the launch that his underwater experience "may yet come in handy" (he was probably referring to a planned spacewalk)—but the spacecraft remained watertight and afloat as the icy winds howled outside. They were advised over the radio to stay inside and wait for rescue.

As chief cosmonaut Shatalov later put it, the rescue operation was "difficult and complicated"—an uncharacteristic understatement if there ever was one. The rescue forces displayed "high courage and heroism" throughout the night, while Moscow news agencies remained silent about the fate of the men. (As hour followed hour in silence, observers began to suspect that some sort of disaster was being covered up.) The first efforts to get a line on the capsule failed, as frogmen struggled with balky connectors and other equipment failures. Amphibious vehicles, brought in by helicopter, were also unable to reach the capsule. Finally a line was secured, but the helicopter could not lift the three-ton Soyuz command module out of the water. Instead, it dragged the capsule toward shore and then across a mile of frozen swamp to where other helicopters could put down safely. Six hours after hitting the water, the men were able to get out of the capsule; four hours later, news of their safe return was released, with a few comments about some minor difficulties during the landing.

The mission objective of the aborted Soyuz-23 must have been important because it was tried again. Four months later, as the Salyut-5's orbit position once again duplicated that which preceded the launch of Soyuz-23, the Soyuz-24 was launched with the backup crew of the failed mission on board. The mission of cosmonauts Viktor Gorbatko and Yuriy Glazkov was characterized by three unusual features: their visit turned out to be unexpectedly brief, only eighteen days; the men, after linking up with the Salyut station on the evening of February 8, 1977, spent the night in their Soyuz ferry ship and did not open the hatch into the space station until the following morning (no other Salyut visitors ever did this before or since); the mysterious detachable recovery capsule of the Salyut was sent back to earth the very next day after the cosmonauts themselves landed (although the Salyut itself remained in orbit, unmanned, until August 8).

While the men were on board, they carried out a few nominal experiments with earth photography, biological specimens and zero-G metal crystallization. They also replaced some electronics modules on the navigation computer, and on February 21, five days after the halfway point of the flight had been announced in Moscow, they replaced the air in the Salyut cabin by opening a drain valve at one end while releasing two hundred pounds of bottled air at the other end.

This air-replacement operation tended to substantiate the *Aviation Week* story that the air in the Salyut had gone bad —although in announcing the operation, Soviet space officials explicitly stated that it was only a test and that the original air was "perfectly good." That this assertion may not have been true is also suggested by that unprecedented (and since then unrepeated) operation of waiting an extra eleven hours before entering the Salyut-5 after docking. Such a step strongly implies that the boarding of the Salyut was expected to be a long and difficult operation requiring a rested crew—which would certainly be consistent with a contaminated air supply.

As to the brevity of the mission, there are several possible interpretations. Plans for a long mission might have been dropped when the cosmonauts determined that whatever was wrong with the Salyut-5 could not be repaired. But the more likely situation is that the mission had always been intended to be short: the landing time for Soyuz-24 was about noon (Moscow time), which was just about perfect, indicating that no premature call-back had occurred; the planned lifetime of the Salyut-5 was probably only about six months originally, and most of the stored food on the station would have gone bad by the time Gorbatko and Glazkov got there eight months after launch; the rushed return of the mystery capsule also strongly suggested that the Salyut-5 was on its last legs and could not be guaranteed fully safe much longer.

Even in disappointment, the 1976–1977 Salyut-5 space-station mission demonstrated the increasing maturity and confidence of the Soviet space team. Two visits had been accomplished and a not inconsiderable amount of technical and scientific research had been carried out. Additionally, the various problems which were encountered forced the flight-control teams to learn flexibility and imagination, and their demonstrated ability to handle such setbacks and still save the lives of the endangered spacemen contributed greatly to their overall self-confidence. Together with the successes of Salyut-4 in 1975, the failures of Salyut-5 must have contributed to the maturation of the Soviet manned space program as it prepared, in mid-1977, to advance to the second-generation Salyut with all of its capabilities and challenges. Cosmonauts and Mission Control specialists felt ready for the mission. And as it turned out, all of their experience and all of their new-found confidence would soon be fully tested —and would meet the challenge.

9

☆

Secret Space Cities

Before every flight into outer space, cosmonauts carry out a strange and solemn ceremony. Each spaceman composes a letter in which he vows to be true to the traditions and standards of his predecessors and to do his best to justify the trust which has been shown in him by his motherland and by the Communist party. He then takes this letter to a quiet room and spends a long time there in silent meditation. Before departing, he leaves the letter on a desk and snaps a salute to an empty chair. Within the hour, he is on an airplane bound for the launch site.

This ceremony of departure takes place in a special room in the Cosmonaut Museum, which is located in Starry Town (Zvezdniy Gorodok), the home of the Soviet cosmonaut detachment. The room is a replica of Yuriy Gagarin's office, containing the exact furniture arranged in precisely the same way things were the moment Gagarin perished in a flight accident at 10:41 A.M. on March 22, 1968. His desk calendar shows his appointments for that day; the wall clock is stopped at the moment of his death; his coat hangs on a wall hook. It had been only a few days after his thirty-fourth birthday.

The village of Starry Town is a world unto itself. Although only forty miles from Moscow, it is enveloped in several layers of secrecy and isolation, and its three thousand inhabitants—cosmonauts, training officials, engineers and their families—might as well live in another world. Many of them may someday do so.

The town is reached by driving northeast from Moscow to the city of Kaliningrad (where the Mission Control Center is located) and then turning east toward Shchelkovo. South of this road lies the sprawling Chkalov Air Force Base aviation complex, hidden from the road traffic by a tall fence. Further down the road, the fences give way to a thick pine forest, and then without warning, an unmarked road turns off to the right into the forest. Anyone curious—or careless —enough to venture down this road finds a guard post just around the bend. The road to Starry Town is barred to outsiders.

For those with legitimate space business—or for high-ranking diplomatic tourists—the road soon comes to a large clearing containing several tall apartment buildings, a few low office buildings and some stores. At one end of the clearing are several small lakes; at the other is a fenced enclosure containing a dozen large structures—the actual cosmonaut training institute.

In the center of the clearing, facing the entrance, stands a statue of a heroic figure, larger than life. The face is modeled after Yuriy Gagarin's, but the character—fearless cosmonaut, devoted communist, perfect father and husband, brilliant engineer, role model for the idealistic youth, charismatic leader—is a creature of legend. As the inspiration for a veritable patron saint of space travel, Gagarin has turned out to be more useful to the Soviet Union dead than alive.

That spirit—as opposed to the man—is nowhere better enshrined than in Starry Town.

Some things look very ordinary on the sidewalks there— shawled *babushkas* push baby carriages and lead toddling grandchildren from home to playground to shops to home again. Construction equipment is parked along many streets, and newly constructed buildings immediately assume the typical decrepit Soviet architectural style. White birches and dark pines rim the meadow where the campus-like village sits.

But there are differences from other towns in Russia. The shops are well stocked with goods. The apartments are larger —the buildings were constructed according to a standard Soviet floor plan, but intervening walls were knocked down and each cosmonaut got a double ration of floor space. Outside, the sound of jet aircraft is almost constantly in the air, since one of the main runways at Chkalov Air Force Base is just through the trees. There are more outdoor sports complexes, and more people using them, than are normal for a village this size. (Soviet cosmonaut training stresses physical conditioning and there is an active program of team sports.) Starry Town is, after all, a special place.

A monument to this uniqueness is found in the Cosmonaut Museum. The replica of Gagarin's study is one room in this building; other rooms hold models of space vehicles and case after case of awards received by Soviet cosmonauts. There is also a large movie theater. The museum hostess is Nina Belyayeva, widow of cosmonaut Pavel Belyayev.

On bulletin boards in the museum and elsewhere are found the private communication systems of Starry Town. Besides memos and announcements, there is the newspaper *Neptune,* a private newsletter full of cosmonaut activities, gossip, accomplishments, jokes and caricatures. The publication is called a "wallpaper" because people have to read the issues tacked to the wall—nobody is allowed to keep personal copies. The information found in *Neptune* is considered top secret: when Americans visited Starry Town during preparations for the ASTP flight in 1975, all they saw were rows of empty bulletin boards with even the tacks packed away. The Americans worked for two years with cosmonaut Aleksey Leonov, who is an amateur artist and the editor and chief cartoonist of *Neptune,* but he never once showed them a copy or even mentioned its existence.

Many different elite standards have been used to admit people to the cosmonaut corps and to residence in Starry Town. For the first ten years of Starry Town's history, it seems that nobody really knew what qualifications made the best cosmonauts—so space officials tried them all.

The twenty young men picked in March 1960, a year before the flight of Vostok-1, were first and foremost medical specimens: they were mostly young—aged twenty-five to twenty-seven—jet pilots in magnificent physical shape. A few were older men with some test-pilot experience, but half of these older would-be cosmonauts were eventually medically disqualified before they could fly. After the initial space flights, the remaining young men were put through the Soviet Air Force Academy in the late 1960s, since they had all originally entered pilot training right after high school.

In January 1963 a new group appeared. It was composed of about a dozen men five to ten years older than the first group, with extensive test-pilot and engineering experience. They would have been the only cosmonauts of the decade who met standards comparable to those used in the American program. Their mission was to have been commanding the multi-crewmen missions of the late 1960s, to the moon and to the Salyut space stations; by that time they would have been in their early forties.

Additional crewmen would come from two more groups picked in 1965–1967. Some of these men were young jet pilots, even younger at their selection than the members of the class of 1960 had been. Others were civilian engineers, men from the engineering and industrial centers where manned space vehicles were designed, built and tested; they were generally in their mid-thirties. The two groups doubled the size of the Soviet cosmonaut corps from about two dozen to more than fifty, just prior to the planned major expansion of cosmonaut flight activities involving moon flights and space stations.

A third group of cosmonauts may have been selected about this same period, but it would have been disbanded following the Soyuz and Salyut disasters in 1967–1973. These men would have been scientist-cosmonauts, specialists in medicine, biology, geology or astronomy, who should have ridden the third seat in the Soyuz (the passenger's seat) and would have been primarily responsible for the scientific research aboard space stations. One such candidate was Rostislav Bogdashevskiy, identified in 1967 to a visiting NBC news team as "trainee cosmonaut," who years later turned out to be an M.D. and expert on space physiology. He never flew in space: when the third seat on the Soyuz was eliminated in 1971 (making room for additional safety equipment), so, too, was the chance of any scientist-cosmonaut flying in space in the 1970s. The men were dismissed from the cosmonaut program and returned to their professional specialties.

The 1966–1968 cosmonauts who were also civilian engineers were difficult enough to train. Unlike the military officers in the cosmonaut program, these civilians already lived in the Moscow area where they had been working for years. They kept their apartments near the spacecraft-design bureaus and commuted to Starry Town by bus, an hour's ride each way.

It was apparently an ordinary commuter bus route, which dropped them off at the unmarked turnoff to Starry Town. Presumably a car would be waiting to take them on the short drive to the training center. Many of the cosmonaut center's employees took that bus, along with dozens of ordinary citizens headed for other stops, so there was nothing special about people getting off at the Starry Town road. But one of the civilian cosmonauts recounted an amusing story: he had taken the bus for three years and nobody had noticed him, but after his first space flight in 1971 all of the other passengers began pestering him so much for autographs that he was forced to take an earlier bus. On this bus, to avoid similar trouble, he disguised himself for a while with a wig and false beard.

The young jet pilots of the 1965–1967 selection had no such commuting problems, since they and their families were given apartments in Starry Town. And they were not pestered by the public: they endured a long anonymity, since it turned out that they would have to wait ten to twelve years for their space missions. The loss of the Soyuz third seat in the 1971 safety redesign meant extra work for them. Normally a man would have made his first space mission in that seat, with a veteran cosmonaut in command and a civilian engineer along as well. Without that third seat, the military pilots had to be ready to command the mission on their first space flight—there was no chance for a warm-up flight. This would—and did—take many additional years of training.

The theory behind the selection of pilot-cosmonauts at the young age of twenty-three to twenty-five seemed to be that no outside experience would really be helpful in learning to become a cosmonaut; the sooner the candidates could be started in training, the better. The high dropout rate such a process would entail (which has never been acknowledged by the Soviets) could be countered by picking two or three times the number needed. For example, only four pilots from the August 1965 selection ever flew in space: Pyotr Klimuk, Gennadiy Sarafanov, Vyacheslav Zudov and Leonid Kizim. (They had all been twenty-three years old when picked.) There may have been as many as ten men in the original pilot group, but the long years of academic training were bound to eliminate some, while inevitable medical complications grounded others. Some, too, may have lost their lives in training-related accidents. We'll probably never know.

It is hoped that these dropouts and casualties have not been forgotten by their more successful colleagues. There seems to be a secret room in the Cosmonaut Museum, off limits to outsiders, where the pictures of these never-to-be cosmonauts are hung on the wall; some of the pictures would no doubt be draped in black crepe. Fidel Castro, on a ceremonial visit to Starry Town, saw this room and referred to it during the 1980 Havana celebrations over Cuba's own (and only) cosmonaut. He called it the "gallery of martyrs," commemorating "many who have died in their attempt to go into space or during their descent from space." Loss of life in those early days, said Castro, had been "relatively high." How high, we still don't know.

The administrative offices at Starry Village have to face another uniquely Soviet question concerning cosmonauts: What to do with retired Russian space pilots? In the United States, former astronauts generally left the program and sought new goals in life. In the Soviet Union, a man is a cosmonaut *for life* and there are no outside options. This is less a way of making use of their experience than of exploiting their government-provided fame. There is always ceremonial work to be done, and why bother the active cosmonauts with it if there are some unemployed veterans available?

However, some semblance of official duties has to be found, even though the men never were chosen for administrative ability. (A few, like Shatalov, surprised everyone and rose very quickly on unexpected managerial merit.) One former cosmonaut is now mayor of Starry Village, and two others are nominally director and deputy director of the Gagarin Cosmonaut Training Center; they all have civilian aides who do the actual work, leaving the former cosmonauts free to do such favorite things as preside over VIP tours or ride the recovery helicopters during spacecraft landings.

By the mid-1970s, Starry Village was undergoing another

expansion. American astronauts who visited the site in 1974 were particularly impressed by the construction going on all over the area. "It's a boom town," astronaut Tom Stafford told newsmen on his return to the United States. "There's no doubt the Soviets have a vigorous ongoing manned space effort planned for the next five or six years." Officials told Stafford that there were eighty to a hundred cosmonauts then in training, indicating another doubling in the size of the space cadre since the late 1960s.

The training center itself, shut off from the village by a tall green wooden fence, is composed of an administrative and classroom complex, a large hall full of spacecraft mock-ups and trainers, a medical center and crew quarantine facility, a gymnasium with an indoor swimming pool, a pressure chamber and assorted support buildings. A big new centrifuge with sixty-foot arms was completed in the late 1970s, and in 1979 a new swimming pool seventy-five feet in diameter was added for spacewalk training. (Floating underwater is the nearest thing to long-duration weightlessness that ground-based facilities can provide.)

Weightlessness can also be simulated in aircraft that fly along parabolic arcs through the sky: for thirty or forty seconds, the aircraft is in free fall, followed by about a minute of twice normal gravity as the plane bottoms out its dive and soars back upward on a new parabolic arc. Stationed at nearby Chkalov Air Force Base, the cosmonaut training air fleet was upgraded in 1979–1980 to use large Ilyushin-76 cargo planes instead of the smaller Tu-104s.

The entire Starry Town complex, including the Gagarin Cosmonaut Training Center, is much more isolated and self-sufficient than the comparable American facility southeast of Houston. There astronauts and other workers live "on the economy" in typical American suburbs; there more than a million tourists walk the grounds annually; there the names of trainee spacemen are listed in public telephone books. But

Starry Town epitomizes the passion for secrecy and security which is a characteristic of Soviet society in general.

Several thousand miles from Starry Town is another isolated and self-contained space community. If anything, it is even more secret than Starry Town—even its name has been expunged from all new editions of Soviet maps (while remaining prominently on the railroad schedules of that region!). It is the home of the Baikonur Cosmodrome workers and their families, a population considerably greater than one hundred thousand people—but even the name of the community is difficult to ascertain.

The spaceport appellation, of course, is a ruse—named after a tiny mining town hundreds of miles to the northeast. The actual town nearest the rocket center is Tyuratam, which lies on a fertile strip of land straddling the Syr Darya River. The small town was inhabited mostly by Kazakhstan natives of a vaguely Turkish origin; when the Russians began arriving in early 1955 they set up their own community a few miles northwest of the native village.

That Russian town has been deceptively referred to in the Soviet press as Baikonur, but its own inhabitants called it Zvezdagrad, or Star City. During ASTP, when American astronauts were given a whirlwind (and severely circumscribed) tour of the launch site, they were told the city was called Leninsk; the Americans were also told that "Star City" was the name of the cosmonaut hometown, and it was by that name (and not the correct translation, Starry Town) that the cosmonaut center near Moscow was identified in all NASA literature. Whether this mislocation of Star City was merely carelessness (perhaps a poor translation?) or a deliberate Soviet attempt at misleading NASA is impossible to determine—but the latter choice is certainly the one more in character.

Star City's central Asian isolation demanded that it provide all necessary services to its inhabitants, since there are no larger cities anywhere nearby. So over the years all the features of a small city were added: a university, a hotel, a concert hall, several theaters, a town hall and giant town square for compulsory political rallies, a soccer stadium, a cemetery and the requisite assortment of shops and restaurants befitting an "elite" Soviet community.

There isn't much available outside of town. The steppes of central Asia, immortalized by Borodin's music (and popularized in the Broadway play *Kismet*), have always been avenues for people trying to get somewhere else: Huns, Mongols, Cossacks and others have swept back and forth over the centuries, and even the very existence of the space center is due only to a desire to use the steppes as an avenue to a new destination. The region is rolling and gravelly, with only nomadic sheep herders in the wastelands away from the river. A few ruined towns and caravansaries might interest amateur archeologists, and treasure hunters might seek the stashed wealth of a generation of civil wars and native uprisings that followed the Bolshevik Revolution (although they would be much more likely to come across now-deserted "islands" of the GULag Archipelago slave camps which once thickly dotted Kazakhstan). But the Kazakh natives, while subdued, would not be described as necessarily friendly to small parties of Russians camped out under the stars—so few citizens of Star City wander far beyond the city limits.

Most of the vast areas north and east of Star City are off limits for reasons of military secrecy. A thousand miles to the east are the nuclear-bomb test areas near Semipalatinsk— also the reported site of Soviet beam-weapon ("death ray") work. Northeast of Star City are the spacecraft landing zones. One, a few hundred miles from the space center, is where the expended stages of the booster rockets hit the desert. (The metal is recovered—many components can be used over again.) Another, centered around the town of Arkalyk, is for space capsules coming back from orbit (occasionally with cosmonauts on board, but nine times out of ten with photographs of Western or Chinese military installations—even though the latter, much greater activity has *never* been admitted by the Soviets).

There are Soviet space facilities which are even more deeply shrouded in secrecy. The Soviet launch center near Plesetsk, a few hundred miles north of Moscow, has never been acknowledged to even exist, although more than two thirds of all Soviet unmanned satellites are launched from there. Most are operational flights with military applications: reconnaissance, communications, navigation and meteorology, as examples. One rare high-trajectory predawn launching on September 20, 1977, led to one of the biggest blunders ever on the part of the Soviet space censorship apparatus. There was nothing particularly unique about the Kosmos-955 spy satellite except that hundreds of thousands of people in northwest Russia saw its contrails—and thought it was an attacking UFO. Their eyewitness accounts were so garbled that censors did not connect the celestial apparition with the top-secret Plesetsk launch—so the story of the UFO was widely published. When the slip-up was discovered, a media campaign was initiated to "explain away" what had become the most exciting UFO story ever heard in the Soviet Union.

One Soviet professor said the UFO must have been "glowing industrial smog," the Russian equivalent of swamp gas. The web of illusion was spun tighter in an attempt to keep the existence of Plesetsk hidden from the Soviet population, and it worked: the consensus was that the light in the sky that morning was really a spaceship—but from another world, not from Russia.

The secrecy and disinformation curtain draped over Soviet space facilities—Starry Town, Star City, Baikonur and Plesetsk—has been developing great rents and holes over the years, and Soviet space spokesmen have become quite adept at sewing on patches. But by now their efforts seem directed mostly at deceiving the Soviet population, since Western observers have penetrated most of the cover-ups (and Western intelligence agencies, of course, know even more). Paint the most flattering image—that's always been the emphasis, whatever the true nature of the reality. And so the great Plesetsk UFO of 1977 flies on in the hearts and minds of ordinary Russian citizens, a fitting symbol of the reliability of official Soviet space spokesmen.

10

☆

The Salyut-6 Breakthrough

"If a Hollywood Central Casting were looking for an actor to play a Russian cosmonaut, they'd choose Georgiy Grechko," remarked a NASA official who knew him. "He's jovial, energetic, ruddy-complexioned, short and stocky. His head is topped by a graying crew cut and is set directly on his shoulders—no neck. His eyes have an Oriental tilt and his cheeks are puffed up from eating potatoes and borscht. And he is a fearsome vodka drinker."

Grechko is also the cosmonaut who was called upon to save the Salyut-6 mission in late 1977 when potential damage to one of the space station's two docking ports threatened to abort the most ambitious Soviet manned space effort to date.

A civilian engineer who had helped run space-trajectory computer programs for every Soviet space shot since Sputnik, Grechko became a cosmonaut in 1966 at the age of thirty-five. His training was delayed by a bad back injury during a parachute mishap, and he did not make his first space flight until 1975, when he spent thirty days aboard Salyut-4.

Two years later, as the preparations for Salyut-6 were

nearly completed, Grechko (now forty-six years old) was busy with a new project: he was probably assigned to the guest-cosmonaut program as a backup pilot for one of the periodic brief "mail runs" being planned as part of long Salyut-6 expeditions. Grechko had just been teamed with an East German pilot named Eberhard Köllner when, in mid-October 1977, more urgent considerations overruled all earlier plans.

Two Soyuz-25 cosmonauts had been launched on October 9, 1977, for a three-month mission aboard the Salyut-6 space station, which would have included a Bolshevik Revolution anniversary linkup with two other cosmonauts; instead, they turned back to earth after their linking attempt failed on October 10. Unlike earlier failures which had involved breakdowns on the Soyuz ferry ship, this failure was more ominous because it seemed to involve the Salyut itself. Soyuz-25 had evidently made several insertions of its nose into the Salyut berth, but the latching equipment had failed to secure the two vehicles together. If the problem was on Salyut-6 and could not be repaired, it could be the most serious Soviet space setback since Salyut-1 six years before.

A new space mission was scheduled to attempt fixing the problem. What was needed for the flight was a cosmonaut intimately familiar with the docking module mechanisms, who could bring a repair kit into space and use it if necessary. There was not enough time to train any of the next-scheduled cosmonauts, but it turned out there was one man available who had helped design the latching mechanisms, who was a space-flight veteran and who was already in training for a Salyut-6 visit: Georgiy Grechko.

By the time the decision was made to send up Grechko on the next three-month attempt, there were less than six weeks until launch. The crew commander was a young rookie named Yuriy Romanenko, thirty-three years old, who had previously spent three years as a backup cosmonaut in the Apollo-Soyuz program. Since 1973, he had been training with a rookie civilian flight engineer named Aleksandr Ivanchenkov. Now, after years of joint preparations, the team was split up to make room for Grechko.

Nobody had asked Grechko, either. As he later confided to a NASA colleague, he did not particularly enjoy the physical sensations of space flight: he had been sick for half his month-long flight in 1975 and had not recovered for some time after his return to earth. (Skylab data had revealed that thirty days is the absolute *worst* duration for a space flight, since the human body has only partially adjusted to weightlessness when it is thrown back into terrestrial conditions.) But now he was the logical choice and was easily replaced in his original assignment by another cosmonaut who had completed a space flight only eight months before and would thus also need minimal remedial training.

So Grechko and Romanenko blasted off aboard Soyuz-26 on December 10, 1977. Since the front door of the Salyut was suspect, they linked up to the back door, a unique second docking port which was the revolutionary design feature of Salyut-6. (Soyuz-25 had not carried enough fuel to try the second port.) Their first order of business was to activate the station's equipment and make sure everything was working; this took a week. Then it was time to tackle the problem of the suspect docking equipment.

On December 20 the two men entered the air-lock module of the Salyut and donned spacesuits. In the nine years since the last Soviet spacewalk, a highly sophisticated new spacesuit had been developed which combined ease in donning, long-duration outside support, high arm mobility and glove sensitivity, and maximum flexibility ("one size fits all" via adjustable straps). The first actual use of such equipment should normally have been at some simple task. Instead, the suits (and Grechko, whose rushed spacewalk training was barely adequate) would have to be trusted without time for a cautious checkout.

The spacewalk had such a high priority that it had to be

scheduled at an inconvenient hour. The best communication orbits across Russia occurred at night, and the cosmonauts began their preparations about six o'clock after an afternoon's fitful sleep. It was midnight by the time the men were ready.

Romanenko and Grechko let the air out of their air-lock chamber and verified that the suits were airtight. They then opened the side hatch and Grechko pulled himself out along handrails. While Romanenko remained in the air lock to monitor the medical readings on Grechko and the performance of his spacesuit, Grechko moved to the suspect docking port, set up a powerful lamp for nighttime operations and began the inspection.

The situation was better than anyone had hoped: there was no visible damage and all of the latches cycled properly when Grechko activated them. He inspected electrical plugs and sockets, contact sensors, guide rods, push rods, locks and sealing surfaces—there was not a sign of trouble. (The Soyuz-25 itself must have malfunctioned in October.) By the time Grechko was ready to head back to the hatch a quarter of an hour later, he knew that Salyut-6 was saved: the second port could be utilized by additional spaceships. Mission Control was jubilant and told the cosmonauts to wrap things up and finish the spacewalk.

The Salyut had passed out of range of Russian radio tracking stations while Grechko was preparing to return to the air lock. He paused to watch the Pacific Ocean pass two hundred miles below him at three hundred miles per minute. Later, he recalled that the most striking impression had been how hot the sun felt even through his suit; he also was struck by the vastness of the sky, and realized that once inside, he'd never see it this way again. Suddenly he was startled to see Romanenko's helmet stick out of the hatch: the other cosmonaut had not been scheduled to leave the air lock, but his curiosity had gotten the best of him and, on impulse, he had decided to depart from the flight plan and take a look outside.

Grechko later recalled being amazed, then alarmed, as

Romanenko drifted further and further out the hatch. Suddenly the young cosmonaut began thrashing violently, his safety line whipping around wildly. It wasn't attached! Grechko leaned over as Romanenko passed and managed to grab the line—and in so doing, saved the other man's life. Had Romanenko been a few more yards away, he would have floated free until his air ran out and he suffocated.

Neither man's pulse was being measured at that moment, but there can be little doubt they reached record highs. Once both men were inside the air lock, they debated whether or not to tell Moscow Mission Control about the incident. But suddenly, as they prepared to refill the air lock, a more urgent problem came up.

According to their instrument panel, the bleed valve through which they had released the air lock's pressure two hours before had not closed. They cycled the control switch several times, but the indicator still read "open." If they released their reserve air supplies, the air lock would stay empty as the gas drained out into space. They were trapped in the vacuum.

During the next half-hour, while waiting to pass within range of a radio site again, the men considered their predicament. Their spacesuit air would be gone soon. There was a slight chance they could go out into space, make their way around the station to their Soyuz spaceship and find a way inside. There were emergency air tanks to repressurize the spaceship, but it was a desperate gamble.

Mission Control personnel were shocked to learn the new developments, since they had expected to hear that the successful spacewalk was over. Ten minutes of frantic conferencing by systems experts confirmed what the cosmonauts suspected: the valve *had* to work; there was no available backup. So their advice to the cosmonauts was to assume that the indicator had failed and that the valve itself had closed properly. Grechko was ordered to let some air into the chamber and see if the slight pressure increase held.

Moments later, Grechko reported triumphantly that the pressure was holding steady: the valve was closed. As the space station passed out of radio range again, the cosmonauts were completing the repressurization successfully. They took off their spacesuits, wiped the sweat from their bodies, checked the status of the rest of the Salyut and then "fell" (to use the term metaphorically) into an exhausted sleep. Somehow the subject of Romanenko's first brush with death had never come up—and the men had decided not to mention it.

In fact, the cosmonauts didn't tell anyone about it for months, even after their return to earth. Grechko eventually figured out a way to present Soviet space officials with a *fait accompli* after which it would be difficult for anyone to discipline either of the cosmonauts for their cover-up: he broke the news at the post-flight news conference to a hallful of journalists. Grechko, at the end of a prepared statement, volunteered to comment on "some details which we did not report to earth," as he termed it. "I hope that the flight directors will not be offended," Grechko said carefully, "but we concealed the fact that it wasn't just me who went out into open space, as was called for in the program, but also commander Yuriy Romanenko. It was very difficult, naturally, for him to restrain himself. It turned out that he had forgotten to fasten his safety line, and I had to grab hold of his line and hold on to him." The Soviet space officials may have been unhappy about this (and the story was kept out of most of the newspapers), but the cosmonauts were apparently not reprimanded.

After the stimulating spacewalk on the tenth day of the flight, the cosmonauts still had a tremendous amount of work to do. Essentially, they were to be medical guinea pigs to test the physiological and psychological effects of ninety-six days in space—which is not to say that they didn't have important scientific and engineering work to do along the way. And even staying alive—ensuring a supply of air, food and water, plus keeping their equipment working—took a large part of their time. But they did it, week after week.

The creation of a totally artificial environment in the space station poses many problems, and some ingenious new solutions were tested on Salyut-6. The basic life-support system included management of atmospheric composition, water supplies and food. Additional measures were taken to maintain both physical and psychological health of the cosmonauts.

Oxygen, for example, is produced via chemical reactions set off by the passage of moist cabin air across thin sheets of potassium superoxide. These sheets are stacked inside canisters about the size and shape of golf bags; each canister produces about five man-days of oxygen before becoming saturated and requiring replacement. The carbon dioxide exhaled by the crewmen is in turn absorbed by granules of lithium hydroxide, which are also packed in canisters that also need periodic replacement.

Each crewman drinks about two to four quarts of water a day; half of this comes out as urine, the other half as moist breath. Since this consumption amounts to 5,000 pounds for two men over a year's time, space engineers have long recognized the need for some system to recover as much of that used water as possible.

Aboard Salyut-6 the urine is dumped overboard, but the moisture in the cabin air is recovered. Cold plates condense the moisture, which is conveyed to storage containers, where it is purified and sterilized. Desired minerals, particularly silver ions, are then added and the water is fit for any use.

Grechko noticed an anomaly with the water system early in January: a substantial amount of water was missing. The cosmonauts knew how much they had drunk, how much they had urinated, how much they had recovered and how much was in the cabin air. A significant quantity was unaccounted for and engineers were concerned that it might have condensed in unpropitious places where it could cause trouble. But careful searches found no trace of abnormal wetness.

As it turned out, the missing water was safe. One of the station's construction engineers noted that the Salyut had been assembled during a hot, dry summer, and that the interior hardwood paneling could be a very effective sponge once it was exposed to a humid atmosphere. Calculations showed that this could account for all of the missing water.

Dining on Salyut-6 was hardly *haute cuisine,* but the cosmonauts were generally satisfied with their fare. Most of the food was canned, but there were ten dehydrated items, too. Either type could be put into a food warmer.

A typical day's diet contained 3,200 calories from a menu along these lines: breakfast of canned ham, white bread, cottage cheese with black-currant jam, cake, coffee and vitamin pills; midday dinner of vegetable soup with cheese and biscuits, canned chicken, plums with nuts and vitamin pills; evening supper of canned steak, black bread, cocoa and fruit juice. The foods had all been tested and approved by the cosmonauts on the ground, but they noticed that their tastes changed in flight: Grechko, for example, found the canned ham much too salty even though he had enjoyed it before the flight—and afterward. Later crewmen developed insatiable cravings for items they hadn't even thought about back on earth: one team couldn't get enough apricot juice and honey, while leaving half its bread in the garbage.

The presence of a second docking port on Salyut-6 enabled visitors to come calling in orbit. Some of these spacecraft brought special food treats to the cosmonauts, with both dietary and psychological benefits. One robot supply ship, for example, had a pantry with fresh fruit, fresh bread and additional spices, such as mustard and horseradish—Grechko and Romanenko having gone through their three-month supply of spices in five weeks. One of the later Soyuz visitors carried a package containing fresh onions, garlic, lemons, apples, milk, Bulgarian peppers, gingerbread, honey, plus such staples as pork and various soups. It was followed by another supply ship, whose cargo included delicacies such as beef tongue in gelatin, quail pâté, miniature sausages, straw-berries—plus more mustard, more honey, more garlic and more onions.

The possibility of growing such spices on board space stations has long been recognized—and Soviet space biolo-gists have been working on the problem since Salyut-1 in 1971, when a suitcase-sized device aptly named "Oasis" was used as a small space garden. On Salyut-4 in 1975, peas were cultivated, but they died after three or four weeks of growth. New techniques were tried on Salyut-5 without success, and Grechko and Romanenko had their own small space gardens on Salyut-6.

But the results were the same: seeds would sprout and develop to a certain stage, but then the plants would die. It proved impossible to obtain a full cycle of development from seed to fruit. Later in 1978, two cosmonauts visiting Salyut-6 were able to nurse an onion to the point of producing a seed stalk, but the rest of the batch of plants were undergrown. Different theories were suggested; the favored one was that weightlessness inhibited the cellular mechanisms whereby waste products were removed.

A year after Grechko's flight, cosmonauts on a 175-day mission used the lessons of earlier failures to nurse new experimental gardens, some in pure weightlessness and some inside a small botanic centrifuge. They were able to grow peas, wheat, cucumbers, parsley, onions, dill, fennel and gar-lic—and even though the plants still would not consistently go to seed, their successful cultivation opened prospects for the in-space production of food, first as a novelty and a nutritional supplement but ultimately as a source of at least half of the bulk diet. (Examination of some space-grown crop samples back on earth showed that weightlessness did not impair protein synthesis; the food value of the plants was still high.) But that was still to come.

Despite the failure of Grechko's garden, the cosmonauts on board Salyut-6 derived other benefits from it. The men tended the green growing things lovingly, even during their free time. Grechko often remarked on the contrast between the warm, green, fertile plants and the cold blackness outside the walls of the space station. The presence of the small garden and a small aquarium with pirouetting tadpoles significantly reduced the psychological stresses on the spacemen.

Not all of the biological experiments were nearly as calming. The space biologists had included the obligatory package of fruit flies among the scientific experiments in an attempt to detect genetic changes over many generations. But the same thing happened on Salyut-6 that has been happening in college genetics laboratories for many years: the container cracked and the flies escaped. Grechko and his roommate at first had great fun chasing them down, trying out different tactics and eventually settling on the use of a small portable vacuum cleaner. The flies, however, proved quite adept at maneuvering throughout the cabin, seeking bright lights and windows. After a week of being pestered at night (when windowshades were installed) by a few holdout renegades, the men were relieved to report that the flies seemed to be all gone—it had long since ceased to be fun to be chasing them. Ground controllers, meanwhile, were extremely nervous that some of the flies might have slipped behind control panels and blocked important electrical switch relays. But after a few weeks, when nothing went wrong, that possibility was dismissed.

Sleeping normally was hard enough without buzzing flies. The cosmonauts used sleeping bags tied to the ceiling of the widest section of the Salyut, "above" the telescope and adjacent to the trash air locks and the exercycle. Grechko recommended that a real bed, with sheets and a pillow, be used in the future, preferably in a special "bedroom" section, which could also provide the privacy that each man occasionally demanded. Some sort of noise attenuation was also found to be desirable: the chattering teletype, whirring ventilation fans, clicking relays, creaking hull (caused by thermal imbalances as it moved between sunlight and shadow), crackling radio speaker and ticking clocks all combined to give a background noise which the men frequently found objectionable. (They had not felt that way during training, and their doctors wondered whether they had become more sensitive or just more irritable.) The sounds of the Salyut's equipment always remained with them, even while they slept, and any unusual sound would wake them up from the deepest sleep. They always had the feeling that something could go wrong at any minute, and this kept their nerves on the alert, never allowing them to fully relax.

When they did dream, it was not surprising that it was usually of woods and rivers and blue skies. But one unexpected theme appeared regularly in Grechko's dreams—skiing. He never quite figured it out, but assumed that it was a combination of the falling sensations of weightlessness, a subconscious realization of the tremendous speed at which he was traveling and the breeze on his face from a wall fan —all synthesized into an image of outdoor winter freedom.

Exercise, of course, was crucial to their safe return to earth's crushing gravity. Without a vigorous regular program of physical activity, the body's muscles and heart-lung system would relax and atrophy, leading to weakness and possible harm following the inevitable landing.

Some physical conditioning did not interfere with their activities, since it involved the wearing of elastic straps which constantly tried to pull the cosmonauts' arms and legs into a fetal posture and thus required a continuous countertension of muscles. (This was nicknamed "the penguin suit" because it made the men waddle awkwardly during ground training.) Other continuous activities were mechanical in nature but still passive, such as wearing reinforced trousers inside of which the air pressure could be lowered, requiring the heart to work harder to pull blood from the lower body. But despite all these countermeasures, the men were also required to put in two hours or more of vigorous exercise every day.

The exercises involved a combination of treadmill (with harness), exercycle and bungee cords. The workouts were strenuous: two hours of exercise was the equivalent of climbing the stairs of a two-hundred-story skyscraper. Grechko complained regularly that the exercise period took up too much time: combined with eating, sleeping and maintenance chores, it left him only a few hours a day for the experiments and observations which were the real purpose of the expedition. He and Romanenko took every excuse to skip the exercises.

It wasn't just the waste of time; the exercises could be physically unpleasant. An hour's work resulted in pools of sweat clinging to the chest and elsewhere, sweat which was hard to dry off and which made their fresh clothes (scheduled to last a week) as smelly as their old ones after only a day or two. The new collapsible plastic shower stall didn't help much, either: they were allowed to use it once a week but soon skipped it more often than not, since their eyes would sting from the soap for almost a full day and it took hours to towel the plastic dry before it could be folded up and put away. When they did wash, it was with disinfectant-impregnated wipes, which they moistened before use.

After sixty days of flight, as they neared the old Soviet endurance record Grechko and Romanenko both began suffering from headaches. Despite this, their work efficiency went up markedly, and they began to feel more at home in the Salyut as the number of technical problems diminished. Yet by eighty-five days, when they broke the American Skylab-4 record, they were suffering from fatigue so deep that sleep did not relieve it, and at that point they had to redouble the exercise program, which they had been seriously neglecting. The flight was within two weeks of ending, and the men felt it was none too soon.

Their on-board medicine chest was of some help. In addition to the bandages, cotton swabs, splints, minor surgical and dental instruments, and other standard equipment, the

Salyut carried a series of drugs: painkillers and tranquilizers, cardiovascular stimulants, stomach and intestinal treatments, vestibular sedatives, water-salt–imbalance counteragents, and anti-inflammation, antibacterial and antiradiation preparations. Vitamin pills and an herb tonic made from Eleuthera tree bark were also available. Grechko made use of some analgesics in mid-January when he had a slight cold, probably caught from one of the recent visiting cosmonauts of Soyuz-27. Both he and Romanenko had a few instances of toothaches, but in each case they responded to medication and emergency dentistry was not required.

The medical condition of the cosmonauts was carefully monitored, since they themselves were one of the most important experiments of the flight: How does the human body react to long periods of weightlessness, and how effective are various countermeasures? Every two or three days the men took electrocardiograms, seismocardiograms and measurements of their breathing rates and volume. Every week or so they devoted an entire day to a much more thorough checkout, which included measurements of the phases of cardiac contraction, heartbeat volume, venous pressure, vascular tone in different parts of the body, blood circulation in the head and lung ventilation. These measurements were taken at rest, after exercising and while wearing the low-pressure trousers (the *chibis,* or lapwing bird) that put a measured stress on the heart. Using such readings, doctors back on earth were able to determine that the cosmonauts' physiological adaptation to weightlessness was essentially completed within thirty days. However, this adaptation went through several interesting stages.

With the absence of gravity, the body's blood and other fluids no longer pool in the legs but become more evenly distributed. Since more blood reaches the heart, autonomous feedback systems register this as an excess, so various body mechanisms are activated to remove "surplus" fluid and materials such as sodium, potassium and calcium salts. With the blood-plasma volume down, other body monitors detect a surplus of red cells, so their production decreases almost to the point of total cessation, but then picks up again in about thirty days, when the correct ratio is established through attrition of original red cells. All of this occurs in parallel with a reduction in energy expenditure in many muscles, which lessens these muscles' needs for oxygen, which lessens the blood's needs for red cells anyhow. This adaptation has the bad effect of reducing the body's capacity to tolerate sudden great physical stresses, such as return to earth. And for some reason the red blood cells which are produced in space tend to be smaller than those produced on earth.

Other body fluids are also redistributed. The cosmonauts described a sensation of fullness of the head, which peaked at about seven to ten days into the flight but which persisted throughout the flight, becoming more pronounced (to the point of discomfort) at the onset of physical work, with fatigue, and after the consumption of large amounts of fluid. Their faces puffed up, accentuating their Oriental appearances (even Skylab astronauts took on a decidedly Mongolian cast to their features); their sinuses felt congested. Together with the ordinary vertigo caused by the short-circuiting of the vestibular system (which the Soviets confessed caused at least half of their Salyut cosmonauts to vomit after some meals on the first few days of their flights), these effects eased with the passage of time but never disappeared.

One other potentially dangerous trend was the gradual lowering of the cosmonauts' immunity response against infection. The physiological cause of this was the reduction in the number of T-lymphocytes in the blood. Soviet space doctors also noticed an alarming increase in the ability of microorganisms to survive on free-floating water droplets inside the cabin, increasing the possibilities of infection. However, a vigorous sanitary program using special antiseptic wipes on the cabin walls made it possible for the Salyut-6 cosmonauts to keep bacterial activity at a tolerably low level.

Research was supposed to occupy five to seven hours daily and was divided roughly into four classes. One third of research time was devoted to earth-surface photography and one third to experiments in "materials processing"; one sixth went to astronomy and physics, and the remaining sixth was utilized for technological and biological experiments. But those activities were themselves only a fraction of the whole day: Grechko found that sleeping, eating, exercising, reading documentation, conducting preventive maintenance and cleanup, and other necessary activities took up an unexpectedly large amount of time, and that actually only three to five hours a day were devoted to the flight experiments.

A "Psychological Support Group" at Mission Control specialized both in monitoring the cosmonauts (primarily through the use of voice-stress analysis) and in organizing activities to avoid the buildup of stress or a feeling of isolation and loneliness. Every week the cosmonauts talked with their friends and relatives. Conversations with their families were not merely for the encouragement of the cosmonauts, revealed Chief Flight Director Aleksey Yeliseyev in an article in *Pravda.* "These contacts not only eliminate questions about the life of their families, which naturally worry the cosmonauts," noted the ex-cosmonaut, "but also their friends and relatives in the talks sometimes can understand more minutely the moods and tastes of the cosmonauts, and can give very valuable recommendations to officials at ground control." The cosmonauts also talked with "special guests" from outside the space program: actors, sportsmen, representatives of youth clubs, sailors—people who were supposed to arouse the cosmonauts' curiosity and interest. Additionally, interviews were set with specialists in the laboratories which were processing the data already sent back to earth. These conversations in particular pleased the spacemen, both because they allowed them to see how future activities could be improved, and because they gave vivid confirmation of the value of the work they were doing—

somebody did care! Last, the cosmonauts regularly received news summaries and short political indoctrination lectures on SALT-2 and other matters.

Extra room on the periodic supply flights was also used for psychological purposes. Letters from home were always welcome, as were surprise boxes of gifts from different teams of specialists. On one flight a guitar was sent up; on another, a set of colored partitions to create more privacy. Beyond the specific contents of each resupply flight, the very fact that new shipments could be expected routinely on a nearly monthly basis was a boost to the crew's morale.

Psychologically, the two men worked well together. Their brief period of joint training and Grechko's seniority in age, experience and education to the man who was nominally his commander might have given rise to personality conflicts. Grechko later discussed that issue in a post-flight interview:

"We were told by psychologists that very often a conflict arises from the presence of two leaders—one appointed and one actual. So we decided that neither of us would press the other, never give orders. Any question is discussed together and the decisions are made together. In this way, we defused potential trouble."

"Competition within a crew is one of the most harmful things," Grechko later recounted, "especially if each starts trying to prove that he is the best one—to prove it to himself, to the earth. In space, you have no psychological outlets. You can't go to the theater or relax with an interesting book. It is much more dangerous there."

Both men tried to forestall problems by carefully observing the other's moods: "When I was going to say something, I first looked to see what mood he was in," Grechko explained. "Perhaps he was busy or deep in thought—it meant I should wait. Another time perhaps I might remember something funny at a time when he was gloomy—I felt that I should keep my joke until the proper moment."

Other possible sources of ill feeling were the unpleasant

cleaning and food-preparation jobs, at which the men were supposed to take turns. Instead, they chose to work together on such jobs.

Grechko explained: "Neither would wait for the other to start a routine job, say, changing the toilet filters—but, rather, he would try to do it himself. So if you see the filter needs changing, you put down your interesting job and start the dirty one. And he does the same. If I see him doing a job that I overlooked, I would drop what I was doing to help him. Again, this sounds like an ordinary thing, but it helps a great deal. We decided we would always have our work in common. If one did something, both were responsible. If a mistake was made, we didn't say, 'He did it.' We would say, 'This is our fault!' "

Each would support the other and provide the psychological strokes needed for self-esteem. It was very important to consider each word or gesture carefully. "For example," Grechko reported, "if you are praised or given just the smallest bit of attention—say, having your tie straightened during a television broadcast back to earth—this is viewed by the other as great concern or attention, even almost a caress, and it produces a very strong impression. On earth you might not pay any attention to that at all. And vice versa, if you did something not quite so well and he looked at you a little bit in the wrong way, you take this as mistrust or as an affront. Everything is felt much more acutely."

A delicate situation arose in January when Romanenko and Grechko were visited by a new pair of cosmonauts, whose mission was to deliver a fresh Soyuz spacecraft and return to earth a few days later in the Salyut crew's original, aging Soyuz ship. During the five-day visit, one of them took Romanenko aside to reveal that Grechko's father had just died. The question was, Should he be told? Romanenko, realizing that diplomacy was more important than candor, decided against it—but he insisted that he be the one to break the news once they were both safely back on earth.

Only days after the departure of the two visiting cosmonauts, Romanenko and Grechko had more company. This time it was the first unmanned robot freighter-tanker ship, called Progress-1. According to Moscow spokesmen, the purpose of the flight was "to blaze the trail for a reliable cargo bridge to ensure a year-long operation by orbital stations." This was to be done by bringing up additional propellant for the Salyut's rocket engines, additional food, water, air and expandable supplies for the cosmonauts, and both replacement and supplemental equipment for the Salyut. (And it worked—over the many months that followed, one Progress freighter after another kept bringing up material until the *new* supplies weighed as much as the entire original space station.)

On Progress-1 the cosmonauts found fresh fruits and bread, more bottled water, a cassette recorder and music tapes, fresh photographic film and new medicines (many supplies originally launched on board Salyut-6 had spoiled during the long delay after the Soyuz-25 docking failure), fresh clothes, linen, air filters and carbon dioxide absorbents, a geographical atlas, a small electrical furnace for melting glass in weightlessness, plus miscellaneous equipment such as seat straps, new attitude-control (or orientation) sensors and an air ionizer. The crew also got newspapers and mail.

The process of transferring rocket propellants (hydrazine and nitrogen tetroxide) from the Progress to the Salyut was a very tricky one, and the Soviet space engineers who worked it out deserve a lot of credit. The highly volatile chemicals are pushed through connecting lines by high-pressure nitrogen gas, but the electrical power required by the compressor pumps is so substantial that it takes several days to carry out the transfer, during which few other instruments on the station can be "powered up." But at the end of the transfer, the Salyut has new supplies good for several months—or even more if, as was demonstrated on Progress-1, the robot ship's own engines were used during the time it was attached to the Salyut. (The fuel is needed to control the pointing direction of the station and to periodically raise its slowly decaying orbit.)

The cosmonauts had a few exciting moments midway through their mission when they were advised that ground-based radar tracking indicated that their spacecraft was being shadowed by a fleet of "flying saucers"—in the words of a Mission Control spokesman. Grechko chuckled to himself, assuming that the psychologists were just trying to stimulate him again. But unable to restrain his curiosity, he floated over to a porthole and looked out—and suddenly shouted for Romanenko to join him.

The startled space crew clearly saw a handful of small, round white objects on the horizon, evidently pacing their spaceship. For a moment the hair on the back of Grechko's neck rose. Flying-saucer stories are very popular in the Soviet Union and the two men had blasted off only weeks after the spectacular Plesetsk UFO attack had become the most sensational flying saucer event ever heard of in Russia. Strange thoughts might have formed during those brief moments before the cosmonauts recognized the "UFOs."

"It's our garbage!" Grechko realized, and their bafflement dissolved into laughter. The crew had recently jettisoned several bags of trash overboard through a small air lock, and these soon-forgotten bags had continued to fly through space on a parallel orbit. One of the men grabbed a camera and took a few pictures. "The bags stayed nearby until we changed course a few days later," Grechko subsequently recalled. The two space-farers continued to chuckle over the incident for weeks; the psychologists in Mission Control were happy too for the unexpected diversion.

Grechko the engineer also became an artist and an entertainer during the flight. He used a set of colored pencils to make very precise drawings of the subtle colorations of the aurora borealis, of the setting of the sun past a cloud-free horizon of the rising of brilliant Venus, and of noctilucent clouds, strange high-altitude wisps whose exact origin is still obscure. Some of these drawings he showed to viewers on the ground via a television camera during communications sessions that were broadcasted over Soviet television. In one of those broadcasts, on February 10, he paid tribute to Jules Verne: "Hello, everyone," he radioed, grinning into the camera. "Today marks the one hundred and fiftieth birthday of Jules Verne, the remarkable French writer. There's hardly a person who hasn't read his books, at any rate not among the cosmonauts, because Jules Verne was a dreamer, a visionary who saw flights in space. I'd say this flight too was predicted by Jules Verne."

This television camera was used for more than just public relations. As a matter of fact, a few days before their spacewalk in December, when their own radio transmitter broke down, the cosmonauts had to signal to earth by charades in front of the video camera, making gestures which the flight control center tried to interpret without the aid of the audio channel. The radio was fixed in a few hours, but they were a tense few hours.

Grechko and Romanenko returned to earth on March 16, 1978, after ninety-six days in space. Their Soyuz command module soft-landed on a wheat field in central Asia, and rescue helicopters touched down nearby within minutes. The cosmonauts were strapped to stretchers and carefully lifted out of the capsule.

Doctors immediately diagnosed a general physical weakness and overall fatigue, which they attributed to the cosmonauts' inadequate exercise regimen: the spacemen had done only one third of the required exercises. Romanenko and Grechko reported that their bodies felt very heavy and that there was an unpleasant sensation that their intestines were about to fall out of their bodies. They were unable to maintain themselves in a standing posture, and any abrupt movements led to vertigo and nausea. On the other hand, they slept well and had good appetites.

Despite the pressures, the constant level of overwork and the fact that the men had been only vague acquaintances six weeks before their blast-off, the psychological results were simply outstanding. Psychologists termed their relationship as "stable and friendly" throughout the mission. Typically, Grechko was more effusive: "Through the flight we became very close," he recalled a year later. "The flight made us friends and the friendship remains. In the past we shook hands when we met. Now we embrace." The flight of the "classics," the "Roman" and the "Greek" (which is what their names mean in Ukrainian), became a classic in space psychology.

Their mission, while medically disappointing because of the crew's inadequate attention to their exercise program, was also a great technological success. They had made an impressive spacewalk, had conducted the first double docking and spacecraft exchange, and had conducted the first in-flight resupply and refueling operation. The medical mistakes of the flight were identified, and improvements were made in schedules, equipment and control procedures. Preflight conditioning of the next crew was reinforced, including vigorous physical exercises, the use of rotating chairs, swings and tilt tables, and sleeping for weeks before the flight on a bed with the head lowered six inches to develop tolerance to increased fluid concentration in the head.

Grechko summed it up nicely: "It *is* difficult to live in outer space—but it *is* possible to work there." As later crews on Salyut-6 explored the possibilities and overcame the difficulties, the records set on Romanenko and Grechko's flight were repeatedly broken. New accomplishments and new problems soon drove the memory of the first Salyut-6 expedition into the background. But theirs had been the hardest flight, the greatest challenge faced by cosmonauts in the nearly twenty-year history of Soviet manned space flight—and the most difficult burdens had been born by Georgiy Grechko, who had been given only six weeks' warning.

11

★

Guests in
Space

Space doctors at Mission Control in Moscow were baffled—
and not a little alarmed—by the first reports of the condition
of cosmonaut Vladimir Remek following his return from
space on March 10, 1978. His hands had turned bright red—
or so the medics at the recovery zone had claimed.

Numerous hypotheses were hastily advanced. Was it some
problem with his circulatory system, manifesting itself in his
extremities? Was it some allergic reaction to space food? Was
it—most serious of all—some fungal infection which even
now was attacking cosmonauts Romanenko and Grechko as
they neared the end of their ninety-six-day marathon?

Unable to reach a conclusion, the doctors waited eagerly
to interview the cosmonaut. As part of the "Interkosmos"
program, Remek was a Czechoslovakian jet pilot who had
received a year's rushed space-flight training in order to
participate (with the actual flying done by a veteran Russian
cosmonaut) in the Salyut program. In space he had performed various experiments prepared by Czechoslovakian
scientists and had made many televised statements about the
value of Czech-Soviet friendship. But now an unexpected

medical complication had come up which at the least would embarrass the Soviets and threaten the political profit of the mission—red hands. How could Remek have gotten red hands in space?

So the doctors asked him when he arrived in Moscow as he was preparing to leave his brief space career for a new profession of public appearances and parades all over Czechoslovakia. Remek looked at his hands, which were still sore, and laughed. "Oh, that's easy," he replied. "On Salyut, whenever I reached for a switch or a dial or something, the Russians shouted, 'Don't touch that!' and slapped my hands." And they reddened.

As it turns out, the red-hands story is apocryphal; it never really happened. But within days of Remek's triumphant return to earth, it was being gleefully passed from friend to friend in Prague, for amusement but also to satirize the political aspects of the flight. "Why weren't *both* Czech cosmonauts on board the two-man Soyuz?" went another joke. The answer was obvious, if slightly bitter: "Because then they would have landed the spaceship in West Germany!"

Outside of being politically reliable and a competent flier, Remek really didn't fit the image of a rugged space hero. His mother proudly recounted how he had loved helping her with the housework as a child. She confidentially told an interviewer that he had been required to lose forty pounds to qualify for the program. In the course of a television show, when asked if he'd do it again, Remek candidly replied, "Well, I'm glad indeed it's over."

Against the genuinely valuable technological accomplishments of the Salyut-6 mission, the guest-cosmonaut program stands out as a propaganda sop to political realities—and it shows that the Soviets continue to be able to manipulate space events for spectaculars at the expense of substantive accomplishments. But in this case, at least, the cost was not high—and the public relations benefits were bound to be impressive, the underground Czech jokes notwithstanding.

The guest-cosmonaut program grew out of an engineering problem. The maximum time a Soyuz spacecraft could be left in orbit safely was about ninety to a hundred days; after that, the propellant tanks and the batteries and other equipment gradually became too unreliable to trust for a return to earth. Yet manned visits to the Salyut space station were planned to last far in excess of that period.

The solution was to send up a fresh Soyuz periodically to replace the aging one. On board the ship would be mail, fresh food and other cargoes; the men aboard the Salyut could use their original Soyuz to send back down to earth the results of their experiments, including exposed film, logbooks, tape cassettes, biological and medical samples, and materials produced in the furnaces.

Sometime in 1976 or so, planners must have realized that these Soyuz replacement flights need not be unmanned, flown entirely on autopilot, as had been the test mission of Soyuz-20 to Salyut-4 in 1975–1976. Instead, two cosmonauts could visit the space crew, cheering them up. Perhaps the copilot's seat could be occupied by a doctor for a cosmic house call to check up on the men's health. Actually, anybody with a few month's training could ride that second seat . . . or just about anybody.

At about this same time, the United States signed an agreement with the European Space Agency, a consortium led by West Germany, France, Great Britain and Italy, according to which the Europeans would build the Spacelab module to be flown inside the cargo bay of the American Space Shuttle sometime after 1980. West European astronauts would be trained to make space flights as part of this project. This idea —of flying foreign guests in a nation's space program—was an attractive one, especially from the diplomatic point of view. The Soviets had realized that the replacement Soyuz was an ideal vehicle to carry their own space guests—prior to Spacelab!

So in mid-1976, the guest-cosmonaut program was announced in Moscow. Representatives of Soviet-bloc countries would participate in Soviet manned space flights between 1978 and 1983. The first contingent, consisting of two pilots each from Czechoslovakia, Poland and East Germany, arrived in Moscow in December 1976. A second group, with men from Bulgaria, Hungary, the Mongolian People's Republic, Cuba and Rumania, arrived in March 1978. Two Vietnamese eventually joined them early in 1979, and cosmonaut candidates from France and India were to show up in 1981. (The French actually reported to the training center in September 1980.)

When the program was announced, the obvious assumption was that qualified scientists and space engineers would be chosen for the flights, since a productive series of scientific earth satellites had been jointly built and operated by a Soviet-led bloc of communist countries since 1969. But as it turned out, the political suspicions with which these Soviet-bloc regimes view their technocrats (perhaps justifiably) ruled out the chance of risking a politically disastrous defection from among the guest cosmonauts—and people were chosen whose primary characteristics were ease in training and political reliability.

To satisfy the first criterion, the men were jet pilots with little or no scientific background. To satisfy the second criterion, they were all party activists who had spent years attending military and political academies within the Soviet Union. Additionally, it helped if they had personal ties to their home country's ruling class: for example, Remek (who had proved his loyalty as a nineteen-year-old flight cadet by touring his country in 1968 lecturing on the necessity of the Soviet invasion of Czechoslovakia) was the son of the Prague Deputy Defense Minister; the Polish cosmonaut was the brother of a top air force general.

But the best laid plans have a way of breaking down, especially in the Soviet manned space program. Due to the rearrangement of the Salyut-6 flight plan following the first linkup failure in October 1977, the first mid-flight Soyuz switch-off was made by an all-Russian crew in January. Despite the fact that the original purpose of the guest-cosmonaut launch was now completed (Romanenko and Grechko were to return to earth in mid-March inside the new Soyuz they received in mid-January), the launching proceeded on schedule; its secondary (political) purpose had moved to the fore.

And so on March 2, for no evident operational or logistic reason, Soyuz-28 was put into orbit. It was piloted by veteran Soviet cosmonaut Aleksey Gubarev, who spent a month with Grechko aboard Salyut-4 three years earlier. The second seat was occupied by cosmonaut-researcher Vladimir Remek, the first non-Russian and non-American to make a space flight. The West Europeans, struggling with delays in the Spacelab and Space Shuttle projects, were years behind—and that was evidently the whole point of the launch.

The purely symbolic nature of these guest flights was underscored by the fact that only one man from each country was to get a chance to fly. Once he had been up, both he and his backup man were removed from the training program permanently. For Remek, the backup man was pilot Oldrich Pelczak, whose space career aborted the moment Remek's mission began. For the Polish cosmonaut Miroslaw Hermaszewski (whose Soyuz-30 visit to the Salyut-6 in June was useless beyond its political value), the grounded backup was Zenon Jankowski. For the East German Sigmund Jähn (whose Soyuz-31 flight in late August 1978 was the only one which served its original purpose: to replace the 140-day-marathon all-Russian-crew's aging Soyuz), it was fellow-pilot Eberhard Köllner. If it were not for the propaganda value of the presence of the East Europeans in space, only the last of these three 1978 flights need ever have been made.

There was one very puzzling aspect of these missions. Something dictated the exact launch dates, even during phases of the long-duration expeditions when such visits

were totally useless operationally. The three 1978 guest-cosmonaut flights were launched at 6:28, 6:27 and 5:51 P.M.
Moscow time (had the last flight gone up a day earlier, it
would have been at 6:15 P.M.)—and although such similarity
cannot be a coincidence, its significance is still obscure. But
since such similar timing only repeats itself every two
months (due to the shift of the space station's orbital plane
by six degrees a day), the particular time a launch opportunity occurs during the flight of the long expedition may not
coincide with a time when an aging Soyuz needs to be exchanged. Nevertheless, the guest launchings were made on
a schedule involving some rigid rhythm we still do not understand. But once the inflexibility of this pattern was recognized by Western experts, subsequent guest visits could be
anticipated with precision.

During the course of the week-long cosmic courtesy calls,
the visitors were not allowed to interfere with the work of the
permanent crewmen. While the visits did provide some excitement and diversion, the long-duration crewmen—like re-
cluses anywhere—did admit to annoyance at having their
accustomed schedules upset. If a rest day fell during the visit,
the visitors were not even allowed into the Salyut; instead,
they spent that day doing experiments in their own Soyuz
spacecraft, with the door closed.

It was probably just as well that the guest cosmonauts did
not interfere with the real work going on aboard the Salyut:
they had a difficult enough time with their own projects. A
good example is the "Syrena" crystallization experiment
conducted by the Polish cosmonaut Hermaszewski in mid-
1978. Although the procedures called for the melting test
runs to be made at night, when the crewmen were asleep and
hence would not shake the samples even slightly, Hermaszewski later confessed that he was so intent on making sure
that the process was running correctly that he got up every
few hours and went over to the small electrical furnace to
check on it.

There is no indication that these unwise moves contributed to the overall disappointing results of the experiment, but by the time the first anniversary of the flight rolled around, the euphoria of the mission had been replaced by a general disillusionment in Warsaw. According to a report published in an underground newspaper, Professor Adam Gierek, son of the former Polish Prime Minister, joked bitterly about the project in a speech to a technical symposium. "The 'Syrena' has brought us back from space to earth with a bump" is how he was quoted. He had really expected the showcase activities to have some practical purpose.

Preparing for the guest-cosmonaut missions was not a trivial task, however simple the actual flights may have appeared. The foreign guests did have to work extremely hard in training and deserve plenty of credit for qualifying.

The minimum Soviet space-flight preparations call for a two-year-long general study program followed by a one- to two-year period of actual preparations for a specific mission. Between those two phases, it was customary for candidate cosmonauts to help more senior crews prepare for and fly their own space missions, and this usually involved serving as test subjects, as "capsule communicators" (that is, the men at the control center or on tracking ships who alone were authorized to talk with cosmonauts in flight) and as backup cosmonauts. Even Soviet space engineers, who had spent five to fifteen years working in spacecraft design and test institutes, needed more than four years to prepare for their own space missions. The pilot cosmonauts, who came from air force and navy jet squadrons, usually accumulated ten years of training and experience before they were allowed to venture into space.

The guest cosmonauts would have to be ready to fly only one year after arriving at the training center. The differences were remarkable: twelve months for the East Europeans, who would be studying in a language not their own; ten to twelve years for the native Russian cosmonauts. The guest-cosmonaut training was bound to be an extremely difficult project.

Vasiliy Lazarev was put in charge of preparing the guest cosmonauts. His own space career was hardly inspiring. Trained first as a doctor and then as a jet test pilot, he joined the cosmonaut detachment in 1965 at the age of thirty-seven after two earlier rejections. He served on several backup crews before he was finally selected to command a Salyut mission, but the space station blew up first. Instead of the long space expedition that his medical and engineering training made him uniquely qualified for, he was assigned the two-day "confidence mission" which followed the deaths of the three cosmonauts of Salyut-1. When he finally blasted off in 1975 for the long-delayed space-station visit, his booster rocket went off course and he nearly lost his life in a crash landing atop a Siberian mountain range. His advanced age (forty-seven) and internal injuries from that accident disqualified him from further space flights and from any chance to achieve what he had striven ten years for. Now he was to "fly a desk" for men whose qualifications were only a fraction of his, but who would, because of a political necessity, be sent on missions denied to him.

The guest cosmonauts would need to learn two things: how to ride on a Soyuz spaceship, and how to live for a week on a Salyut space station. They would also have to be familiar with the scientific equipment on the Salyut and with the special experiments that were being developed by scientists in their native countries. Toward these ends, Lazarev had available vast resources used by Russian cosmonaut trainees: experienced lecturers, special tours of factories and institutes, the wide array of mock-ups and simulators at the Gagarin Cosmonaut Training Center and survival schools in Siberian forests, in deserts and swamps, in Cuban jungles and at the Black Sea. But this was all too time-consuming for the pace of the guest-cosmonaut program.

First off, Lazarev had to dispense with all "superfluous"

training. Survival school, for example, was cut to a bare minimum—forest and ocean only. All spacewalk instruction was useless—cut it out. Medical equipment connected with long space flights—irrelevant. The systems engineering of the Soyuz and Salyut—teach them only how to push the buttons, since there always would be a Russian along to fix anything that wasn't working right. Mathematical theory of orbital rendezvous and atmospheric reentry—no, just teach them how to follow a checklist. Operating-control procedures for the space station—no, they would only be guests and could rely on their Russian hosts.

The whole idea was to stick to basics and speak in simple sentences. "This is a schematic of the Salyut space station," an instructor would enunciate carefully. "There are three independent pressurized modules: the main module here, the transfer module here, which serves as an air lock, too, and the aggregate equipment module here at the aft end. These are the two docking ports, one at the transfer module and one at the aggregate module. Look at the drawing."

At the training center, the guest cosmonauts could see the outside of the Salyut. There were the solar power wings, which generated 4,000 watts in full sunlight. Much of that had to go into the banks of nickel-cadmium batteries, which supplied electrical power during the third of each orbit spent in earth's shadow. The wings could be tilted to catch the maximum sunlight; that was controlled by an on-board computer ("Don't touch that!"). Here at the thicker, aft end of the Salyut were the rocket engines. Two propulsive engines, mounted near the rim of the back end and pointing aft, would be used to push the Salyut into a new orbit. Four clusters of small engines, mounted along the outer edge of the cylindrical station right near the aft end and pointing sideways, would be used to change the orientation of the whole space station. In the center of the aft end was the second docking port.

The practical needs of the visiting flight would have to be

stressed. The Soyuz docking would always be at the aft end of the Salyut, where most of the navigation aids were installed. (The main crew's own Soyuz would be at the forward port.) Once aboard the space station, the visitors would have to swap their customized acceleration couches from their new Soyuz to the old Soyuz at the forward port—since they would be flying *that* one home, leaving their fresh spacecraft attached. The visitors would also go over a cargo of things to carry back to earth: exposed film, processed-materials ampules, logbooks, biological and medical specimens, personal mail and other items. Specialists on earth would have to specify the right stowage lockers in the Soyuz, to keep the ship's center of gravity within limits.

The basic process could be accomplished in about two days, but for purposes of psychological support and to provide time for the visitors to conduct special experiments, the length of the visit would be seven days. The first two days would be devoted to the exchange procedures, and the last day would be left for checking out the landing craft. Half of the intermediate time would go toward ceremonial activities and socializing. That left two full days for joint experiments, if the visitors weren't nauseous with "space vertigo" (as half were bound to be).

The Salyut mock-up, in the large hall in the Gagarin Training Center, could be used for showing the guest cosmonauts the layout of the space station. Amidship was the spacecraft control panel ("Don't touch that!"), and right across from it the fold-down dining table and food preparation equipment. ("Use these elastic straps to hold down the food packages," they would be told. "Use this tube to pump hot water into the dehydrated food packets.")

Over there, guest cosmonauts are told, is the STROKA teletype, which will print out changes in your daily flight plan—ask a cosmonaut how to pull the paper out. This switch on the radio activates the phase inversion circuit, which makes the voice signal unintelligible to any eavesdroppers. (Use it when discussing personal medical problems.) Over here is the "massmeter": it measures a cosmonaut's weight by oscillating his body up and down on a calibrated spring and then converting the period of oscillation into a mass value.

Forward of the control panel is the section where the life support equipment is located. Behind this panel (don't touch that!) are chemical canisters which react with cabin humidity to give off pure oxygen; one golf-bag–sized canister is used up every day of a guest space visit. Behind that panel are lithium hydroxide canisters; they absorb carbon dioxide and also have to be replaced regularly. The air is pumped through charcoal filters to remove odors; then it goes through a condenser, where moisture is extracted, concentrated, purified and stored for reuse.

At the far end of the cylinder, behind the telescope, is the hygiene station. Before using the toilet, be sure to turn on the air suction—it's the only way the material will go where you want it. If you make a mess, here are the towels—you clean it up. When you are done, the toilet filters get wrapped up and stashed in a trash bag, along with food wrappers and soiled clothing. The bags are sealed, placed in one of two side-by-side trash ejection air locks and jettisoned by pulling this lever (don't touch that!).

The biggest piece of scientific equipment in the station is the 1,500-pound BST-1M, or on-board submillimeter (infrared) telescope—and it's none of the guest cosmonaut's business, since only the Russians are allowed to operate it. However, since it extends from floor to ceiling and nearly blocks the widest section of the Salyut, even visitors do need to know a little about it. Here's the control panel (don't touch that!), and here's where the magnetic tape of the observation data is mounted. This is the cryogenic unit, which produces liquid helium at $-445°F$, to cool the infrared sensors to their operating temperatures (but since the compressor needs the full power output of the station, the machine can only be used a few times a month). Targets for study include the moon, stars, nebulas, the gas clouds of the galactic center and the layers of earth's own atmosphere (an extra ultraviolet receptor helps with this last target).

Two of the regular on-board devices are available for use by the guest cosmonauts, although they would probably be set up by the Russian crew, who would let the guest push the start buttons. One device is the MKF-6M, the multi-spectral camera six-bands, modified, which observes earth's surface in six different wavelengths of light; the other is a family of electrical furnaces used to melt metals, glass and various composite substances for subsequent cooling and crystallization without the disruptive effects of gravity. These pieces of equipment are among the busiest on the Salyut; hardly a day passes when the crew isn't exposing a pack of film over some ground target or running one or more furnaces through their cycles. Most of the film and most of the crystal ampules are produced on order from users in industrial organizations. In that sense, the Salyut-6 has already become primarily an *operational* facility rather than a *research* facility, since most of the work of the cosmonauts is directly utilized by Soviet industry.

The MKF-6M camera system is as good as anything ever flown on American spacecraft—and it's better than anything the Russians can build. (The unit was obtained from the Zeiss factory in Jena, East Germany; what, if anything, the Soviets paid for it has never been disclosed.) The camera takes six simultaneous photographs of a one-hundred-square-mile area directly below the space station; four of the images are in visible light and two are in infrared. By studying the varying brightness of objects in different color bands, experts can identify crops (and incipient crop diseases), locate and measure ground water supplies, chart pollution and trace geological structures, such as fault lines. Each guest cosmonaut will be given a chance to photograph his native country during his week-long sojourn.

Other devices are also available to survey the planet's surface. There is the KATE-140, a specialized mapping camera designed to provide topographers with precisely calibrated photomaps. There is also a collection of hand-held cameras for shots out the portholes and a pair of binoculars. To aid in cataloging the data obtained, the space station carries special logbooks, maps and color index albums. Verbal observations can be recorded on tape. When a button by the window is pushed, the on-board navigation computer records the time and the geographic location of the station —for future reference.

There are two different electrical furnaces on the Salyut: the SPLAV ("alloy") and the KRISTALL ("crystal") units. SPLAV is a fifty-pound device which uses 300 watts of electrical power to heat samples to temperatures of 2,000°F; the sample can be cooled uniformly or from one side to the other, with the temperature profile controlled by a twenty-pound mini-computer. KRISTALL, which was brought up on a cargo flight in July 1978, is about the same size and power as the first furnace but is used for glass and for thin films of semiconductor material. Dozens of different combinations of materials are being processed in these furnaces, and each guest cosmonaut will bring a package of ampules for further processing.

The space career of the first group of guest-cosmonaut trainees was completed in September 1978, when Sigmund Jähn returned to earth. A second group of candidate cosmonauts had been in training for six months already, and if another visit to the Salyut-6 proved possible, the new group would have only six more months to produce an adequately trained guest cosmonaut together with his countryman-backup pilot. The rushed training schedule was accelerated even more.

Salyut-6 did hold out, and the guest cosmonauts did complete their highly abbreviated training program in time. On

April 10, 1979, the Soyuz-33 blasted off in a fierce windstorm (which seems to have delayed the lift-off by two days) and soared away on a day-long space chase. A Russian cosmonaut was in command, and Bulgarian pilot Georgi Ivanov was along for the ride.

But a random failure intervened and the rendezvous was canceled. The main maneuvering rocket had broken down only two miles short of the docking, and the mission was ordered aborted. The crew wanted to try backup procedures, but Mission Control overruled them: first, their training had not been thorough enough to expect them to be able to cope with such an emergency; second, a docking would have been futile since there was no way the damaged Soyuz could have been swapped out in orbit. No, the best course would be a quick return to earth—and the cosmonauts reluctantly agreed. Mission Control tried to cheer up the crew with some good-natured kidding: "Before the Bulgarian closes his faceplate," Shatalov advised them, "be sure he tucks his mustache inside." The cosmonauts forced a few chuckles.

Since the inoperative maneuvering engine was also used for returning to earth, the Soyuz-33 crewmen were in genuine danger of being trapped in space until their air ran out in a few days. In fact, the commander (a veteran of the Apollo-Soyuz project named Rukavishnikov, who spoke fluent English) later admitted to thinking briefly about an American science fiction novel he had once read—*Marooned,* by Martin Caidin—which was about space-station astronauts trapped in orbit by a faulty rocket engine.

But the Soyuz also had an emergency backup engine, which worked adequately even though its timer failed and the cosmonauts had to shut it down by hand. Their subsequent return to earth was along an emergency high-G path that subjected them to more than ten times the force of the equivalent of gravity. But they made it. Out of a cloudless night sky, under a full moon, their capsule was spotted by the pilot of a recovery plane, the Soyuz's heat shield still glowing red hot. The capsule hit the ground and rolled over, and the men scrambled outside to await rescue helicopters. "It may have been only two days," the Russian cosmonaut remarked later, "but it seemed like a month."

The reaction of the Bulgarians to the failure was predictable but interesting. After the launching, while things were still going well, the Premier of Bulgaria underscored the political significance of the flight in terms that soon turned ironic: "This event, which has historic significance for our country, became possible because Bulgaria is an indivisible part of the cooperation among the socialist countries. This is why, during these moving hours, we express our admiration for the genius of the Soviet scientists and specialists as well as of the Soviet people, who were the first to penetrate space. The Soviet scientists and specialists have created a technology that allowed a country such as Bulgaria to send its worthy son into the depth of space." The Bulgarian cosmonaut, Georgi "Gosho" Ivanov, expressed similar sentiments in a pre-flight statement: "Now every citizen of my country well realizes that it is only due to friendship with the Soviet Union that Bulgaria could appear in space orbits. The road to outer space has been paved for us by socialist integration." Yet when the mission failed (the "genius of the Soviet scientists" was evidently lacking), the Bulgarians hailed it as proof of the courage of their man Ivanov: "Further convincing and outspoken evidence has been given," trumpeted *Radio Sofia,* "of the strength of internationalism and of the mutual benefit from fraternal cooperation. Part of the planned flight program has been accomplished. However . . ." But the broadcast ended on an even more upbeat note: "The Bulgarian cosmonaut has proved that he was worthy of joining the large, friendly family of cosmonauts by showing manliness and heroism. The two cosmonauts worked correctly and the operations were completed in a precise manner. [The flight] made a further step in the peaceful research of outer space. Welcome to earth, heros!"

There had been some question about whether or not the Bulgarians should be given a second chance. If not, the purely symbolic nature of the flight would be underscored: the Bulgarian really had never been needed on board at all. But if so, then the Bulgarians would get two cosmonauts to the other countries' one. (This would have been somewhat alleviated by sending the same crew back up—which never had been done before, either.)

The Hungarians would have been next, but the Soyuz problem needed to be analyzed and solved. Just to be on the safe side, the next replacement Soyuz (the one the Hungarian guest cosmonaut should have ridden) was sent up on autopilot in June and made a successful automatic linkup (thus proving that the actual presence of men on board was not required for any operational reason). The Bulgarians were sent home and the Hungarians (and everyone else) were told to wait another year—a respite that allowed them to complete their training program fully.

Bertalan Farkas, the Hungarian, finally made his flight in May 1980. Reportedly the next man in line would have been the Rumanian, followed by the Cuban—but the next flight happened to fall during the tarnished Moscow Olympics. (The date was dictated by the orbital path of the space station, and every Western commentator who reported that the flight had been "obviously timed for the propaganda value" just didn't know what he was talking about.) To fully exploit the public relations possibilities, and to send a message to the recalcitrant regime in Bucharest, Kremlin officials were supposed to have ordered that the Rumanian cosmonaut be replaced by the Vietnamese candidate—even though he was a full year behind everyone else in training. The Soviet Union evidently wanted the world's first non-white spaceman to provide the best possible publicity; it also evidently wanted to improve Vietnam's international image after the bad press of the boat people, the Laotian and Cambodian incursions, and the skirmishing on Thai and Chinese borders. Sending a man into space was a wonderful way to distract attention from embarrassing earthbound realities, as Soviet officials could testify based on decades of experience!

The twenty-nine-year-old Vietnamese, Pham Tuan, had spent half his adult life in military schools in the Soviet Union. A fighter pilot during the Christmas 1972 B-52 raids over North Vietnam, Tuan had nearly died when his aircraft hit a bomb crater on a runway during one emergency landing. The following night he allegedly became the first Vietnamese pilot to shoot down a B-52, a claim which U.S. Air Force spokesmen later disputed with the assertion that all bombers lost over Hanoi were hit by surface-to-air missiles. But whatever the truth to the conflicting claims (the U.S. Air Force account seems more trustworthy here), the Soviets advertised their latest space guest as the first cosmonaut to have killed "American imperialists" in action. It was an unkind response to the U.S.-led Olympic Games boycott!

Late in September—right on my schedule, projected according to the identical-launch-time restriction—the next guest cosmonaut went up. He was a Cuban, Arnaldo Tamayo-Mendez, the first black man in space. That surprised some observers, but back in the May 1976 issue of *Spaceflight,* I had mentioned that if the Soviets followed their standard propaganda policies, the Cuban cosmonaut would be picked on racial grounds. The title of the article was *First Negro Cosmonaut?*

Despite the fact that Cuba is one of the loveliest regions of our planet when viewed from orbit, the Cuban cosmonaut never got the chance to see it: all the Salyut's passes across the island were in darkness! Due to the station's orbital motion, launching Tamayo a few weeks earlier or later would have allowed daylight flights over Cuba—but the Soviet passion for methodical invariability ruled out any modification in the launch countdown. The Cuban's space comrades promised to take some photographs and mail them to him.

As it turned out, the whole flight was pure showmanship anyway. (The Cuban even brought up a vial of "holy" sand from the Bay of Pigs, site of the 1961 ill-fated anti-Castro invasion, whose failure had contributed substantially to the U.S. decision to send men to the moon.) This fact was underscored when the visitors—Tamayo's chauffeur was Yuriy Romanenko, who had spent ninety-six days aboard the Salyut almost three years earlier—returned to earth in their own Soyuz, not even bothering to switch out spaceships with the marathon crew—who didn't need one anyhow, since they were returning to earth in a few weeks. So there wasn't a single operational reason to launch the Cuban's ship, but then, such rational justifications have rarely been needed in the cosmonaut program, as we've seen!

By late 1980, more candidate space guests were on their way to the Gagarin Cosmonaut Training Center. Two French pilots, Jean-Loup Chrétien and Patrick Baudry, went to Moscow for a mission planned for the spring of 1982. Two Indian pilots, slated to fly in mid-1982, were supposed to join them. (Sanjay Gandhi, son of the Indian Prime Minister, was reportedly the leading candidate at the time of his death in an aircraft accident in mid-1980.) The program had reaped the public relations harvests that Soviet officials had anticipated, and new invitations to new countries were bound to follow.

All the speculation about the political significance of the order in which the guest cosmonauts were being launched was dispelled late in 1980 when Russian-space-watcher Maarten Houtman of Amsterdam figured out the real Soviet pattern: the guest cosmonauts of the 1978–1979 class were being launched purely in alphabetical order! In Russian alphabetical order, with Russian names, the countries were Bolgaria (Bulgaria), Vengria (Hungary), Vietnam, Kuba (Cuba)—to be followed by Mongolia and Rumynia (Rumania). The irony was that in a program whose very existence depended on political propaganda purposes, the Sovi-

ets evidently backed off from being forced to rate the loyalty
of their allies in launch sequence—and chose the politically
neutral alphabetical order as the ultimate test of who would
go up when. And the scheme still allowed Moscow to make
the recalcitrant Rumanians wait until the end of the line!

12
☆
Through the Zero-G Barrier

The two spacesuited figures waited in the dark, underneath a dome full of stars that moved across the sky at an unnaturally rapid rate. Below them, other lights would cross from horizon to horizon in only five minutes. There were flickering smears of lightning-lit thunderclouds, jewel-like single beacons of ships at sea, then the webs of city streets as the cosmonauts crossed over the Pacific coast of South America.

One man, Sasha, stood on a work platform alongside the air-lock hatch; the second man, Vladimir, stood in the hatch, his body halfway out. The thirty-five-minute-long nightside pass was an opportunity to rest between more active phases of the spacewalk. There were some spotlights installed at the work platform, but Sasha had turned them off so the men's eyes could adjust to the darkness.

A sudden flare of light—and a gasp from Vladimir—made Sasha jump. As he turned to look, he noticed his shadow moving across the side of the work platform. Something very bright and very fast was passing them.

Vladimir had been staring out into the distance when the fireball flared into life, moving across their bow in a slightly descending path. "It was like an blow torch," he later recalled. Sasha turned in time to glimpse the fireball flicker out —its total lifetime had been about five seconds. "How close was it?" Vladimir wondered to himself, his eyes still dazzled. He suddenly remembered something and, still blinded, fumbled for it where he had attached it to his spacesuit—his camera. There it was, right where he had placed it and right where he had left it during the meteor's passage.

Their eyes never did adapt to the dark again because dawn approached—or, more accurately, they flew into the dawn at 18,000 miles per hour. At sunrise they were crossing the coast of west Africa and soon were above the red-yellow-white-purple splotches of the Sahara. For the next hour the two cosmonauts retrieved scientific equipment from mounts at the work platform, replacing the units with fresh modules; they detached meteor-dust collectors and a pack of organic polymers called Medusa (designed to see if living cells could survive unprotected voyages across interplanetary space to "infect" nearby planets); they installed a new set of radiation sensors; they photographed earth's surface as they soared across the Black Sea, Kazakhstan and China.

Just before going out of radio range, they heard from Moscow Mission Control one last time: "If you have nothing more to do, then you may get back in." But Vladimir, enjoying the view now that the work was done, called back: "We would just like to take our time, since this is the first time in forty-five days that we've gone out into the street for a stroll." Before anyone could disagree, they were out of range. For the next twenty minutes they watched the ground roll by: south China, the Philippines, New Guinea, the Coral Sea and Australia's Great Barrier Reef, and finally sunset over New Zealand, as the South Island's mountains cast long shadows on rosy clouds to the east. The space station passed into earth's shadow, and the two men reluctantly entered the air lock and closed the hatch.

They had been in space a month and a half—and they had more than three months to go.

The spacewalk had been a tremendous psychological boost for the men, and they had needed it. Since their launching aboard Soyuz-29 on June 15, 1978, cosmonauts Vladimir Kovalyonok and "Sasha" Ivanchenkov had been carefully marshaling their energies for the marathon record-breaking flight—but previous Soviet space experience suggested that there was a good chance they would fall short of their goal.

They were both determined to succeed. For Kovalyonok, it was his second chance: he had been the commander of the aborted Soyuz-25 linkup attempt the previous October. For Ivanchenkov, who had trained with Yuriy Romanenko for five years only to be bumped at the last moment by Georgiy Grechko, it was an opportunity to demonstrate that he would have done just as well as—or better than—Grechko if the crew assignments had not been scrambled.

The challenge was tough: 140 days in space. Nobody, Russian or American, had been up for anywhere near as long or had kept a space station operational for so many months after launch. They were venturing into genuinely unknown territory, physiologically, psychologically and technically.

Many lessons from the 96-day flight of Romanenko and Grechko were incorporated into the scheduling of activities for the 140-day flight. Romanenko and Grechko had worked a six-day week followed by one rest day, but as they grew more fatigued they were allowed to have one rest day after five working days. On this, the next expedition, Kovalyonok and Ivanchenkov were to be given two rest days after five work days—although they were expected to do light duties, such as documentation updates or cabin disinfecting, during their "weekends."

Food was improved. Halfway through the 96-day flight, Romanenko and Grechko had had a noticeable decrease in appetite, attributed to boredom with the repetitious menu, which was recycled every six days. On this longer mission, changes were made: enriched wheat bread was added; at dinner each day, a second freeze-dried dish was included; a new assortment of products appeared, including fruit and berry juices. The crewmen liked the changes, but there was still work to be done. Ivanchenkov, for example, had a selectively decreased appetite during the second half of the flight, not finishing his meat dishes but scrounging all the cheese, juice and other liquids he could from Kovalyonok's menu. During that period he had a significant weight loss, which was reversed only during the last few weeks of the flight.

The men adjusted to weightlessness well, but had difficulty sleeping during the first five or six weeks. Ivanchenkov would have trouble falling asleep, while Kovalyonok would doze off almost immediately—but then would wake after four or five hours and would be unable to get back to sleep. He tried various tranquilizers, including a drug called eunoctin— which gave him bad headaches and a generally sickly feeling. But eventually both men's sleeping problems cleared up.

The work schedule was heavy enough that it should have ensured a good night's sleep. They would wake at seven in the morning, spend half an hour checking the space station and reviewing the day's schedule, then spend an hour on their morning hygiene and breakfast. They would then work for two hours and exercise for another hour, followed by more work and then dinner. Four more hours of work filled the afternoon, with another hour of exercise preceding supper. In the evening they had three hours for their meal, for reviewing the following day's schedule and for "free time." They were scheduled to get to bed by ten or eleven o'clock, but often worked until past midnight on balky equipment and confused documentation.

Outside of problems of general fatigue, the men had to stay healthy. In this they were quite successful: their only significant complaints during the entire flight were of an infected

Red Star in Orbit

fingernail that Kovalyonok got after taking a blood sample (it was treated successfully with antibiotics, sulfamide and ointments) and a bad earache for Ivanchenkov (taken care of with a warm alcohol compress). In the second month of the flight, the men developed headaches on three separate occasions when the carbon dioxide in the cabin built up—even though doctors had felt that such a level should still have been tolerable. Once the cause had been identified, the crew was directed to change their air purifiers more frequently. The problem did not reoccur.

The cosmonauts introduced one new operational capability during their expedition. On the second of two guest-cosmonaut visits, the visitors had left their fresh Soyuz parked at the aft docking port and had flown the crew's original Soyuz back to earth. (The first visit, only a week after their launching, had been purely symbolic and there had been no Soyuz exchange.) In order to clear the aft end for subsequent robot Progress freighter linkups, the cosmonauts got into the new Soyuz, cast off from the Salyut and flew around to the front end, where they redocked. It was a neat trick—but just in case the redocking might have failed, the crew had packed their Soyuz with the results of their experiments for a contingency landing, if needed. But nothing went wrong and the men had another enjoyable outing, a "drive in the country" to add to their earlier spacewalking "stroll down the street."

Pacing themselves for the full twenty weeks in space was a problem. After about 60 days, Kovalyonok and Ivanchenkov both began to get tired: their voices on the radio showed clear signs of fatigue. But as they approached the "old" record, their spirits picked up and they got their second wind. By the time they passed 100 days, everyone was pleased with their energy and good spirits. At 120 days, doctors noticed a new adaptation: the cosmonauts' pattern of day-night pulse rate and temperature fluctuations (the so-called circadian rhythm) leveled off abruptly, although their sleep cycles were not affected. And toward the end of the flight, they began to get hints that the calcium loss from their bones might have been easing—but they landed before the results could be confirmed.

Kovalyonok, a young White Russian pilot with the chin, blond hair, and slate-blue eyes of a movie star, later described the gradual change in his attitude as month followed month: "The length of the flight is not just the qualitative growth of knowledge," he wrote in a magazine article in 1979. "It is useful and interesting to fly for a long time. The whole expedition may be divided into several periods. In the first month, one becomes accustomed to flight conditions and adjusts to them. The second month, one gradually begins to gain knowledge and collect facts. In the third month, one begins to analyze them more deeply and many questions arise. One begins to feel like a real researcher in the full sense of the word."

An example of this kind of genuine research (as opposed to monkey-mode button-pushing) was the visual observation of earth's surface. The men looked at snowcaps and glaciers in the Pamir Mountains and reported seeing features, such as a glacier crater less than a hundred feet in diameter, which specialists were certain should have been invisible. At one point, brightly colored ground cloths were laid out near the edge of a convenient glacier, and the cosmonauts were asked to estimate just how near. After several passes overhead, Kovalyonok reported that he thought the markers were about seven hundred feet from the edge—and that was close enough to make believers out of the ground experts.

Observing the oceans was equally fascinating. The men could distinguish the borderline between cold and warm water, which led to the location of rich plankton beds in the northwest Pacific—and fishing fleets later reported a rich yield of mackerel. A number of typhoons occurred during the flight (Agnes, Virginia, Hector and others) and the cosmonauts watched them develop. Over calm water, they found they could detect submerged islands, including some which didn't show up on their charts. They watched icebergs in the Southern Hemisphere and found it was easy to distinguish an old, disintegrating iceberg from a sturdy, fresh one: the old ones were surrounded by halos of fresh water, which stood out plainly. The cosmonauts found that their color-differentiation capabilities were vastly enhanced: they had a chart of 192 colors designed for oceanographic observation, but found it inadequate.

Kovalyonok joked about not seeing anything strange over the Bermuda Triangle and about not running into any flying saucers, like Grechko had. In a more serious vein, he was depressed by the vast preponderance of desert and wasteland over cultivated land, and made a comment based upon his own ideological background. "It is a pity that development is neglected," he told a reporter during an in-flight radio interview, "because of the current arms race instigated by imperialists." Or at least that quotation appeared in the newspapers, attributed to him.

Kovalyonok and Ivanchenkov developed the Progress re-supply operations to perfection. "The ground training procedures were not helpful," Ivanchenkov later commented. "The only real training was *experience*. Our first unloading took a week, but our third took only two days." It was more than just a matter of manhandling a few tons of cargo through a hatch; the new equipment had to be checked off on a cargo manifest and properly stowed inside the Salyut, while broken equipment and expended air canisters were put in the emptied places in the Progress cargo hold (about the size of a station wagon).

The contents of Progress-4, launched on October 4, 1978 (twenty-one years to the day after the first Sputnik), are illustrative. There was the usual amount of rocket propellant in special tanks, as well as photographic films, music tape cassettes, ampules for the materials-processing furnaces, mail, air filters and regeneration canisters, and clean clothing. A hundred-pound picnic box contained food items: sausages, beef tongue, freeze-dried beef, fruit sticks, assorted canned meats, strawberries, fresh milk, onions, garlic, curds with nuts and two boxes of candy. There were two new "penguin suits," since the old ones' straps had broken. There were two pairs of fur-lined boots (the cosmonauts had complained that their toes were cold) and two pairs of slippers (the old ones had been worn out on the treadmill). There were dividers to be installed inside the Salyut to partition off areas for privacy. There were new electric razors, a new tape recorder, a new repair tool kit and clean sleeping-bag liners. There was a medical kit with special drugs to be used as stimulating agents just prior to the return to earth. The crew off-loaded a total of 3,000 pounds of cargo and replaced it with 2,000 pounds of discarded equipment that had been cluttering up the space station. It was destined for incineration when the Progress dove back into the atmosphere.

In November the last big hurdle loomed: the landing, after 140 days in space. The cosmonauts switched the Salyut to automatic control, loaded the experimental results into the Soyuz, deactivated the station's life-support systems and cast off for earth. The descent through the atmosphere and final touchdown were routine. At last they were lying on their form-fit couches inside a space capsule sitting on the ground.

The exercise and improved medical preparations paid off: both men climbed out of the Soyuz themselves, waving away helping hands. Standing by the capsule, Kovalyonok smiled, bent over, picked up some dirt and smelled it joyfully as he stood straight again. The symbolic gesture took all his energy, he later admitted—but he wanted to demonstrate graphically the success of the anti-weightlessness countermeasures.

The doctors confirmed it. "The condition of the men after their 140-day flight is better than the condition of cosmonauts Grechko and Romanenko after their 96-day flight," reported Dr. Anatoliy Beregovkin, chief physician of the cosmonaut training center. There were some oddities, however. The cosmonauts at first reported difficulty in talking. When Kovalyonok drank two cups of tea at the hospital, he felt he had a heavy weight in his stomach. When the men moved their heads, everything around them seemed to rock back and forth. Nevertheless, their recovery astounded the medical experts. The day after the landing, they swam in the hospital pool; the next day, they insisted on a stroll in the park. Before the week was out, their blood mass and distribution were back to normal, and they were spending hours in outdoor walks. A few days later, they were jogging.

Space official Feoktistov paid tribute to the men: "In their hard and strenuous work, the Soviet cosmonauts once again showed the best of human qualities—will, endurance, courage and heroism." And these qualities paid off: after forty-five days back on earth, there was no medical evidence that the cosmonauts had ever been in space at all. And the Salyut-6 space station flew on, temporarily empty.

The American reactions to the Salyut-6 space-station successes were varied. NASA sent the obligatory congratulatory telegrams as American-held records were broken repeatedly. Astronauts expressed their personal good wishes too. Skylab veteran Jerry Carr welcomed the development: "I'm pleased the Soviets are still pushing ahead, putting the pressure on the frontier. We've established our beachhead in space and now we're going to consolidate it." By "we" he meant human beings, since it was Russia which was now carrying the ball.

NASA administrator Robert Frosch took several public positions on the Soviet successes. Following the first double docking in January 1978, he felt that the feat showed that "the Soviets are really trying to do exactly what they said they will—set up a space station occupied continuously for a year or more. It is a matter of continuing their technical program." Yet months later, he expressed puzzlement about their motivations: "The Soviets have decided they want to try for very long stays," he told the UPI after the 140-day flight. "I'm not sure why." But by early 1979 he was telling Congress that the impact of a permanent Soviet space station "could be severe in the sense that suddenly there would be a change from experimentation to some kind of operational status." Concluded Frosch, "I think people in general would consider it a serious event."

The 96- and 140-day missions in 1978 had fulfilled the prime objectives planned for Salyut-6, but space officials were pleased to find that the station was still in good shape. The possibility of additional expeditions had always been present and now real plans were laid.

A new visit would have several purposes. It would extend the flight duration beyond 140 days and confirm the effectiveness of the countermeasures. It would extend the experimental program and include new investigations which had not been available earlier. Most important, it would test the ability of cosmonauts to refurbish an aging space station via repairs and replacement of old equipment. This last activity would have great significance for the long-term operation of permanent space stations.

In February 1979 the Soyuz-32 blasted off, carrying Vladimir Lyakhov and Valeriy Ryumin. They were bound for 175 days in space, nearly half a year, during which they would once again encounter unexpected technical problems and once again demonstrate the value of the human presence in space.

Until this flight, repair work on Soviet spacecraft had been limited to replacing plug-in modules, air regenerators and filters, light bulbs and similar equipment. Now the cosmonauts were equipped with the most sophisticated tool kit ever used in space: various pliers and screwdrivers, special vices, clamps and bolts, electrical diagnostic meters, and a soldering gun and tin solder. With such equipment, they set to work: they replaced many electronic units; they changed the read/write head on their videotape unit; they replaced cables and headsets for their radio, clocks on their control panels, the plastic curtain on their shower and worn parts on their exercycle. New equipment to be installed included a new massmeter, a linen drier, additional body restraints, improved carbon monoxide detectors, a new audio tape recorder, a new portable gamma-ray telescope and one major improvement in earth-to-space communications: the first ever on-board television screen, to be used for displaying family interviews, instruction sequences, video entertainment and visual material such as blueprints and maps.

And they learned a lot. At one point, the engineer Ryumin complained that some instruments that needed work were not designed to be opened in space—the prospect of in-flight repair had been ignored. Another time, the new equipment had unexpected effects on other spacecraft functions: when the men turned on a new glass furnace, all their medical telemetry readings stopped, and it took a few days to find out that some crossed wires were causing intermittent interference. The most serious repair job involved spinning the whole space station slowly to clear propellant from a storage tank that had become contaminated. It could not be fixed, but it was "safed" and isolated, and the two remaining tanks were adequate to continue the mission.

Like their predecessors, Lyakhov and Ryumin adjusted well to space conditions. Lyakhov remarked that at first the small size of the cabin had bothered him, "but as our floating in weightlessness was becoming the normal state," he recalled later, "the compartments of the station seemed more and more convenient and spacious." After several months of flight, the men were working at an efficiency at least three times greater than that of short-duration crewmen.

A remarkable document came to light early in 1980, when free-lance journalist Henry Gris returned from a series of interviews in Moscow. It appeared that he had obtained a copy of Ryumin's in-flight personal diary, an extraordinary acquisition—and both the circumstances and content of the document testified to its authenticity.

Ryumin comes through in this account as an extremely cautious man who was always anxious about one thing or another. Before launch, he mused over the prospects of half a year in space: "Didn't O. Henry say, 'All one needs to effect a murder is to lock two men in a cabin eighteen feet by twenty and keep them there for two months'?" During the launching he had worried about crashing back to earth in some remote corner of Siberia and freezing to death; during the docking phase he was concerned about a second failure which would probably end his space-flight career forever.

The adaptation to weightlessness also seemed unpleasant, as described by Ryumin: "Our faces have begun to swell, so much that looking into the mirror I fail to recognize myself. I feel dizzy, nauseous. My movements lack coordination. I keep bumping into things, mostly with my head. Objects float away from my hands. Chaos in a teapot!"

Ryumin on exercises: "I hate them. Loved exercises on earth. But here, each time I have to force myself. Boring and monotonous, and heavy work."

Ryumin on food: "For some reason, we have lots of candies aboard, but we hardly touch them. We would rather have something salty. They keep forgetting to send it up."

Ryumin on his health: "My worst fear during this stay in space has been over a possible appendicitis attack. I still have my appendix and one never knows. And another: that I may get a toothache requiring dental help. In space? One night I dreamed that I *was* having a toothache and I woke up in a cold sweat. And one tooth *was* indeed sensitive. But by morning, the toothache was gone."

Occasional visits by guest cosmonauts would have probably aided the crew's psychological stamina, and several such visits were planned. But they all had to be canceled. In April a routine mail run and Soyuz exchange mission was launched, flown by the Russian engineer Rukavishnikov and by Georgi Ivanov, the Bulgarian guest cosmonaut. But as detailed in the last chapter, the Soyuz-33 was forced to turn back because of rocket failure, and the chance for possible later visits by Hungarian and Cuban guest cosmonauts was lost.

Lyakhov and Ryumin had been watching eagerly out of a porthole as their would-be visitors approached, end forward, preparing for one last braking rocket blast. They saw the engine light, then flicker, change colors and go out, followed a minute later by the Soyuz-33 zipping by when it should have slowed down. The linkup mission was a failure—although it took almost a day for Moscow press officials to announce that.

"Something had gone dangerously wrong," Ryumin wrote in his diary. He stayed awake all night plotting a way for himself and Lyakhov to take their own Soyuz and attempt a rescue if the endangered men were really stranded. Then he began worrying about the engine in his own Soyuz.

The Soyuz-33 failure led to many months of investigation by space engineers before the Soyuz could again be certified safe for cosmonauts. This meant that for the entire 175-day flight, Lyakhov and Ryumin would go without other human company. They began to regard this as an "extra psychological experiment." And such it was: there will probably not be a similar period of solitude for spacemen until the first manned voyages are sent off to the planets.

As the months passed, the men found that their adjustment to space was more than just physical and psychological. They also gained experience in the mechanics of everyday life, and in the problems of observing earth's multifaceted surface.

Ryumin described this latter process in a diary entry for June 25, the 121st day of the flight. "Only now," he wrote, "have we acquired what I like to call 'space sight,' an ability to discern sites on earth as they go below us. We used to lose them as soon as we thought we had located them. . . . At night we can easily pick out city lights. In Europe, France looks best to us or, more precisely, Paris. And North America is brightest of all at night, making me want to get into a car and race one of its straight-as-an-arrow highways."

A steady parade of robot supply ships kept them provisioned and equipped. The first Progress, sent up only two weeks after their launching, carried consumable supplies and replacement parts as well as new astronomical and botanical equipment. The second Progress, in May, brought up the usual assortment of cargo plus new control panels and a fascinating botanical experiment—a tulip. In June an unmanned Soyuz (which except for the April failure would have carried a Hungarian copilot, but Soviet space officials wanted to play it safe) brought up four hundred pounds of food delicacies and new biological samples. The cosmonauts loaded their old Soyuz with experimental results, sent it back to earth on autopilot and then flew the new Soyuz around from the aft hatch to the forward hatch. This cleared the way for yet another Progress docking, late in June, which carried new radio equipment and a new materials-processing experiment designed to produce very thin films of metals and plastics.

When this last Progress freighter unlatched from the Salyut's back end, it uncovered a special device which the cosmonauts had installed in the transfer tunnel: a folded radio dish antenna, which immediately unfurled to a full thirty-five-foot diameter. A series of tests, including some radio-interferometry experiments with a large radio telescope in the Crimea, were then run. This impressive technological accomplishment was somewhat marred when, after three weeks of operations, the planned jettisoning of the radio dish failed. Instead of falling free, the mesh wire of the antenna tangled in a protruding piece of equipment at the back end of the Salyut. The cosmonauts rolled the station back and forth, but the six-hundred-pound dish antenna only flopped around. It stayed securely attached.

The men still could return to earth safely, since their Soyuz was at the other end of the Salyut, but the problem would have forestalled any future use of the aft hatch. So with only a few days left in space, the decision was taken to allow the cosmonauts to make a spacewalk, during which one of them would use wire cutters on the balky antenna. This decision was a risky one for a number of reasons: the men had been in space for a very long time; the problem was at the opposite end of the station from the air lock and that section had never before been visited by spacewalkers; the only tools available were jury-rigged ones; the spacesuits had already long exceeded their design lifetime and could not be guaranteed. This last concern was accentuated during the spacewalk rehearsal when it was discovered that the radio relay unit in the air lock had malfunctioned, cutting off all voice communications to the cosmonauts once they were inside their spacesuits.

In preparing for the spacewalk, the cosmonauts took several unusual steps. They had thoroughly checked out the spacesuits and gone over their own plans, but there was still a chance of something going disastrously wrong. Consequently, they completed the packing of their Soyuz, loading it with film, logbooks, and biological and metal samples so that it could return "with or without us" (as Ryumin noted in his diary). One more item was added at the last moment: each man wrote a letter to his family. "We did the latter without much ado," Ryumin wrote, "just in case we would not return from the spacewalk. We knew there was such a possibility."

On August 15, the men entered the air lock, donned the spacesuits and let out the air. But when the time came to open the hatch, it refused to budge. Both men leaned hard against it, and it finally popped open. Their spacewalk had only begun and already they were behind schedule and overworked: Ryumin, the one who would do the actual cutting, had a pulse rate of 134. By the time they had installed handrails at the open hatch, the sun was setting, requiring another half-hour delay.

When the hatch had opened, Ryumin had looked straight down two hundred miles. He *knew* it was safe, but it still bothered him: "To be honest, I didn't care for it," he confessed to his diary the following day. "I was scared. To get out of the hatch I had to face outward into the void. And while this doesn't matter in a state of weightlessness, I was not happy about it!"

The men rested in the darkness, anticipating the view of the stars. They were not disappointed: "They look like huge diamond pins on black velvet," Ryumin remembered thinking. "We saw stars so close it seemed we could reach out and touch them."

Ryumin hung in space, attached to the side of the Salyut with a safety belt. He looked toward the east, where the spacecraft's motion made sunrise approach at a rate sixteen times as fast as on earth's surface: "First a slim greenish-blue line on the farthest horizon," he recounted later, "turning within a couple of minutes into a rainbow hugging the earth, and it in turn exploding into a golden sun. You're out of your mind, I was telling myself—hanging on to a ship in space, and to your life, and getting ready to admire a sunrise." He turned his attention to the task at hand.

At sunrise Ryumin moved hand over hand along the handrails, while Lyakhov remained at the hatch and played out his friend's sixty-foot safety line. Ryumin stopped at the rear edge of the Salyut and peered over; he could see where the antenna was snagged (at a T-bar mounted on a pole, which served as an optical docking target), but it was well out of reach and there were no handrails there on the back end. So he began cutting wires nearer to him in the hope that the mesh would unravel.

Meanwhile, the sun was shining right into his eyes. Ryumin closed the glare shield across the faceplate, but then the glass cooled, allowing condensation from his rapid breathing to cloud over most of the faceplate. He quickly raised the sun visor and squinted through sweat-soaked eyes, cutting methodically at the wires within reach.

Very soon his strategy worked, and he could see the snag fall away. With a pole he pushed the antenna free and, satisfied that it had cleanly separated, made his way back to the hatch. Ryumin was so exhausted that he hardly had energy to unsnag his own backpack when it got stuck in the hatch —but he did, and he soon had enough breath to report to Mission Control that their spacewalk had been a success. The men on earth stood and cheered; Ryumin managed a smile as the sound of applause filled his helmet.

Even before this achievement, the whole lesson of the 175-day mission had been that men were needed in space to conduct both preventive and restorative repairs, and this spacewalk further underscored that lesson. Chief cosmonaut Shatalov referred to such operations in a summary report a few months later when he wrote: "It can be said with complete assurance that the prolonged operation of the Salyut-6 station became possible only due to the cosmonauts."

Four days after the spacewalk, and almost six months after blasting off, the men returned to earth. They landed within six miles of their target point, a bull's-eye by Soviet standards, and were greeted by doctors within three minutes. The cosmonauts stumbled out of the capsule and lay down on special reclining chairs. Ryumin was handed a bouquet of flowers; he loved the smells, but felt the bouquet was crushing his chest. Lyakhov, the pilot, had vestibular disorders and elevated blood pressure, and Ryumin reported trouble speaking. Their pulse rates ranged from 100 to 112. The doctors characterized them both as "active, even slightly euphoric," but found nothing to worry about.

Ryumin, in fact, had not lost any weight over the course of the flight and was so fit that he was strolling in the hospital park the next day and by the third day was jogging. He was proud to have made the flight, but was happy to be back on earth.

The doctors were, if anything, even happier. The post-flight checkups confirmed and extended the medical results of the 140-day flight: the collection of countermeasures had apparently succeeded in preventing any additional physical changes beyond those observed on the first, 96-day expedition. The heart-lung systems of the cosmonauts had remained strong. Most significantly, the insidious calcium loss which had threatened to turn the spacemen's bones to jelly had been found to be self-limiting: there was little difference between the decalcification levels of the 96-day, 140-day and 175-day missions. The drop seemed to level off and would not pose any danger for even longer flights, according to chief Soviet space doctor Oleg Gazenko.

Gazenko, interviewed in April 1980 issue of *Soviet Union*, exuded optimism. There were no pathological changes found in the 175-day crewmen, he reported, and their period of readaptation was shorter and easier than either of the two earlier Salyut-6 expeditions. The bone-deterioration problem, while not solved, was manageable: "The calcium loss was moderate, about 8 percent," Gazenko noted. "American astronauts lost about the same amount [actually, 6.8%] after the eighty-four-day Skylab space mission: However, even if the loss were to reach 16 percent, the result could be considered normal. Clinical observations have shown that a loss of over 20 to 25 percent is dangerous."

The final verdict of the long flights was that potential medical problems had been exorcised. "I believe that humankind can be as happy in space as on earth," Gazenko concluded. The cosmonauts themselves may have felt such a sweeping boast was just a euphoric exaggeration: they still recalled the fatigue, the anxiety, the frustration, the grueling exercise regimen. Living in space was still a far cry from living on earth. But due to the cosmonauts' efforts, the gap had narrowed significantly.

The one man who demonstrated that medical barriers to long space missions had been overcome was Valeriy Ryumin. Only eight months after his record-breaking orbital marathon in 1979, he was sent back up into space for an even longer mission.

It happened this way: Ryumin's flight in 1979 had been a "bonus mission" since the two long visits (96 days and 140 days) in 1977–1978 had accomplished the original objectives set for Salyut-6. But since the space station was still in good shape, one additional mission was made to study the mechanics of repairing and revitalizing the worn-out on-board equipment. This flight lasted 175 days. At the end of it, space officials were amazed at the continuing good health of the Salyut, so they proceeded with the option of making a *second* bonus mission in 1980.

Most of the cosmonauts from the 1977–1978 missions had already been reassigned to new projects, so the 1980 flight crew (who had been the stand-in crew in 1979) was assigned two relatively inexperienced cosmonauts as understudies— with the assumption that since this was to be the last long Salyut-6 visit, the understudies would have another year or two to prepare for their eventual *real* space missions. Ryumin, meanwhile, was assigned to direct the training of the primary 1980 crew, which consisted of jet pilot Leonid Popov and veteran civilian cosmonaut Valentin Lebedev.

But only a month before the early spring 1980 launch of Popov and Lebedev aboard Soyuz-35, disaster struck. Lebedev smashed his knee during a trampoline mishap and was rushed to a hospital. Surgery followed, and the doctors grounded the injured cosmonaut.

The normal procedure would have been for Lebedev's backup cosmonauts to step in, but officials hesitated. The bonus and double-bonus missions had used up the best-trained cosmonauts assigned to Salyut-6 (there were many other cosmonauts, of course, but they were working on different projects), and Lebedev's backup man was judged unready to make such a demanding flight. Who could step in?

We don't know how Ryumin, the crew's training director, came to get the job. Perhaps he was an obvious choice and cosmonaut corps officials prevailed upon him to take the opening; perhaps he personally concluded that the backup engineer was not qualified, and reluctantly volunteered; perhaps he eagerly sought to replace the still-anonymous rookie whose position was precarious. We don't know—nor do we know the feelings of the rejected replacement: Was he relieved? Was he bitterly disappointed? Was he grateful to Ryumin or resentful? That side of the cosmonaut story is hidden from us.

The bottom line was that Ryumin learned he would fly again—with only a few weeks to go before blast-off—on a mission for which he had not even been a designated crewman. But he did fly, and space records were broken again: by late September 1980, when the Salyut-6 celebrated its third birthday in orbit, Ryumin had just returned safely to earth with another 185 days of flight experience. (His grand total was only three days shy of a full year.) He had become at home in orbit—and he would be only the first of many Russians to feel that way.

13
☆
Things to Come

Soviet space successes on Salyut-6, coincident with extensive delays in the American Space Shuttle program, have understandably raised a compelling question: Has the United States fallen behind the Soviet Union in a new round of the space race? The string of new Soviet space records—and the apparent lack of any significant American response—has been used by Moscow propagandists to support their latest claims of Soviet space supremacy. Many Western observers, and many ordinary citizens, seem to agree.

But it would be a mistake to view recent space events in simplistic statistical terms or to draw alarmist conclusions from them. The manned space efforts of the United States and the Soviet Union are currently proceeding along parallel paths but are temporarily pursuing different short-range goals, goals which are based on the different needs of the two countries. The rationale for one country's effort would be irrelevant to the other country, and vice versa—so far.

The United States, Canada and the European Space Agency are together developing a "space transportation system," consisting of the Space Shuttle, the Spacelab research module, and a family of rocket engines to be carried aloft in and launched from the Shuttle. The immediate goal is to establish easy and economical access from earth into space and back, and to conduct frequent scientific sorties into orbit with a large variety of scientific instruments and earth observation equipment. Such capabilities could, toward the end of this decade, lead to the creation of one or more permanently occupied space stations of considerable size.

The Soviet Union, on the other hand, is now developing a small basic space-station module first, in order to gain long-term experience in space operations with a limited amount of research equipment. Later in the decade the Soviets will probably introduce reusable systems akin to the NASA Space Shuttle, but at present they are relying on tried-and-true expendable boosters and capsules while concentrating their developmental efforts on extending the capabilities of the space-station system itself.

Most experts feel that the United States does not at present need a permanent manned space station, since sophisticated unmanned systems, supplemented by brief but well-equipped Spacelab orbital sorties, can conduct useful work in space—while defining the types of tasks which will eventually justify the creation of a permanent space base. The Soviet Union, in its turn, does not seem to need a cheaper space transportation system, but instead needs to extend the useful space life of vehicles already launched into orbit—and a manned space platform is one logical way to meet that requirement. So both countries are developing space systems based purely on their own internal needs, not in response to some perception of a common goal toward which both nations can race. In that sense, the space race really is over—just as the competition to find ways to exploit space for practical benefits is getting fiercer and fiercer.

The first step in the Soviet plan is the establishment of permanently occupied space outposts orbiting just beyond the atmosphere. The goal has been an officially acknowledged one for years, and is explicitly expressed in a near-religious litany which is repeated after each new Soviet space success (and there have been a lot of them lately): "We believe that continuously inhabited space stations in near-earth orbits will be humanity's main road out into the universe."

No more breakthroughs are needed. All of the pieces have been tested and verified. Men have proved their adaptability and durability during the long expeditions on Salyut-6; the machines have shown that they, too, can function, as long as men are available to refurbish and repair them. Salyut, Soyuz, Progress—they add up to Kosmograd, the code word for Space Colony Number One, made in the Soviet Union.

The approach to be used in building this Kosmograd has been described in specific terms by numerous Soviet spokesmen. The basic theory was expounded several years ago by Boris Petrov, chairman of the Interkosmos Council for scientific space research: "When it comes to creating large stations, it will obviously be expedient to carry out their assembly from component parts in one or two dockings." Sergey Grishin, a leading official of the Soviet flight-control center, told reporters in mid-1979 that such a course had been chosen: "Orbiting stations of future generations will consist of separate, independently launched modules. The main module will offer more comfortable conditions for crews; it will have control consoles for all of the orbiting station's systems. Other modules, which may fly detached from the main module, will contain scientific apparatus and technological equipment that require special orientation of the modules and total absence of vibration and gravity forces." Salyut designer and former cosmonaut Konstantin Feoktistov wrote in mid-1978 that "as in the Salyut-6 station, one can envision replaceable modules docking with a space factory or orbiting laboratory to supply new or improved equipment." The unanimity of these descriptions betokens the official blessing which this approach must have received.

The intended use of such equipment is not mysterious,

explained chief cosmonaut Vladimir Shatalov in late 1979: "We are close to the constant operation of orbital stations—to around-the-clock, year-round work of cosmonauts aboard them, replacement of crews directly aboard the stations and regular delivery of the necessary materials into orbit." Nor is it any secret how long the space-duty tour should last: chief rocket designer Valentin Glushko told an *Izvestia* reporter recently that it would seem "reasonable" to have crews work in space for as long as one year. In this regard, Glushko pointed to the experience of twenty-four Arctic and twenty-three Antarctic expeditions which had changed crews annually. Chief Soviet space doctor Oleg Gazenko endorsed this view in March 1980 when he told a Hungarian newspaper that flights lasting a whole year "could realistically be envisaged for the near future."

So the development of a permanent Soviet space station is entirely feasible in the 1981–1982 time period. Three or four men could work aboard it in orbit for a year at a time. Periodically, new Soyuz replacement vehicles would be brought up by visitors, who would include guest cosmonauts as well as Russian scientist-cosmonauts. Add-on modules would provide temporary specialized labs. The core Salyut module could be operational for at least five years.

And, of course, such a station will be only the first step in the spaceward migration prophesied by Tsiolkovskiy.

A key element in setting up large permanent space colonies and in preparing years-long manned expeditions to other planets is a system for recycling air, water and some food. Such a "closed-loop" life-support system could use a combination of mechanical, chemical and biological processes to grossly reduce the amount of fresh supplies needed to keep space-farers alive.

Water on Salyut-6 was already 50 percent recycled via a mechanical system which extracted humidity from the cabin air. The next step is a urine still, which could increase reusability to 90 percent or better. Such equipment is doubtlessly in an advanced stage of development.

Air on Salyut-6 was purified via chemical reactions with various substances, but this required chemical canisters of great bulk and weight. Banks of chlorella algae have already been tested in space—they could help absorb carbon dioxide and give off fresh oxygen, achieving a recycling of better than 80 percent.

Food on Salyut-6 was imported in canned or dehydrated form. Space gardens have produced some edible plants, first as a novelty but later as a significant dietary supplement (primarily for vitamins). Space gardens of the near future will be able to produce fruits and vegetables to the extent that 20 to 40 percent of the bulk food consumed in orbit will be grown in orbit.

This area of research is one which has already been vigorously pursued by Soviet engineers, both in space and in earthbound laboratories. The payoff is so promising that continued efforts—and continued progress—can be counted on. But it is not an easy line of research, as experience on Salyut-6 has shown: scientists are still trying to determine why it has been impossible to produce a complete plant-development cycle on board a spacecraft and why plants grown from seeds have failed to bloom or to produce seeds of their own.

Other studies have been more productive. Chlorella experiments have shown that these algae cells grow much faster in space, although they exhibit a different cell morphology whose significance is not understood. In any case, scientists have calculated that a tank with ten to fifteen gallons of chlorella in suspension would be sufficient to resupply one crewman with adequate air, protein and fresh water. As for food crops, Soviet botanists are investigating both traditional plants (wheat, cucumbers, cabbage) and unusual ones (flax, chrysanthemums, wild onions). Different methods of providing nutrients to the plants are also under investigation, including hydroponics, "aeroponics," capillary systems and aerosol methods. The only way to advance in this technology is to experiment in flight, and that is exactly what the Soviets are doing.

Throughout the 1980s, Soviet space stations will grow in size beyond the intermediate ones holding two to six crewmen. Boris Petrov wrote in 1977 that "scientists are already busy designing larger stations, for a crew of twelve to twenty, with a lifespan of up to ten years, which would replace the present small stations. This will happen as soon as it is clear that the present stations have exhausted all their possibilities." Space experts are even predicting the appearance of "space towns" with several thousand people, perhaps by the end of the century. Konstantin Feoktistov reported that conditions there would not just be acceptable, but even be "very attractive."

Although the Soviets stopped talking about sending cosmonauts to the moon back in 1969, when Apollo-11 landed and the Soviet effort failed, recent statements from space officials suggest that new man-to-the-moon plans have been made.

For example, space official Georgiy Narimanov gave the following account to a newspaper reporter in 1979: "I think that stations designed for lunar studies will figure prominently in future space exploration. With such stations put into lunar orbit, it will be feasible to periodically take cosmonauts to the lunar surface aboard small expeditionary ships. Such stations will be assembled in earth orbit and then sent to the moon." Dr. Boris Petrov, head of the Interkosmos Council for international space cooperation until his recent death, had frequently echoed Narimanov's words: "In the future, there will be a need for a lunar orbital station, which could be assembled in near-earth orbit and then towed into lunar orbit."

Given the kinds of space capabilities which are being developed for earth-orbital operations in the 1980s, a Soviet manned lunar program looks more and more feasible. Soviet manned lunar flight could progress over several plateaus, each more difficult—and rewarding—than the last. A fully fueled Soyuz with beefed-up heat shield could link up in orbit with a Proton-launched rocket unit, which would push the complex out to the moon. There, the Soyuz could maneuver into an orbit around the moon for a month-long scientific survey.

Permanent space stations could be set up in lunar orbit. This would require a specialized Salyut module, a Proton-launched rocket unit and a third Proton launch carrying additional propellant for the rocket unit. Once the Salyut reached lunar orbit, cosmonauts could be sent to it on board stripped-down Soyuz capsules launched aboard single uprated Proton boosters.

Other Proton launches could each emplace two or three tons of supplies directly on the lunar surface. With such equipment caches already set up, cosmonauts could descend from the semipermanent lunar-orbit space station on board minimum-weight "space scooters"—perhaps even just sitting on an open rocket platform in spacesuits. Soviet cosmonauts would then have reached the moon via a series of steps that ensured continuous (even permanent) manned activity around the moon.

Flights to Mars and other planets have also been the topic of official speculation, and while no timetables are given, the impression is that such feats are possible before the end of this century. Soviet space experts have made repeated assertions that their long-term space stations are paving the way for interplanetary flight.

For example, at the beginning of the Salyut-6 mission, cosmonaut Georgiy Beregovoy wrote that such long-duration space stations were important for many reasons: "Their successful development is creating the necessary conditions for interplanetary flights." Cosmonaut Grechko put it in a broader perspective in late 1978 when he wrote that "in less than twenty years the duration of space flight has increased from little more than an hour to many months. This progress will continue, and soon we will be able to stay in space for two or three years. Specialists would not be surprised if men land on Mars [in the next twenty years]."

Late in 1979 cosmonauts Georgiy Beregovoy and Valeriy Ryumin told Soviet radio listeners that manned Mars missions could begin in ten or fifteen years. A year later, after returning from his second six-month space flight in a row, the forty-one-year-old Ryumin announced his readiness to go up again: "If an expedition to Mars were being prepared and it should be necessary to hold a year-long stay in space as an intermediate step, I think that we would readily agree to such work." Chief Soviet space doctor Oleg Gazenko told European scientists the same thing in November of 1980: "It is difficult to give an exact date for a flight to Mars. But I think the basic prerequisite for such a flight exists now . . . Whether the flight happens in ten, fifteen or twenty years, I cannot say. But I believe it will be before the year 2000."

Such flamboyant forecasts are solidly based in good, sound engineering logic. Salyut is just the kind of module needed for a two- or three-year-long round trip to Mars in the mid-1990s. Current and near-future orbital operations are generating precisely the kinds of test data needed to design manned interplanetary spacecraft. In fact, the kinds of equipment which will be installed on permanent space stations will not differ significantly from the kinds of equipment needed for a Mars expedition. The life support (with most water, air and food recycled), the crew systems, the communication systems, the navigation computers—all will be ready, after having been used operationally on orbital space flight for years.

So to the question, Do the Soviets plan to send men to the moon and planets?, the answer is clear: while such flights are several years away, the Soviets today are testing equipment which would be needed to support such flights. Frequently such equipment and techniques are more sophisticated than those that would be needed merely for earth orbital operations. Soviet pronouncements on such distant goals, then, are more than just daydreams: cosmonauts and space engineers are doing their homework now to allow those dreams to be realized.

Important new information on Soviet manned space plans was revealed by *Aviation Week* magazine in mid-1980 when its space editor, Craig Covault, published what appeared to be an account of a high-level briefing from U.S. intelligence agency officials. SOVIETS DEVELOPING 12-MAN SPACE STATION was the title of the article; the lead paragraph summed it up: "Soviet Union is developing a 220,000-lb. military/scientific space station to be manned permanently in earth orbit by about 12 cosmonauts following launch in the mid-1980s on board a 10–14 million-lb. booster more powerful than the U.S. Saturn 5." Covault continued with the prediction that "the massive new booster and space station will provide the U.S.S.R with a solid base on which to mount the first manned missions to Mars in addition to initial Soviet manned lunar flights."

The news that the Soviets have resumed development of their superbooster (which was a dismal flop in the 1969–1972 period) is confirmation of a claim from Europe last year. There, German rocket expert Rolf Engel, writing in his book *Moskau militarisiert der Weltraum* (*Moscow Militarizes Space*), alleged that his own East European contacts had informed him that the big booster was being reconsidered and that the launch pads were being overhauled.

Aviation Week suggested that the first launch could come as early as 1983 and that the booster could be operational by 1985. Its payload capacity would be about as much as the Saturn-5 (its higher thrust would be offset by less efficient engines): more than 200,000 pounds in low earth orbit; about 100,000 pounds to the moon; a bit more than that in geosynchronous orbit and a bit less than that on an interplanetary trajectory.

By the time the heavy space station is to be launched,

Aviation Week suggests that a winged "space shuttle" (launched on an expendable Proton booster) would also be available to transport crew and cargo to the station. New systems to support Soviet cosmonauts on the moon would have to appear a few years later.

Covault's article did not avoid making some value judgments which bordered on editorializing: "Explosive expansion of Soviet space program activity over the past several years, especially in the manned area, has been possible because the Russians have been providing their program with real funding increases of 3–5 percent per year, a sharp contrast to the U.S. congressional and presidential attitude toward the U.S. program since the end of the Apollo project.... These new Russian developments of expanding booster power with a Saturn-5–class vehicle, development of a permanent space station larger than Skylab and planned use of winged, reusable space transports indicate that the decades the 1980s and 1990s will be full of intense Russian manned space activity. Many managers in the U.S. space program hope the military strategic and scientific significance of this major Russian development push will not be lost in planning for the space shuttle and will stimulate full use of its capabilities."

The aerospace magazine closed the article with a quotation from a presidential briefing prepared by the National Security Council in late 1979: "The currently operational military and civil Soviet manned program could provide them with significant scientific, technical, political and strategic advances.... If we do not expend the thought, the effort and the money required, then another more progressive nation will."

Soviet space vehicles will be flying in great numbers over the next several years. Their current launch rate of one hundred satellites a year (compared to the United States rate of twenty) will doubtlessly continue, but such numbers—and the different types which they break down into—will be of interest mainly only to statisticians. For the Western public, these

Soviet space shots are both invisible (they aren't newsworthy enough) and uninteresting (what news is printed consists of dry facts without any context or analysis).

Furthermore, there's little reason to expect the quality of American news-media coverage of Soviet space activities to improve much, either. For weeks in 1978, Western correspondents in Moscow kept repeating how wonderful it was that the Progress-1 robot tanker had transferred "liquid oxygen and kerosene" onto the Salyut-6 space station; but it hadn't (the fuels were nitrogen tetroxide and hydrazine), and no Russian source had ever said it had. Later in 1978 a leading New York newspaper science editor described how the dying Skylab space station might soon be followed to a fiery doom by the "empty derelict Salyut-6"; the description would have startled the two cosmonauts who had been happily working on board the station for weeks, unknown to the science editor. When Salyut-6 cosmonauts turned their infrared telescope toward the moon, darkened by earth's shadow during a total lunar eclipse, Western wire services related how the earth-orbiting space station had changed course to allow it to photograph the hidden far side (the "dark side") of the moon. (It hadn't; the reporters had confused "dark side" with "far side.") Similarly, when a network television news program showed films of a 1975 Soviet space flight while claiming they were current shots of the Salyut-6 mission three years later, the science editor responded to complaints by demanding, "How should I be expected to tell Russian cosmonauts apart?"

No, the facts and figures of this decade's Soviet space spectacular are bound to be mind-boggling enough without the additional garble factor introduced by Western journalism. And the really fascinating side of these space activities will be the human angle, the personal triumphs and tragedies, the practical jokes, the ironies, the disasters. If the past is any indication, this aspect will not easily make itself known to us: official Soviet spokesmen will spare no effort to exploit, distort or hide such events, depending on how the events might affect the image which is supposed to be projected.

The establishment of a permanent Kosmograd space colony is bound to be an exciting human adventure. There will be cases of unexpected breakthroughs in research; there will be fights among crewmen. Some cosmonauts may come to spend more time in space than they do on earth—and it may have something to do with their wives or bosses.

The second Soviet woman cosmonaut will go up in this decade, possibly just a few months before the first American woman astronaut. Guest-cosmonaut flights are bound to continue, with representatives from a long string of countries (Sweden, Korea, Palestine, Yugoslavia, Finland, Afghanistan?)—perhaps including a teen-aged Young Pioneer (a Soviet Boy Scout). Along the way, Moscow might decide to send up representatives of non-Slavic Soviet nationalities, such as Lithuanians, Armenians, Kazakhs, Estonians, Azerbaijanis; whether or not they would be *more* politically reliable than East Europeans is a question for the Kremlin to ponder. The most significant guest-cosmonaut flight will be the one on which a second citizen of any of the cooperating nations gets to fly—he (or she) will have to earn that ticket via personal (not political) merit.

The appearance of another Russian spacewoman (and an elitist one, too—she'll probably be a doctor or a biologist) will take the public relations pressure off the Nikolayev-Tereshkova marriage, which might then break up. Meanwhile, their daughter Yelena will be old enough to get married in the mid-1980s. Other space offspring may have inspiring accomplishments: we'll probably see at least one cosmonaut candidate whose father was a cosmonaut. That, too, would be an appealing popular development.

More top Soviet space officials will die and thus allow us to learn their names. Authorized biographies of them, as well as of already publicized space officials, such as Glushko and Kosberg, will provide additional insights—and additional

carefully designed deceptions. Perhaps the future will reveal
documents that would truly set the record straight on Soviet
space history—and the still-missing memoirs of Korolev
would be the greatest prize. The Soviet underground press,
the *samizdat,* may produce some fascinating items along
these lines in the next decade; new defectors will add their
own insights.

Other glimpses behind the official Soviet space façade can
be provided by the guest cosmonauts. It isn't necessary for
one to defect (although that possibility certainly exists and
will grow stronger); later participants will be from countries
not under Soviet control—and with news agencies not subject to Soviet censorship. They are sure to see and hear a lot
of fascinating things during their sojourns in Starry Town.

A higher volume of manned space activities is bound to
exact its price: sometime in the 1980s, a breakdown on a
Soviet spacecraft may lead to the deaths of its crewmen. Even
if not, at least a few emergency landings would be likely;
perhaps several days of drama could follow an unexpected
splashdown in a distant corner of an ocean. And with a large
number of working people permanently in space, the odds go
up that one or two will die there, from medical complications
or accidents (probably on a spacewalk—one of the most
dangerous activities and, as it becomes more commonplace,
likely to be conducted with less training, caution and rigid
safety standards).

Back on earth, some of the earlier cosmonauts (and astronauts) will be approaching the age bracket in which actu-
arial tables predict an increasing frequency of natural deaths.
There is every reason, therefore, to expect the 1980s to witness additional cosmonaut funerals—but by then these
events may not be earthshaking enough to warrant such
high-level honors as interment of ashes in the Kremlin Wall;
the nearby Novodevichy Cemetery may have to be sufficiently honorable.

Attitudes of space-farers are also bound to evolve. Space

flight will no longer be a once-in-a-lifetime thrill. For many of the space specialists aboard Soviet space stations a decade from now, working in space will be just another technological profession. Even the carefully cultivated hero worship which the Soviet Union wraps around its space conquerors will be lost: future Soviet cosmonauts—by virtue of their sheer numbers—will probably not be known by face to the average Soviet citizens. Such cosmonauts, back from a year-long tour in space, will be able to walk the streets of Moscow unrecognized. And someday the Soviet practice of issuing posters, portrait postcards and authorized inspirational biographies of every cosmonaut will just become too tedious and too uninteresting to the Russian public: outstanding heroes and martyrs will continue to get the publicity, but most working cosmonauts will fade into obscurity. A hint of this may come with the first Soviet manned space shot that does *not* appear on the front page of *Pravda.* (Already a few "routine" launches have been demoted to below the fold.)

Gradually, a few of the more perceptive and adventurous people living on these Soviet space habitats may come to see outer space as their normal environment. The periodic rotations earthside would be temporary interruptions in an ordinary state of space habitation. Some older cosmonauts may feel this way—and with no dependents on earth (their children would be grown, their spouses assigned on space stations as well), they could come to accept space as home. In parallel with these conceptual changes, there would be people for whom medical complications (a serious injury, a disease or an unexpectedly severe adaptation to pure weightlessness) would bar the door for any safe return to the crushing gravity of earth. Such causes could lead to the first true "space colonists"—people who for any number of reasons expect to live out their lives in space.

By the turn of the millennium, there could be a few hundred people distributed among a dozen Soviet space outposts (including ships between here and Mars or the asteroids, or on Mars and the asteroids themselves). Many of these people will be able to think of themselves as permanent space settlers. They will be the parents of the first babies born in space.

This would all be in fulfillment of the dreams of Tsiolkovskiy a century earlier. The Russians steadfastly believe in that dream and have loyally cherished it; they have worked and sacrificed for it and now they are moving to harvest its reality. These accomplishments may be remembered long after the propaganda and political motivations have been forgotten—and in the long run, perhaps that's only fair.

Appendices

Biographies

Aksyonov, Vladimir (b. 1935, c. 1973*). Former air force pilot (1953–1957), now a civilian engineer-cosmonaut specializing in test flights of new equipment, including the first use of the MKF-6 survey camera on Soyuz-22 (1976) and the first manned flight of the upgraded Soyuz-T (1980). (Russian)

Andreyev, Boris (b. 1940, c. 1970). Civilian engineer-cosmonaut on backup team for Apollo-Soyuz (1973–1975). Has apparently since then been grounded. (Russian)

Artyukhin, Yuriy (b. 1930, c. 1963). Military engineer-cosmonaut on crew of first successful Salyut mission (1974), since retired. (Russian)

Belyayev, Pavel (b. 1925, c. 1960, d. 1970). Commander of Voskhod-2 spacewalk mission (1965), then apparently tagged to fly first Soviet man-to-moon mission, later canceled. Died after surgery for peritonitis. (Russian)

Beregovoy, Georgiy (b. 1921, c. 1964). Veteran WWII fighter pilot, later test pilot. Was oldest man ever to enter cosmonaut training. Flew first successful Soyuz mission (1968), is now cosmonaut training official. (Ukrainian)

*c. denotes year became cosmonaut.

Bykovskiy, Valeriy (b. 1934, c. 1960). Flew Vostok-5 (1963), was to have commanded Soyuz-2 (1967), but was mysteriously grounded for almost a decade. Then commanded Soyuz-22 (1976) and Soyuz-31 (1978—East German visit to Salyut-6) and is in line for additional missions. (Russian)

Chelomey, ? (b. 1910?). Soviet rocket engineer whose political instincts kept him in favor with Stalin, and who was one of Korolev's enemies. Ran his own rocket center specializing in military missiles.

Dobrovolskiy, Georgiy (b. 1928, c. 1963, d. 1971). Commander of first-ever Salyut space crew, perished during return to earth when air leaked out of Soyuz-11 capsule. (Ukrainian)

Dyomin, Lev (b. 1926, c. 1963). Military engineer-cosmonaut on aborted Soyuz-15 mission to Salyut-3 (1974), now retired. (Russian)

Dzhanibekov, Vladimir (b. 1942, c. 1970). Backup pilot-cosmonaut for Apollo-Soyuz (1973–1975), commander of Soyuz-27 (1978), transferred to guest-cosmonaut program (1979–1981). (Russian, adopted wife's Kazakh name)

Feoktistov, Konstantin (b. 1926, c. 1964–1965). Leading spacecraft designer, was passenger on three-man Voskhod (1964) and is now a top official in Salyut space-station program. (Russian)

Filipchenko, Anatoliy (b. 1928, c. 1963). Pilot-cosmonaut, commanded Soyuz-7 (1969) during the triple spacecraft mission, commanded Soyuz-16 (1974) dress rehearsal for Apollo-Soyuz mission, is probably now retired. (Ukrainian)

Gagarin, Yuriy (b. 1934, c. 1960, d. 1968). First man in space (1961), spent five years on ceremonial duties, returned to train for Soyuz mission, but was killed in training jet crash along with flight instructor Vladimir Seryogin. (Russian)

Gazenko, Oleg (b. 1909). M.D., leading Soviet space-medicine expert.

Glazkov, Yuriy (b. 1939, c. 1965). Military engineer-cosmonaut, visited Salyut-5 aboard Soyuz-24 (1977). (Russian)

Glushko, Valentin (b. 1908). Leading Soviet rocket-engine designer, long-time friend and colleague of Korolev's.

Gorbatko, Viktor (b. 1934, c. 1960). Pilot-cosmonaut, last of his cosmonaut class to fly (Soyuz-7, 1969), then visited Salyut-5 aboard Soyuz-24 (1977) and visited Salyut-6 with Vietnamese copilot (Soyuz-37, 1980). (Ukrainian)

Grechko, Georgiy (b. 1931, c. 1966). Civilian engineer-cosmonaut, spent a month aboard Salyut-4 (via Soyuz-17, 1975) and three months aboard Salyut-6 (via Soyuz-26, 1977–1978), during which he made a courageous mission-saving spacewalk. (Russian)

Gubarev, Aleksey (b. 1931, c. 1963). Pilot-cosmonaut, commanded first visit to Salyut-4 (via Soyuz-17, 1975) and flew first guest-cosmonaut mission to Salyut-6 (Soyuz-28, 1978, with Czechoslovakian copilot). (Russian)

Ivanchenkov, Aleksandr (b. 1940, c. 1970). Civilian engineer-cosmonaut assigned as backup during Apollo-Soyuz (1973–1975), then flew 140-day mission on Salyut-6 (via Soyuz-29, 1978). (Russian)

"Ivanov," Dmitriy (b. 1930, c. 1960–1969). Pilot-cosmonaut who was backup commander of Voskhod-2 (1965), then was medically disqualified in 1969, after which his face was airbrushed out of official pictures. Identified only by first name in 1978 book; "Ivanov" is Russian equivalent of "Jones" and will have to do until Soviets tell more.

Kamanin, Nikolay (b. 1912?). Soviet air hero and WWII veteran, became first commander of cosmonaut corps in 1960, overseeing training, recruitment and ideological reliability. After disasters and fatalities in 1967–1971, was retired involuntarily and replaced by Shatalov.

Khrunov, Yevgeniy (b. 1933, c. 1960). Pilot-cosmonaut, walked in space from Soyuz-5 to Soyuz-4 (1969), then was grounded for ten years before returning to flight status in guest-cosmonaut program. (Russian)

Klimuk, Pyotr (b. 1942, c. 1965). Outstanding member of new generation of cosmonauts, commanded three space missions by age thirty-six: Soyuz-13 (1973), Soyuz-18 visit to Salyut-4 (1975), Soyuz-30 visit to Salyut-6 with Polish copilot (1978). (Byelorussian)

Komarov, Vladimir (b. 1927, c. 1960, d. 1967). Leading cosmonaut of first group, was tasked to command first multi-man flight (Voskhod, 1964) and first planned space linkup (Soyuz-1, 1967), on which flight he died. (Russian)

Korniev, Ivan (b. 1942?). Name given to Western newsmen in 1967 of a recently selected candidate cosmonaut; has never shown up. Presumably—but not proven—was one of the "six to eight" dead cosmonaut trainees admitted to by a leading Soviet cosmonaut in 1974.

Korolev, Sergey (b. 1906, d. 1966). Ukrainian rocket engineer and space-flight visionary who survived Stalinist labor camps to emerge as chief designer of the Soviet space program, persuading politicians to pay for space missions but in exchange having to perform frequent space stunts and often taking bold gambles.

Kovalyonok, Vladimir (b. 1942, c. 1967). Pilot-cosmonaut, flew aborted Soyuz-25 (1977) and was given second chance aboard Soyuz-29 (1978), spending 140 days aboard Salyut-6. (Byelorussian)

Kubasov, Valeriy (b. 1935, c. 1966). Civilian engineer-cosmonaut, rode on Soyuz-6 (1969), trained for aborted Salyut missions (1971–1973), then flew on Apollo-Soyuz space-linkup mission (Soyuz-19, 1975); commanded Soyuz-36 visit to Salyut-6 with Hungarian copilot (1980). (Russian)

Lazarev, Vasiliy (b. 1928, c. 1966). Test pilot and flight surgeon (M.D., 1952), was ideal choice to command long-duration Salyut mission, but never did: missions were canceled or cut back (Soyuz-12, 1973) or crashed back to earth (unnumbered Soyuz, 1975). Was finally grounded and assigned to supervise training of guest cosmonauts. (Russian)

Lebedev, Valentin (b. 1942, c. 1972). Civilian engineer-cosmonaut, made astrophysics observations on Soyuz-13 (1973), trained for Salyut-4 and Salyut-6, was to have flown on Soyuz-35 (1980), but broke knee in training and was replaced by Ryumin. (Russian)

Leonov, Aleksey (b. 1934, c. 1960). First man to walk in space (Voskhod-2, 1965), was trained for abortive man-to-moon program and Salyut missions (1971–1973) and was finally assigned to command Soviet half of U.S.-U.S.S.R. space linkup (Soyuz-19, 1975). (Russian)

Lyakhov, Vladimir (b. 1941, c. 1967). Pilot-cosmonaut, commanded 175-day mission on Salyut-6 (1979). (Ukrainian)

Makarov, Oleg (b. 1933, c. 1967). Civilian engineer-cosmonaut, flew on two-day Soyuz-12 (1973), aborted unnamed Soyuz (1975), first double-docking mission (Soyuz-27 to Salyut-6, 1978), and Soyuz T-3 repair flight (1980). (Russian)

Malyshev, Yuriy (b. 1941, c. 1967). Soviet pilot-cosmonaut, commanded first manned mission of new model Soyuz-T (1980). (Russian)

Maslennikov, Anatoliy (b. 1934?, c. 1960–1962). Rumored name (unconfirmed) of Soviet candidate cosmonaut known to have been dropped from program for medical reasons or for academic or ideological shortcomings. Face has been erased from official photographs.

Nedelin, Mitrofan (b. 1902, d. 1960). Soviet artillery general who organized Strategic Missile Forces in 1957–1959 and was directly responsible for all Soviet rocket programs; ordered the inspection of a rocket that subsequently exploded, killing himself along with dozens of engineers, technicians and guards.

Nikolayev, Andrian (b. 1929, c. 1960). Pilot-cosmonaut, former lumberjack, flew Vostok-3 (1962) and Soyuz-9 (1970), now a cosmonaut-training bureaucrat. (Russian-Chuvash)

Nikolayeva, Yelena (b. 1964). Only child of cosmonauts Nikolayev and Tereshkova.

Nikolayeva-Tereshkova (*see* Tereshkova)

Patsayev, Viktor (b. 1933, c. 1967, d. 1971). Civilian engineer-cosmonaut on first manned space-station mission (1971). Perished during return to earth due to cabin air leak. (Russian)

Popov, Leonid (b. 1945, c. 1970). Pilot-cosmonaut, commanded 185-day Salyut-6 mission (via Soyuz-35, 1980). (Ukrainian)

Popovich, Pavel (b. 1930, c. 1960). Pilot-cosmonaut, flew Vostok-4 (1962). Activities from 1964 to 1972 are unknown. Commanded first successful Salyut mission (Salyut-3 via Soyuz-14, 1974). (Ukrainian)

Romanenko, Yuriy (b. 1944, c. 1970). Pilot-cosmonaut, was backup crewman for Apollo-Soyuz project (1973–1975), then commanded first visit to Salyut-6 (via Soyuz-26, 1977–1978), where he nearly lost his life in a spacewalk mishap. Then was transferred to guest-cosmonaut program, where he flew Soyuz-38 (1980) with a Cuban copilot (the first black in space). (Ukrainian)

Rozhdestvenskiy, Valeriy (b. 1939, c. 1965). Military engineer-cosmonaut, supported Salyut-3 mission (1974) and rode aborted

Salyut-5 visit (aboard Soyuz-23, 1976), which was the first and only manned Soviet spacecraft to land in water (accidentally). Was main radio communicator ("CAPCOM") for Salyut-6 (1977–1980). (Russian)

Rukavishnikov, Nikolay (b. 1932, c. 1967). Civilian engineer-cosmonaut, frustrated in attempt to visit Salyut-1 aboard Soyuz-10 (1971). Flew Apollo-Soyuz dress-rehearsal mission (Soyuz-16, 1974), then became first civilian to command a space mission (the aborted Soyuz-33, with Bulgarian copilot, 1979). (Russian)

Ryumin, Valeriy (b. 1939, c. 1973). Most experienced civilian engineer-cosmonaut. Accumulated 362 days of flight experience on three missions to Salyut-6 (Soyuz-25 in 1977, Soyuz-32 in 1979, Soyuz-35 in 1980). (Russian)

Sarafanov, Gennadiy (b. 1942, c. 1965). Pilot-cosmonaut who commanded abortive Soyuz-15 linkup mission to Salyut-3 (1974). Present status unknown. (Russian)

Sevastyanov, Vitaliy (b. 1935, c. 1967). Civilian engineer-cosmonaut aboard Soyuz-9 (1970) and Soyuz-18 visit to Salyut-4 (1975). Now assigned to Soyuz-T program. (Russian)

Shatalov, Vladimir (b. 1927, c. 1963). Three-time space veteran (commanded Soyuz-4 and Soyuz-8 in 1969 and Soyuz-10 in 1971). Replaced Kamenin as head of cosmonaut corps in 1971, has re-formed flight-training programs and become ideological spokesman and watchman for cosmonauts. (Russian)

Shonin, Georgiy (b. 1935, c. 1960). Pilot-cosmonaut who commanded Soyuz-6 (1969). Current status and whereabouts unknown. (Ukrainian)

Tereshkova, Valentina (b. 1937, c. 1961–1963). First and only woman in space, was one of four trainees (other three were dismissed after mission). After flight, became diplomatic and propaganda activist, married cosmonaut Nikolayev (one child, a daughter), from whom is possibly now separated. (Russian)

Titov, Gherman (b. 1935, c. 1960). Pilot-cosmonaut on second Soviet orbital flight (1961), later grounded due to medical problems. Current status and whereabouts unknown. (Russian)

Volkov, Vladislav "Vadim" (b. 1935, c. 1966, d. 1971). Civilian engineer-cosmonaut on Soyuz-7 (1969) and on first Salyut space mission (1971), during which he perished due to air leak. (Russian)

Volynov, Boris (b. 1934, c. 1960). Pilot-cosmonaut who commanded Soyuz-5 linkup (1969) and Salyut-5 military reconnaissance mission (via Soyuz-21, 1976). (Russian)

Yangel, Mikhail (b. 1911, d. 1971). Soviet rocket designer. Ally of and later successor to Korolev.

Yegorov, Boris (b. 1937, c. 1964–1965). Space doctor, passenger aboard the first multi-man spacecraft (Voskhod, 1964). Now heads flight-medicine laboratory. (Russian)

Yeliseyev, Aleksey (b. 1934, c. 1966–1972). Civilian engineer-cosmonaut, made three space missions with Shatalov (in 1969–1971). Now is leading official at Soviet Mission Control Center near Moscow. (Russian)

Zholobov, Vitaliy (b. 1937, c. 1963). Military engineer-cosmonaut aboard Salyut-5 reconnaissance mission (via Soyuz-21, 1976). May have since been grounded for medical problems. (Ukrainian)

Zudov, Vyacheslav (b. 1942, c. 1965). Pilot-cosmonaut who commanded aborted Soyuz-23 linkup with Salyut-5 (1976) and made forced landing on a lake during a midnight snowstorm. (Russian)

Guest Cosmonauts

Czech, Polish and East German guests began training December 1976; Bulgarian, Hungarian, Cuban, Mongolian and Rumanian guests in March 1978; Vietnamese in March 1979; French in September 1980.

Czechoslovakia (Soyuz-28, 1978): Vladimir Remek (b. 1949), with backup Oldrich Pelczak

Poland (Soyuz-30, 1978): Miroslaw Hermaszewski (b. 1941), with backup Zenon Jankowski

East Germany (Soyuz-31, 1978*): Sigmund Jähn (b. 1937), with backup Eberhard Köllner.

Bulgaria (Soyuz-33, 1979—failure): Georgi Ivanov (b. 1939), with backup Aleksandr Aleksandrov

Hungary (Soyuz-36, 1980*): Bertalan Farkas (b. 1946), with backup Bela Magyari

Vietnam (Soyuz-37, 1980*): Pham Tuan (b. 1951), with backup Bui Thanh Liem

Cuba (Soyuz-38, 1980): Arnaldo Tamayo-Mendez (b. 1941) with backup Jose Lopez-Falcon

*Achieved Soyuz switch, returning to earth in older Soyuz.

Mongolia (Soyuz-39, 1981): Jugderdemidiin Gurragcha (b. 1947), with backup Maidarjabyn Ganzorig

Rumania (Soyuz-40, 1981): Dumitru Prunariu (b. 1952), with backup Dumitru Dediu

France (due mid-1982): Jean-Loup Chrétien and Patrick Baudry

India (due 1982)

Soviet Man–Related Space Shots

Name	Launch	Duration	Crew (Backup) and Call Sign	Comments
Sputnik	Oct. 4, 1957	3 months	unmanned	First artificial satellite
Sputnik-2	Nov. 3, 1957	5 months	one dog	First animal in orbit
Luna-1	Jan. 2, 1959	forever	unmanned	First successful moon shot
Spaceship	May 15, 1960	4 days	unmanned	Reentry guidance failed
none	July 1960	0	two dogs?	Reported launch failure
Spaceship-2	Aug. 18, 1960	1 day	two dogs	Successful recovery
Spaceship-3	Dec. 1, 1960	1 day	two dogs	Burned up on reentry
none	Dec. 1960	0	two dogs?	Reported launch failure
Spaceship-4	Mar. 9, 1961	1½ hours	one dog	Successful single orbit
Spaceship-5	Mar. 25, 1961	1½ hours	one dog	Successful single orbit
Vostok	Apr. 12, 1961	1½ hours	Gagarin (Titov) "Cedar"	First manned space flight
Vostok-2	Aug. 6, 1961	1 day	Titov (Nikolayev) "Eagle"	First eat, sleep in space

	Date	Duration	Crew	Notes
Vostok-3	Aug. 11, 1962	4 days	Nikolayev (Bykovskiy) "Falcon"	Longest flight
Vostok-4	Aug. 12, 1962	3 days	Popovich (Komarov) "Golden Eagle"	Joint flight with Vostok-3
Vostok-5	June 14, 1963	5 days	Bykovskiy (Volynov) "Hawk"	Longest flight
Vostok-6	June 16, 1963	3 days	Tereshkova (?) "Seagull"	First and only woman in space
Kosmos-47	Oct. 6, 1964	1 day	unmanned	Voskhod precursor
Voskhod	Oct. 12, 1964	1 day	Komarov (Volynov) "Ruby" Feoktistov (?) Yegorov (?)	First multi-man vehicle
Kosmos-57	Feb. 22, 1965	1 day	unmanned	Air-lock deployment test
Voskhod-2	Mar. 18, 1965	1 day	Belyayev ("Ivanov") "Diamond" Leonov (Khrunov)	First spacewalk
Kosmos-110	Feb. 22, 1966	22 days	two dogs	Voskhod bio-satellite
Kosmos-133	Nov. 28, 1966	2 days	unmanned	First Soyuz test, success?
Kosmos-140	Feb. 7, 1967	2 days	unmanned	Soyuz precursor
Kosmos-146	Mar. 10, 1967	?	unmanned	Lunar program test, on Proton
Kosmos-154	Apr. 8, 1967	?	unmanned	Ditto
Soyuz-1	Apr. 23, 1967	1 day	Komarov (Gagarin) "Ruby"	Pilot killed
Soyuz-2	Apr. 24, 1967 —canceled		Bykovskiy (Belyayev?) "Hawk" Yeliseyev (Kubasov?) Khrunov (Gorbatko?)	Linkup/spacewalk planned
Kosmos-186	Oct. 27, 1967	4 days	unmanned	Soyuz linkup chase ship
Kosmos-188	Oct. 30, 1967	3 days	unmanned	Soyuz linkup target ship
none	Nov. 1967	0	unmanned	Reported moon-shot launch failure
Zond-4	Mar. 2, 1968	6 days?	unmanned	Practice moon shot
none	Apr. 1968	0	unmanned	Reported moon-shot failure

Name	Launch	Duration	Crew (Backup) and Call Sign	Comments
Kosmos-212	Apr. 14, 1968	5 days	unmanned	Soyuz linkup success
Kosmos-213	Apr. 15, 1968	5 days	unmanned	Soyuz linkup success
Kosmos-238	Aug. 28, 1968	4 days	unmanned	Soyuz precursor or target?
Zond-5	Sept. 15, 1968	6 days	unmanned	Successful circumlunar flight
Soyuz-2	Oct. 25, 1968	3 days	unmanned	Rendezvous target
Soyuz-3	Oct. 26, 1968	4 days	Beregovoy (Shatalov) "Argon"	First successful Soyuz
Zond-6	Nov. 10, 1968	6 days	unmanned	Successful circumlunar flight
Zond	Dec. 1968 —canceled		Belyayev (Leonov?) "Diamond"	Man-around-moon voyage
Soyuz-4	Jan. 14, 1969	3 days	Shatalov (Filipchenko) "Amur"	Linkup with Soyuz-5
Soyuz-5	Jan. 15, 1969	3 days	Volynov (Shonin) "Baykal" / Yeliseyev (Kubasov) / Khrunov (Gorbatko)	Two men spacewalk to Soyuz-4
none	June 1969	0	unmanned	Reported super-booster disaster
Zond-7	Aug. 7, 1969	6 days	unmanned	Successful circumlunar flight
Soyuz-6	Oct. 11, 1969	5 days	Shonin (?) "Antaeus" / Kubasov (?)	Engineering experiments
Soyuz-7	Oct. 12, 1969	5 days	Filipchenko (?) "Snowstorm" / Volkov (?) / Gorbatko (?)	Joint flight with Soyuz-6, 8
Soyuz-8	Oct. 13, 1969	5 days	Shatalov (Nikolayev) "Granite" / Yeliseyev (Sevastyanov)	Docking with Soyuz-7 fails

Spacecraft	Date	Duration	Crew	Notes
none	Nov. 1969	0	unmanned	Reported moon-ship hardware failure
Soyuz-9	June 1, 1970	18 days	Nikolayev (Lazarev) "Falcon" Sevastyanov (Makarov?)	Longest flight
Zond-8	Oct. 20, 1970	6 days	unmanned	Successful circumlunar flight
Kosmos-379	Nov. 24, 1970	?	unmanned	Moon-ship equipment test?
Kosmos-382	Dec. 2, 1970	?	unmanned	Proton-launched moon-ship (?) test
Kosmos-398	Feb. 26, 1971	?	unmanned	Moon-ship equipment test?
Salyut-1	Apr. 19, 1971	6 months	unmanned	First space station
Soyuz-10	Apr. 22, 1971	2 days	Shatalov (?) "Granite" Yeliseyev (?) Rukavishnikov (?)	Docking with Salyut-1 fails
Soyuz-11	June 6, 1971	24 days	Dobrovolskiy (?) "Amber" Volkov (?) Patsayev (?)	Visit Salyut-1, die on return
none	June 1971	0	unmanned	Reported super-booster failure
Kosmos-434	Aug. 12, 1971	?	unmanned	Moon-ship equipment test?
Kosmos-496	June 26, 1972	6 days	unmanned	Soyuz requalification
none	July 29, 1972	0	unmanned	Reported Salyut launch failure
none	Nov. 1972	0	unmanned	Reported super-booster failure
Salyut-2	Apr. 3, 1973	22 days	unmanned	Out-of-control Salyut
Kosmos-557	May 11, 1973	20 days	unmanned	Out-of-control Salyut
Kosmos-573	June 15, 1973	2 days	unmanned	Soyuz requalification
Soyuz-12	Sept. 27, 1973	2 days	Lazarev (Gubarev) "Ural" Makarov (Grechko)	Test Soyuz improvements

Name	Launch	Duration	Crew (Backup) and Call Sign	Comments
Kosmos-613	Nov. 30, 1973	60 days	unmanned Soyuz	Salyut-4 ferry precursor
Soyuz-13	Dec. 18, 1973	8 days	Klimuk (?) "Caucasus" Lebedev (Sevastyanov?)	Astrophysics observations
Kosmos-638	Apr. 3, 1974	10 days	unmanned	ASTP precursor
Kosmos-656	May 27, 1974	2 days	unmanned Soyuz	Salyut-3 ferry precursor
Salyut-3	June 24, 1974	3 months	unmanned	Military space station
Soyuz-14	July 3, 1974	16 days	Popovich (Volynov) "Golden Eagle" Artyukhin (Zholobov)	First successful Salyut mission
Kosmos-670	Aug. 6, 1974	3 days	unmanned Soyuz	New autopilot test?
Kosmos-672	Aug. 12, 1974	6 days	unmanned	ASTP precursor
Soyuz-15	Aug. 26, 1974	2 days	Sarafanov (Zudov) "Danube" Dyomin (Rozhdestvenskiy)	Linkup with Salyut-3 failed
Soyuz-16	Dec. 6, 1974	6 days	Filipchenko (Romanenko) "Snowstorm" Rukavishnikov (Ivanchenkov)	Dress rehearsal for Apollo linkup
Salyut-4	Dec. 26, 1974	2 years	unmanned	Scientific space station
Soyuz-17	Jan. 10, 1975	30 days	Gubarev (Lazarev?) "Zenith" Grechko (Makarov?)	Successful visit to Salyut-4
Soyuz-X	Apr. 5, 1975	15 minutes	Lazarev (Klimuk) "Urals" Makarov (Sevastyanov)	Launch abort, crew nearly killed
Soyuz-18	May 24, 1975	63 days	Klimuk (Kovalyonok) "Caucasus" Sevastyanov (Lebedev?)	Successful visit to Salyut-4
Soyuz-19	July 15, 1975	6 days	Leonov (Dzhanibekov) "Union" Kubasov (Andreyev)	Linkup with American Apollo

Mission	Date	Duration	Crew	Description
Kosmos-772	Sept. 29, 1975	2 days	unmanned Soyuz	New autopilot test
Soyuz-20	Nov. 17, 1975	90 days	unmanned	Automatic docking, long duration
Salyut-5	June 22, 1976	1 year	unmanned	Military space station
Soyuz-21	July 6, 1976	49 days	Volynov (?) "Baykal" / Zholobov (?)	Visit Salyut-5, return early
Soyuz-22	Sept. 15, 1976	8 days	Bykovskiy (Malyshev) "Hawk" / Aksyonov (Strekalov)	Earth photography in most northern orbit
Soyuz-23	Oct. 14, 1976	2 days	Zudov (Gorbatko) "Rodon" / Rozhdestvenskiy (Glazkov)	Linkup with Salyut-5 fails, splashdown in lake
Kosmos-869	Nov. 8, 1976	18 days	unmanned Soyuz-T	First Soyuz-T test flight
Kosmos-881/882	Dec. 10, 1976	1½ hours	two unmanned ships	Unexplained Proton launch
Soyuz-24	Feb. 7, 1977	18 days	Gorbatko (?) "Terek" / Glazkov (?)	Short mission to close down Salyut-5
Kosmos-929	July 17, 1977	200 days	unmanned Salyut	Probable Salyut-6, Progress precursor
none	Aug. 1977	0	two unmanned ships	Reported unexplained test failure
Salyut-6	Sept. 29, 1977	to the present	unmanned	Second-generation space station
Soyuz-25	Oct. 9, 1977	2 days	Kovalyonok (Romanenko) "Photon" / Ryumin (Ivanchenkov)	Salyut-6 linkup fails
Soyuz-26	Dec. 10, 1977	96 days	Romanenko (Kovalyonok) "Taymyr" / Grechko (Ivanchenkov)	Successful Salyut-6 visit
Soyuz-27	Jan. 10, 1978	6 days	Dzhanibekov (Kovalyonok) "Pamir" / Makarov (Ivanchenkov)	First exchange of Soyuz after double docking
Progress-1	Jan. 20, 1978	19 days	unmanned supply ship	Resupply mission
Soyuz-28	Mar. 2, 1978	8 days	Gubarev (Rukavishnikov) "Zenith" / Remek (Pelczak)	Propaganda spectacular

Name	Launch	Duration	Crew (Backup) and Call Sign	Comments
Kosmos-997/998	Mar. 30, 1978	1½ hours	two unmanned ships	Unexplained single orbit, Proton launch
Kosmos-1001	Apr. 4, 1978	11 days	unmanned Soyuz-T	Possible failure
Soyuz-29	June 15, 1978	140 days	Kovalyonok (Lyakhov) "Photon" Ivanchenkov (Ryumin)	Successful Salyut-6 visit
Soyuz-30	June 27, 1978	8 days	Klimuk (Kubasov) "Caucasus" Hermaszewski (Jankowski)	Propaganda junket
Progress-2	July 7, 1978	28 days	unmanned	Supply ship for Salyut-6
Progress-3	Aug. 7, 1978	16 days	unmanned	Supply ship for Salyut-6
Soyuz-31	Aug. 26, 1978	8 days	Bykovskiy (Gorbatko) "Hawk" Jähn (Köllner)	Soyuz exchange, plus politics
Progress-4	Oct. 4, 1978	21 days	unmanned	Supply ship for Salyut-6
Kosmos-1074	Jan. 31, 1979	60 days	unmanned Soyuz-T	Long solo test flight
Kosmos-1100/1101	May 22, 1979	1½ hours	two unmanned ships	Unexplained Proton launch
Soyuz-32	Feb. 25, 1979	175 days	Lyakhov (Popov) "Proton" Ryumin (Lebedev)	Successful Salyut-6 visit
Progress-5	Mar. 12, 1979	24 days	unmanned	Supply ship for Salyut-6
Soyuz-33	Apr. 10, 1979	2 days	Rukavishnikov (Romanenko) "Saturn" Ivanov (Aleksandrov)	Rendezvous fails
Progress-6	May 13, 1979	27 days	unmanned	Supply ship for Salyut-6
Soyuz-34	June 6, 1979	74 days	unmanned (returned manned)	Replacement-and-supply mission
Progress-7	June 28, 1979	22 days	unmanned	Supply ship for Salyut-6

Mission	Date	Duration	Crew	Purpose
Soyuz-T	Dec. 16, 1979	100 days	unmanned	Test linkup to Salyut-6
Progress-8	Mar. 27, 1980	30 days	unmanned	Supply ship for Salyut-6
Soyuz-35	Apr. 9, 1980	185 days	Popov (Kovalyonok) "Dniepr" Ryumin (Strekalov?)	Successful Salyut-6 visit
Progress-9	Apr. 27, 1980	20 days	unmanned	Supply ship for Salyut-6
Soyuz-36	May 26, 1980	8 days	Kubasov (Dzhanibekov) "Orion" Farkas (Magyari)	Soyuz exchange, plus politics
Soyuz T-2	June 5, 1980	4 days	Malyshev (Kizim) "Jupiter" Aksyonov (Makarov?)	Test new, improved manned spacecraft
Progress-10	June 29, 1980	22 days	unmanned	Supply ship for Salyut-6
Soyuz-37	July 23, 1980	8 days	Gorbatko (Bykovskiy) "Terek" Tuan (Liem)	Soyuz exchange, plus politics
Soyuz-38	Sept. 18, 1980	8 days	Romanenko (Khrunov) "Taymyr" Tamayo (Lopez)	Propaganda junket
Progress-11	Sept. 28, 1980	60 days	unmanned	Supply ship for Salyut-6
Salyut-6	Sept. 29, 1977 to the present		unmanned	Second-generation space station
Soyuz T-3	Nov. 27, 1980	13 days	Kizim (?) Makarov (?) Strekalov (Savinykh)	Repair Salyut-6
Progress-12	Jan. 24, 1981	49 days	unmanned Savinykh (Ivanchenkov?)	Supply ship for Salyut-6
Soyuz T-4	Mar. 12, 1981	90 days	Kovalyonok (Romanenko?) "Photon" Dzhanibekov (Lyakhov)	Fifth Salyut-6 long expedition
Soyuz-39	Mar. 22, 1981	8 days	Gurragcha (Ganzorig)	Propaganda junket
Kosmos-1267	Apr. 25, 1981		unmanned Salyut	Third-generation space module
Soyuz-40	May 14, 1981	8 days	Popov (Romanenko*) "Dniepr" Prunariu (Dediu)	Propaganda junket

*Probably replaced Bykovsky, backup crew sent up.

Annotated
Bibliography

Bergaust, Erik, *The Russians in Space,* G.P. Putnam's Sons, New York, 1969. Children's book almost entirely derivative of Sheldon studies, without attribution.

Daniloff, Nicholas, *The Kremlin and the Cosmos,* Alfred A. Knopf, New York, 1972. Excellent overview of political significance of Soviet space activities through Salyut-1 disaster.

Dmitriyev, A., et al., *From Spaceships to Orbiting Stations,* Moscow, 1971 (NASA translation, 1973). Soviet account of how wonderful all their space vehicles are, even if they kill cosmonauts on occasion.

Ezell, Edward, and Ezell, Linda, *The Partnership: A History of the Apollo-Soyuz Test Project,* NASA, Washington, DC, 1978. Complete and honest account of the political, technical and personal aspects of the U.S.-U.S.S.R. "space handshake," but little insight into the actual Soviet program itself.

Froelich, Walter, *Apollo-Soyuz,* NASA, Washington, DC, 1976. The space linkup as détente-minded diplomats would like to have had it happen—all sweetness and light and cooperation.

Golovanov, Yaroslav, *Sergey Korolev: The Apprenticeship of a Space Pioneer,* Mir Publishers, Moscow, 1975 (in English). Fairly honest account of early years of Korolev's life, with a candid personal appraisal that was cut out of the Russian-language editions.

Gurney, Gene, and Gurney, Clare, *Cosmonauts in Orbit,* Franklin Watts, New York, 1972. Modest and readable account of Soviet space explorers for younger readers, but superficial and lacks insight.

Harvey, Mose L., Harvey, Dodd L., and Ciccoritti, Linda C., *U.S.-Soviet Cooperation in Space: A Documentary,* Center for Advanced International Studies, Washington, DC, 1975. Excellent but dry chronology of U.S.-Soviet negotiations, position papers and propandizing about "space cooperation" and "space competition" from before Sputnik right up to just before ASTP.

James, Peter N., *Soviet Conquest from Space,* Arlington House, New Rochelle, NY, 1974. Based on excellent information from the U.S. intelligence community, this is intriguing but quite over-alarmist in its exaggeration of Soviet military manned activities in space.

Johnson, Nicholas L., *Handbook of Soviet Lunar and Planetary Exploration,* American Astronautical Society, Univelt Publishers, San Diego, CA, 1979. Up-to-date and exhaustingly complete chronology and spacecraft description of Soviet deep-space probes, written for the space-history buff or the engineer.

———, *Handbook of Soviet Manned Space Flight,* American Astronautical Society, Univelt Publishers, San Diego, 1980. Complete summary of Soviet manned spacecraft descriptions and accomplishments, organized in a confusing way.

Killian, James R., Jr., *Sputnik, Scientists, and Eisenhower,* MIT Press, Cambridge, MA, 1977. Memoirs of man chosen to be U.S. "missile czar" following Sputnik shock.

Lebedev, L., *et al., Sons of the Blue Planet,* Political Literature Press, Moscow, 1971 (NASA translation by Amerind Publishers, New Delhi, 1973). Political guidance based on personal glimpses of Soviet cosmonauts, stressing how they were perfect communists and devoted patriots and worthy role-models for Soviet youth.

Medvedev, Zhores A., *Soviet Science,* W.W. Norton, New York, 1978. Emigrant's account of Soviet science establishment, including details of Urals nuclear disaster in 1958 and of Nedelin catastrophe of 1960.

Penkovskiy, Oleg, *The Penkovskiy Papers,* Avon Books, New York, 1965. Controversial documents purporting to be memoirs of top Soviet defense official who was actually a CIA agent, the book contains erroneous reports of pre-Gagarin cosmonaut fatalities and a highly distorted account of the Nedelin catastrophe.

Popescu, Julian, *Russian Space Exploration—The First 21 Years,* Gothard House, London, 1979. An absolute disaster of a book, chock-full of errors and fantasies which any proofreading should have caught but didn't, leaving readers alternately bored, confused and misinformed.

Riabchikov, Evgeny, *Russians in Space,* Doubleday, New York, 1971. The Soviet manned space program as a Soviet author would like Westerners to imagine it. The deliberately deceptive text is counterbalanced by excellent photographs.

Romanov, A., *Spacecraft Designer,* Novosti Press Agency Publishing House, Moscow, 1976 (in English). Official version of Korolev's life, on the occasion of what would have been his seventieth birthday.

Schauer, William H., *The Politics of Space,* Holmes and Meier, New York, 1976. Good discussion of politics of space race, in an academic style.

Sheldon, Charles, II, *et al., Soviet Space Programs, 1976–1980,* U.S. Government Printing Office, Washington, DC, 1981. Survey by staff of Library of Congress, it is the authoritative U.S. document on all details of the current Soviet space effort.

———, *Soviet Space Programs, 1971–1975,* U.S. Government Printing Office, Washington, DC, 1976. Covers the entire Soviet space research, applications and military activities, with in-depth political and economic analyses, for the period from Salyut-1 through ASTP.

———, *Soviet Space Programs, 1966–1970,* U.S. Government Printing Office, Washington, DC, 1971. Covers the height of the space race, the Apollo triumph and the evidence for a Soviet man-to-the-moon program, and ends with the Salyut-1 disaster.

Shelton, William, *Soviet Space Exploration: The First Decade,* Washington Square Press, New York, 1968. Readable and insightful overview of the period from Sputnik to the death of Komarov on Soyuz-1.

Smith, Marcia, *Astronauts and Cosmonauts: Biographical and Statistical Data,* U.S. Government Printing Office, Washington, DC, 1978. From a Library of Congress report, covers all known space pilots, listing flights, records and other data, with portraits.

Smolders, Peter, *Soviets in Space,* Taplinger Press, New York, 1974. Informed and well-illustrated survey of Soviet space program that suffers slightly from author's evident desire to give Soviet official claims "the benefit of the doubt" far too frequently.

Talbott, Strobe (editor and translator), *Khrushchev Remembers: The Last Testament,* Little, Brown, Boston, 1974. Contains long section on Soviet missiles and space probes, including a detailed account of the Nedelin catastrophe.

Vladimirov, Leonid, *Russian Space Bluff,* Tom Stacey, London, 1971. Much-maligned unfairly by Western reviewers, this insider's account of pre-1966 Soviet space technology and space politics is a valuable mine of insights if the author's justifiable but highly visible anti-Soviet biases can be filtered out.

Sources of Current Information

Aviation Week and Space Technology, McGraw-Hill, 1221 Avenue of the Americas, New York, NY 10020. Keeps up with Soviet launches, announcements and speculations on future activities. Weekly, $35/year.

Foreign Broadcast Information Service: Soviet Union. Transcripts of translations of Soviet news broadcasts, including several pages per week on space activities. Available from National Technical Information Service, 5285 Port Royal Road, Springfield, VA 22161. Issued daily, costs $165/year.

Spaceflight, British Interplanetary Society, 27/29 South Lambeth Road, London SW8 1SZ, GB. Undoubtedly the authoritative chronicle of all aspects of the Soviet space program as researched by dedicated and inspired amateurs. Monthly, approximately $26/year.

Open Questions: An Invitation to Readers

In many areas of Soviet cosmonaut activities, current research has only just scratched the surface. Here are some additional open items whose answers may lead to new insights and revelations. Anyone out there—defectors, observers, analysts—is invited to send potentially useful material to the author in care of the publisher.

Korolev's rumored second imprisonment in a *sharashka*, 1948–1952—how real was it, and what are corroborative details?

What kind of ICBM, satellite and moon-shot launch failures occurred in the 1956–1960 time period?

Are there additional names and details connected with the October 1960 Nedelin disaster, which killed dozens of rocketeers?

What are the biographical details and what became of the photographs of purged cosmonauts of the 1960–1963 period—the three Valentins, plus Anatoliy, Ivan, Dmitriy, Grigoriy and Mars? Of the "six to eight" men killed in training?

Is there any further information on the three lost women-cosmonauts who backed up Tereshkova in 1963—Irina, Tanya and "X" (code-named here, purely for reference, as "Ludmilla")?

What are the identities and biographical details of the backup passenger-cosmonauts for the October 1964 Voskhod three-man space mission?

What are the details of the Voskhod-2 off-course recovery in the Urals in March 1965? Are there first-person accounts?

Are there unofficial (and unprintable) personal glimpses of cosmonauts and their families, including any accounts of disciplinary actions taken against them?

The August 1968 launch of Kosmos-238—was it intended for a rendezvous with the manned Soyuz-3, but aborted?

What data exist on the rumored 1967–1968 scientist-cosmonaut team which included Bogdashevskiy but which was evidently disbanded in 1971?

What of the ill-fated superbooster program, 1969–1971—its failures, design features, personnel involved, cost estimates?

What were the true purpose and results of the mysterious Luna-15 unmanned moon orbiter, sent up only days before Apollo-11's launching in July 1969? Was it a sample return attempt?

The mystery Kosmos series of 1970–1972, including Kosmos-379, 382 and others like them—what kind of man-related moon-flight hardware was tested?

The cosmonauts assigned with Belyayev to train for the Zond round-the-moon flights of 1967–1970—who were they?

What has become of launch photographs of the Salyut space station, any Salyut?

What are the engineering details, any details, of the Proton launch vehicle, first flown in 1965 but never described in the Soviet literature?

Who were the backup cosmonaut crews for Soyuz-6 and 7 (1969), Soyuz-10 and 11 (1971) and Soyuz-13 (1973)?

Who was that vaguely imaged "third man" in the Leonov-Kubasov team training for a Salyut mission in 1971? And what became of him?

What has become of the photographs and drawings of the "military Salyut" variations, Salyut-2 (1973), Salyut-3 (1974) and Salyut-5 (1976)? And of the photographs of on-board activities or ground training for the cosmonaut crewmen?

What are the details of the "detachable module" on Salyut-3 and Salyut-5, which returned "experimental materials" to earth after the departure of the last visiting crew? How big was it? Where was it attached? What was its capacity? Could it be automatically loaded?

What are the details of the configuration and mission of Kosmos-929, the Salyut-sized precursor of the Salyut-6 mission, launched in July 1977 and deliberately de-orbited six months later? What was it doing in space? What did it look like?

Where is ASTP cosmonaut Boris Andreyev? Has he been purged from the program? What of ASTP Soviet CAPCOM cosmonaut Illarionov?

The twin "once-around" missions launched atop Proton boosters in 1976–1979—what did they look like? Were both payloads identical or substantially different? What were their purposes?

Development problems in the Soyuz-T program—was the second unmanned test (disguised as Kosmos-1001) a failure with a premature termination after only eleven days in space? What about these reentry control problems reported on Soyuz T-2 in June 1980?

Index

Adzhubei, Aleksey, 59
air, in "closed-loop" life-support system, 226
Aksyonov, Vladimir, 239
Aldrin, Edwin, 124
Aleksandrov, Aleksandr, 246
Andreyev, Boris, 239, 263
Apollo space program, 77, 84, 90, 99, 100, 101, 112, 113, 116, 117, 120–21, 122, 125, 126, 127
Soyuz linkup with Apollo (Apollo-Soyuz Test Project), 109, 136–37, 138, 139–44
Artyukhin, Yuriy, 132, 239
Astashenkov, Pyotr, 25
Aviation Week and Space Technology, 260
on military Salyuts, 130
on Soviet manned space plans, 230–31
on Soyuz-21 mission termination, 146, 148

Baikonur Cosmodrome (Zvezdagrad), as secret Soviet space city, 158–60

deception about, 56
See also Plesetsk; Starry Town
Baudry, Patrick, 200
Belyayev, Pavel, 74, 80, 82, 118, 119, 120, 152, 262, 269
Benedict, Howard, 114
Beregovkin, Dr. Anatoliy, 209
Beregovoy, Georgiy, 99, 228, 229, 239
biological experiments on board Salyut-6, 171
Bogdashevskiy, Rostislav, 154, 262
Braun, Wernher von, 59
Brezhnev, Leonid, 25, 27, 78, 85, 99
Bui Thanh Liem, 246
Bykovskiy, Valeriy, 67, 97, 240

cameras, on-board Salyut space station, 194–95
Carr, Jerry, 210
Castro, Fidel, 156
casualty rate among cosmonauts, 10–12. *See also* deaths
catastrophe, Nedelin, xii, 39–49, 261
accounts of, 40–44

catastrophe, Nedelin, (cont'd)
  death toll, 47
  fuel-feed system of rocket, 47–48
  "launch window," 39, 45
  scenario of events, possible, 45–46
  survivors of, 46–47
Cernan, Eugene, 82
Chelomey (Soviet engineer), 21, 27, 240
chibis (low-pressure space trousers), 174
Chkalov Air Force Base, 151, 152, 157
chlorella experiments, "closed-loop" life-support system and, 226
Chrétien, Jean-Loup, 200
Chronicle of Current Events, Korolev repression and, 19
circadian rhythm of cosmonauts in space, 206–7
"civilian" and "military" Salyuts, 129–30
"closed-loop" life-support system, as problem for space colonies, 225–27
  air, 226
  food, 226–27
  water, 225–26
Collins, Michael, 118, 124
color-differentiation abilities of cosmonauts, 208
Cosmonaut Day (1980), 9–10, 12
Cosmonaut Museum, 150, 152, 156
cosmonauts
  circadian rhythm of, in space, 206–7
  color-differentiation abilities of, 208
  deaths of, 10–12, 56–60, 62–63, 91–93, 95, 96, 97–98, 102–5, 108–9, 110, 234
  disappearance of, first manned space flights and, 60–62
  exercise in space by, 172–74, 181, 209
  fatigue of, on Salyut-6, 173, 181
  future numbers of, 234–35
  guest program for, 183–201
  immunity response of, on Salyut-6, 175
  oceanographic observations by, 207–8
  physiological and psychological effects of space on, 78, 167–68, 174–75, 176–78, 181–82, 219–21
  qualifications for becoming, 153–55
  radio interferometry experiments by, 215
  "space sight" of, 214–15
  space spectaculars by, 83–84, 110, 115, 232–33
  spacewalks by, 79–82
  weightlessness problem and, 36, 174–75, 205, 209–10, 213
  women, 63–72
Covault, Craig, 230–31
Cronkite, Walter, 113

deaths, space and, 10–12, 91–93, 95, 96, 97–98, 102–5
  future space programs and, 234
  rumors about, 56–60
  Steep Road into Space (1972), 108–9, 110
  in training, 62–63
decalcification process, prolonged space flights and, 4
Dobrovolskiy, Georgiy, 101, 102, 108, 240
Dyomin, Lev, 240
Dzhanibekov, Vladimir, 240

Eisenhower, Dwight D., 34, 40
Engel, Rolf, 230
European Space Agency, 185, 222
exercise by cosmonauts in space, 172–73, 174, 209

Farkas, Bertalan, 198, 246
Feoktistov, Konstantin, 77, 210, 224, 227, 240

Filipchenko, Anatoliy, 240
food, in "closed-loop" life-support
system, 226–27
chlorella experiments and, 226
*Foreign Broadcast Information Ser-
vice,* 260
Frosch, Robert, 210–11
Fulbright, Senator William, 35
furnaces, on board Salyut space station, 195

Gagarin Cosmonaut Training Cen-
ter, 156, 157, 190, 192, 200
Gagarin, Yuriy, xi, 9, 11, 50, 52, 53,
54, 55, 56, 58, 63, 64, 72–73, 84,
91, 94, 96–97, 98, 101, 103, 150,
151, 152, 240
Gandhi, Sanjay, 200
gardens, space, 170–71, 226
Gazenko, Oleg, 219, 225, 229, 240
Gemini space program, 75, 76, 77,
90
Ghali, Paul, 41
Gierek, Adam, 189
GIRD (Group Studying Rocket
Propulsion), 17, 18
Glazkov, Yuriy, 148, 149, 240
Glushko, Valentin, 21, 22, 225, 233,
240
Goddard, Robert, 18
Golovanov, Yaroslav, 20, 22–23,
26
Golyakhovskiy, Vladimir, 88, 89
Gorbatko, Viktor, 148, 149, 240–41
Grechko, Georgiy, 162–74, 176,
177–82, 187, 204, 208, 209, 228,
241
Gris, Henry, 212
Grishin, Sergey, 224
Gruening, Senator Ernest, 69
Gubarev, Aleksey, 187, 241
guest-cosmonaut program ("Inter-
kosmos"), 183–201
equipment, use of, 192–95
in future, 233
knowledge of Soviet programs
from, 234

launching times of, 187–88
list of, by nationality, 246–47
political purposes of, 184, 186, 187
preparations for, 189–90
qualifications for, 186
space careers of different nationalities, 195–201
"Syrena" crystallization experiment and, 188–89
training of guests, 190–92
Gvay, Ivan, 43

Hermaszewski, Miroslaw, 187, 188,
246
Houtman, Maarten, 200

Ilyushin, Vladimir, 51, 53
"Interkosmos." *See* guest-cos-
monaut program
Interkosmos Council, 224, 227
International Astronautical Feder-
ation (FAI), 54, 55, 56, 90
Ivanchenkov,   Aleksandr
("Sasha"), 164, 204–10, 241
"Ivanov," Dmitriy, 241
Ivanov, Georgi, 196, 197, 213, 246

Jähn, Sigmund, 187, 195, 246
Jankowski, Zenon, 187, 246

Kamanin, General Nikolay, 59,
90–91, 97, 104, 241
KATE-140 mapping camera, 195
Kennedy, John F., 84, 90, 103, 111,
121
Khrunov, Yevgeniy, 94, 241
Khrushchev, Nikita, 16, 17, 24, 25,
26, 28–30, 33–34, 35, 36–38,
39, 40, 42, 43, 44, 45, 46, 48, 63,
64, 65, 66, 69, 71, 72, 75, 76, 79,
84, 90, 94, 118, 120
Klimuk, Pyotr, 137, 155, 241
Köllner, Eberhard, 187, 246
Komarov, Vladimir, 91, 92, 93, 94,
95, 96, 97, 98, 103, 117, 241
Korda, Sergey, 26
Korniev, Ivan, 242

Korolev, Sergey ("Sergeyev"), xi,
  xii, 16–38, 39, 45, 46, 47, 48, 49,
  50, 53, 54, 63, 66, 75, 76, 78,
  84–86, 90, 91, 115, 116, 118, 234,
  242, 261
  death of, 87–89
  rehabilitation of, 24–25
  repression of, 19–24
Kosberg, Simon, 47–48, 233
Kosmograd (Space Colony Number One), 224, 233
Kosmos-557, 106–7, 108, 129–30
Kosmos-929, 263
Kosmos-955 spy satellite, as UFO,
  160–61
Kosygin, Aleksey, 85, 93
Kotenkova, Nina (Korolev's second wife), 24
Kovalyonok, Vladimir, 204–10, 242
KRISTALL electrical furnace, 195
Kubasov, Valeriy, 109, 110, 242

landing technique, of first manned
  space flight, 54–55
"launch window," 39, 45, 117
Lazarev, Vasiliy, 128, 134, 135, 136,
  190, 242
Lebedev, Valentin, 5, 220, 242
Leonov, Aleksey, 70, 74, 75, 79, 80–
  81, 82, 83, 99, 109, 110, 118, 153,
  242
linkup/spacewalk, Soviet, 98–100
Lopez-Falcon, Jose, 246
Luce, Clare Booth, 69
Luna-15 space probe, man-on-
  moon race and, 124–25, 126
Lyakhov, Vladimir, 4, 211, 214–19,
  242

Magyari, Bela, 246
Makarov, Oleg, 128, 134, 136, 242
Malyshev, Yuriy, 243
manned flights, 52–72
  disappearances of cosmonauts,
    60–62
  International Astronautical Fed-
    eration's (FAI) certification
    of, 54, 55, 56

landing technique of, 54–55
launch site hoax, 55–56
psychological concerns about,
  52–53
rumors about deaths, 56–60
training deaths, 62–63
women cosmonauts and, 63–72
See also Voshkod space programs
man-on-moon race, 120–27
  cover-up story by Soviets, 126–27
  Luna-15 probe, 124–25, 126
  "moon buggies" (Lunokhods),
    125
  robot "scooper ships," as Soviet
    alternative to, 125
  Soviet plans for, 121, 227–28,
    229–31
  space maneuvers by Soviets and,
    123–24
  space stations, permanent, 228
  superbooster, Soviet, 121–22,
    230–31
  technical capability of Soviets
    and, 122–23
  termination of, by Soviets, 124
  See also moon race
Mars
  probes by Soviets, failure of, 39,
    42, 45
  Soviet plans for flight to, 228–30,
    235–36
Maslennikov, Anatoliy, 243
Medusa experiment with organic
  polymers, 203
Medvedev, Zhores, xii, 42–43, 44,
  88
Mercury program (U.S.), 51, 63, 75
"military" Salyuts. See "civilian"
  and "military" Salyuts
Ministry for Medium Machine
  Building, 24
"missile gap," launching of Sputnik
  and, 35–36
Mission Control Center (Moscow),
  5, 6, 7, 96, 117, 134, 138, 140, 142,
  146, 149, 151, 166, 176, 180, 183,
  196, 203, 218

MKF-6M camera system, 194
"moon buggies" (Lunokhods), 125
moon race, Soviet intentions about,
    111–27
    Apollo-8 success, 117, 120
    evidence of Soviet intentions to
        win, 114–120
    Khrushchev's memoirs and, 118
    man on moon and, 120–27
    nonlaunch by Soviets, mystery
        about, 119–20
    official Soviet position on, 112–13,
        117–18
    *Soviet Encyclopedia of Space
        Flight* and, 117
    U.S. views on Soviet intentions
        about, 113–14, 126–27
    Zond probes by Soviets and, 114–
        17, 118–19, 120

Narimanov, Georgiy, 227
NASA, xi, xii, 56, 69, 82, 107, 113,
    116, 117, 121, 141, 144, 162, 164,
    210
National Security Council (USA),
    231
Naval Research Laboratory, 15–16
Nedelin, Field Marshal Mitrofan,
    xii, 34, 38, 40–45, 47, 48, 243.
    See also catastrophe, Nedelin
Neptune (cosmonaut newspaper),
    152–53
news coverage, U.S., of Soviet
    space program, 232
Nikolayev, Andrian, 67, 71, 99, 243
Nikolayeva-Tereshkova. *See* Ter-
    eshkova
Nikolayeva, Yelena, 243
Nixon, Richard, 121, 139

Oberth, Dr. Hermann, 37, 59
oceanographic observation by cos-
    monauts, 207–8
Ogden, Dennis, 51–52, 53–54
outposts in space, Soviet plans for,
    223–27
    "closed-loop" life-support sys-
        tem, as problem for, 225–27

Kosmograd   (Space   Colony
    Number One), 224
    size of, 227
    "space colonists," 235–36
Ozerov, Georgiy A., 88

Parry, Albert, 40
Patsayev, Viktor, 101, 102, 108,
    243
Pavlovskiy, Nikolay, 41
Pelczak, Oldrich, 187, 246
Penkovskiy, Oleg (*Penkovskiy Pa-
    pers*), 41, 42, 44, 59
Petrov, Boris, 224, 227
Petrovskiy, Dr. Boris, 88–89
Pham Tuan, 199, 246
physiological   and   psychological
    effects of prolonged time in
    space, Salyut-6 experiments
    and, 7–8, 167–68, 174–75, 176–
    78, 181–82, 219–21
    circadian rhythm in space, 206–7
    first manned space flights and,
        52–53
    Lyakhov-Ryumin 175-day mis-
        sion, as "extra psychological
        experiment," 214
    "Psychological Support Group,"
        176
Plesetsk, as secret Soviet space city,
    160–61. *See also* Baikonur Cos-
    modrome; Starry Town
politics, Soviet, space programs
    and, 28–30, 33–34, 35, 36–38,
    39–40, 43, 63–64, 65, 66, 69,
    71–72, 75, 78, 100, 108, 139, 184,
    187, 200
Popov, Leonid, 3, 5, 6–9, 13, 220,
    243
Popovich, Pavel, 55, 66, 67, 132, 243
Progress   robot   freighter-tanker
    ships, 7, 179
    during   Lyakhov-Ryumin   175-
        day mission, 215
    perfection of, 208–9
propaganda, Soviet, space program
    and, 33–34, 68, 69, 71–72, 84,
    110, 126, 184

Proton rocket boosters, 89–90, 100, 106, 114, 115, 116, 122, 228, 262

"PS" (test satellite), launching of Sputnik and, 31–32 psychological effects of space. *See* physiological and psychological effects

radio interferometry experiments by cosmonauts, 215

Red Army, 18, 28, 29, 33

Remek, Vladimir, 183, 184, 186, 187, 246

repairs in space, preventive and restorative, 218

Reston, James, 33

Riabchikov, Evgeny, 55

Romanenko, Yuriy, 163–67, 169, 170, 173, 174, 178–82, 183, 187, 200, 204, 209, 243

Romanov, A., 19, 25

R-1 (all-Russian ballistic missile), 22

Rozhdestvenskiy, Valeriy, 146, 243–44

R-7 rocket *(semyorka)*, 27–30, 35–36, 47

Rukavishnikov, Nikolay, 196, 197, 213, 244

Rynin, Nikolay, 14

Ryumin, Valeriy, 3–13, 211, 212–21, 229, 244

Salyut-6 space station, as Soviet success, 3, 6–13, 162–82
American reactions to successes of, 210–11
bleed valve crisis, as danger to cosmonauts, 166–67
biological experiments, 171
docking-module mechanism problem, 163, 164, 165
exercise on board, 172–73, 181
fatigue of cosmonauts, 173, 181
food on board, 169–70, 178
garbage disposal, 180
immunity response of cosmonauts, 175
Kovalyonok-Ivanchenkov 140-day mission, 202–10, 211
Lyakhov-Ryumin 175-day mission, 211–19
medicines on board, 173–74
oxygen production, 168
physiological and psychological effects and, 167–68, 174–75, 176–78, 181–82
Progress-1 robot freighter-tanker ship and, 179–80
research experiments on board, 176
Romanenko's near death, 165–66, 167
Ryumin's 185-day mission, 219–21
sleeping on board, 171–72
space garden, 170–71
television, use of, 181
uncleanliness on board, 173, 177–78
water supply, 168–69
weightlessness, medical condition of cosmonauts and, 174–75
See also space-station program

Sarafanov, Gennadiy, 155, 244

"scooper ships," Soviet, 125

Scott, David, 118

semyorka. See R-7 rocket

"Sergeyev." *See* Korolev, Sergey

Sevastyanov, Vitaliy, 137, 244

Shatalov, Vladimir, 70, 97, 147, 156, 196, 218, 225, 244

Sheldon, Dr. Charles, II, 60

Shonin, Georgiy, 61, 62, 244

Skylab, 100, 101, 104, 106, 107, 108, 109, 110, 143, 144, 164, 175, 231, 232
endurance data from, 164

Slayton, Deke, xi, 141, 143

Solzhenitsyn, Aleksandr, 17, 20, 23

Soviet Academy of Sciences, 24

Soviet Encyclopedia of Space Flight, Zond probes and, 117
Soyuz space programs, 3–6, 75, 76, 79, 84, 85, 90–110
Apollo-Soyuz Test Project (ASTP), 136–37, 138, 139–44
deaths and disasters in, 91–93, 95, 96, 97–98, 102, 105, 108–9
emergency landing problem of Soyuz-23, 146–48
equipment failures, 95–96
linkup/spacewalk, 98–100
linkup with Salyut-6, 130–36, 137–38
mission of Soyuz-24, 148–49
as space spectaculars, 94–95, 110
space stations and, 100–9
Spaceflight, 260
Spacelab, 185, 187
space race, status of, 222–23
Space Shuttle, American, 144, 185, 186, 222, 223
"space sight," cosmonauts' observation of earth as, 214–15
"space spying," 129–30, 143
space-station program, Soviet, 100–9, 128–49
Apollo-Soyuz Test Project (ASTP), 136–37, 138, 139–44
camera on board, MKF-6M, 194
"civilian" and "military" Salyuts, 129–30
equipment on later Salyuts, 192–95
future size of, 227
Kosmos-557, 106–7, 108
lifespan of Salyut-4, 138–39
Mars and, 228–30
permanent, in Soviet plans for man on moon, 228
Salyut-5, problem with, 144–46, 148–49
Salyut-6 success, 3, 6–13, 162–82
Salyut-Soyuz linkup, 130–34
Soviet's current uses of, 223

Soyuz-18/Salyut-4 setback, 134–36, 137–38
Soyuz replacements, 185
telescope, on-board submillimeter infrared, 193–94
"space transportation system" of West, 222–23
space vehicles, number of Soviet launches of, 231–32
spacewalk, first, 79–82
spectaculars, Soviet cosmonaut, evaluation of, 83–84, 110, 115
future, 232–33
SPLAV electrical furnace, 195
Sputnik, birth of, 14–38
clues about, 14–15
follow-on launchings, 36–37
Khrushchev's role in, 16, 25–26, 28–30, 33–34, 36–38
Korolev's role in, 16–33, 36–38
launching of "PS" (test satellite), 16, 31–32
propaganda uses, 33–34
R-1 and, 22
R-7 rocket and, 27–30, 35–36
V-2 rocket research and, 21–22
West's reaction to, 34–35
"spy satellites," Kosmos-955 as, 160–61
Stafford, Tom, 103, 141, 143, 157
Stalin, Josef, 18–19, 22, 24, 25
Starry Town (Zvezdniy Gorodok, U.S.S.R.), as secret space city, 150–58
Cosmonaut Museum at, 150, 152, 156
cosmonaut qualifications for, 153–55
description of, 151–53
facilities at, 157–58
retired cosmonaut problem, 156
See also Baikonur Cosmodrome; Plesetsk
Steep Road into Space (Soviet film), 108–9, 110
STROKA teletype on Salyut space station, 192

Sullivan, Walter, 15
"super booster," Soviet ("Webb's giant"), man-on-moon race and, 121–22, 230–31

Tamayo-Mendez, Arnaldo, 199, 200, 246
technology, Soviet space, appraisal of, 83
telescope, on-board submillimeter infrared (on Salyut space station), 193–94
Tereshkova, Valentina, 64–65, 66, 67, 68–69, 70–71, 72, 73, 99, 101, 244, 261
Titov, Gherman, 118, 244
Tolubko, V.F. (*Nedelin: First Chief of the Strategics*), 44
Tsiolkovskiy, Konstantin, 14, 18, 30, 37, 225, 236
Tukhachevskiy, Mikhail N., 18–19
Tupolev (Soviet airplane designer), 17, 20, 21, 25

UFO, Kosmos-955 spy satellite as, 160–61, 180
unmanned tests, 50–51
U.S. Information Agency, 35
Ustinov, Dmitriy, 25

Verne, Jules, 181
Vick, Charles, 119
Vishnevskiy, Dr. Aleksandr, 89
Vladimirov, Leonid, xii, 19, 38, 113
Volkov, Vladislav, 101, 102, 108, 244
Volynov, Boris, 145, 245
Voskhod space programs, 76–85
conversion of Vostok spaceship, 77
dog experiment and, 89
landing mishap, 82–83
launch escape system of, 79
longevity of flight, 78–79
politics and, 78
spacewalk and, 79–82
as spectaculars, 83–84
technology of, 83
Vostok spaceships, 50–51, 52, 53, 54, 55, 56, 63, 64, 67, 75, 76–77
See also manned flights
V-2 rocket research, 21–22

water, in "closed-loop" life-support system, 225–26
Webb, James, 121
weightlessness in space, medical effects on cosmonauts and, 36, 174–75, 205, 209–10, 213
women cosmonauts, 63–72, 233
chauvinism and, Soviet, 70–71
propaganda purposes of, 68, 69, 71–72
U.S. reaction to, 69–70

Yangel, Mikhail, 45–46, 110, 245
Yefremov, Dmitriy, 41, 44
Yegorov, Boris, 77, 245
Yeliseyev, Aleksey, 94, 176, 245

Zander, Friedrich, 17
zero-G barrier, breaking of, 202–21
Kovalyonok-Ivanchenkov 140-day mission, 202–10, 211
Lyakhov-Ryumin 175-day mission, 211–19
perfecting Progress resupply operations, 208–9, 215
physiological and psychological lessons from, 214, 219–21
Ryumin's 185-day mission, 129–31
weightlessness and, 205, 209–10, 213
See also space-station program
Zhukov, Marshal, 28, 29, 33
Zholobov, Vitaliy, 145, 245
Zond probes, Soviet, moon race and, 114–17, 118–19, 120
Soviet Encyclopedia of Space Flight on, 117
Zudov, Vyacheslav, 146, 155, 245
Zvezdagrad. *See* Baikonur Cosmodrome
Zvezdniy Gorodok. *See* Starry Town